The History of Valley Center, California:

The Homestead Years, 1860-1900

The History of Valley Center, California:

The Homestead Years, 1860-1900

by
Petei McHenry

Foreword by Raymond Brandes, Ph.D.

Second Paperback Edition

GP Marketing, Escondido, California

The History of Valley Center, California:
The Homestead Years, 1860-1900.
Valley Center Historical Society Special Edition

By Petei McHenry

Published by: GP Marketing
            PO Box 1091
            Valley Center, CA 92082 U.S.A.

First Paperback Printing 1998
Second Paperback Printing 2007
Museum Edition printed for the Valley Center Historical Society 2007
Printed by Vanard Lithographers, San Diego, California USA

Publisher's Cataloging-in-Publication Data
(Provided by Quality Books, Inc.)

McHenry, Petei.
        The history of Valley Center, California : the homestead
    years, 1860-1900 / by Petei McHenry ; foreword by Raymond
    Brandes. — 1st ed.
        p. cm.
        Includes bibliographic references and index.
        Preassigned LCCN: 98-85039
        ISBN 0-9660789-1-8 (pbk)

1. Valley Center (Calif.)   —History—19th century.
I. Title.

F869.V35M34 1998   979.49804
                                          QBI97-41366

TABLE OF CONTENTS

LIST OF TABLES

LIST OF FIGURES

LIST OF FIGURES CONTINUED

LIST OF CHARTS

FOREWORD

by Raymond Brandes, Ph.D.

As Valley Center enters the 21st century, newcomers will find a remarkable history of the region. The fascination of the area to date has largely been dictated by the archaeologists following pipeline excavations or sites where the Native Americans lived at some time in the past. As in most parts of the West, the interest of the historic past has been eschewed by those who dig in the soil to speculate with conclusions about the Indian past.

Within the last 40 years with the introduction of historical archaeology, that is the excavation of sites where ranches, old military forts, stagecoach stations and even small ghost towns has taken place, a new breed of public historians or applied historians with some archaeological or historical research experience has taken place.

These are the individuals who not only see above or below in the soil the remains of the past, but by detective-like work know how to find the paper that helps to verify what was previously unknown. They may be called historians, historical archaeologists, or archivists, because their University and practical training has made it possible to do what people in all professions must do, and that is to solve problems.

Petei McHenry embarked on a monumental task when she began to write the history of Valley Center. I had known this area as a small country region with farming and ranching as the major focus. I had also known of some of the "characters" who had come out West for all the reasons easterners do: the weather, their health, to look over the next hill, to begin life anew, or to escape from something.

Until she had begun the research for the first volume in this four volume series, Petei could not have realized the full impact of the remarkable undertaking which lay before her. The necessity for her to have lived 100 years ago in Valley Center was not relevant. She became a pioneer abetted by her training, her intuitiveness and skills. In this way Petei McHenry solved the first major problem: where to find the information that would help her solve the problem--what was the authentic history of Valley Center? She did not want to write another anecdotal history of some town in San Diego County filled with the mythical stories of the great and famous.

Ms. McHenry found maps, knew where to look for the deed books, the homestead claims, mortgages, building records, court cases, Justice

Court documents, and newspaper accounts of events which could be cross-documented. Her's was a treasure hunt for she found diaries, journals, accounts and papers, and photographs of some of early residents. Through paper transactions the tracing of ownership of property became another test of her patience and ability to document her primary resources.

What is emerging, therefore, is a chronicle about Valley Center, California-- in which time, place, people, and events emerge in a well written chronological fashion. This won't have to be done again. Such a record will be invaluable not only for the descendants of the early settlers, but for those newcomers who will realize that they are staking out their own claims to a rather remarkable piece of the American West.

PREFACE

My interest in the history of Valley Center, California, began as a result of my participation in an archaeological study conducted in 1994. The subject became the focus of my Master's thesis completed for the University of San Diego in 1997.

It was surprising to learn that a formal compilation of the history had never been completed. Several residents had written personal memoirs, but were not published. Therefore, information was difficult to obtain due to the fact that all data had to be researched using primary sources. Old maps were studied for original land owners supported by the original homestead documents. The historical files in the Valley Center Library and the Escondido Pioneer Room proved to be valuable resources which provided photographs, newspaper articles, and personal information regarding the early settlers of the valley.

The following book is the first of a four-volume set on the history of Valley Center. It contains information regarding the pioneer settlers during the homestead years, 1860-1900. The end product is intended to be a research tool for future historians or descendants of the early pioneers. Resources are documented and cited for ease in data retrieval. Further investigation will be conducted and written to complete the history and bring the reader up to the present time in volumes two and three. The second volume will include the war years from 1900-1945. The third volume will include the baby boom years from 1945-present. Volume four of this set will be presented as a family album and include photographs and memorabilia of Valley Center. Each volume will be preceded by a limited hardcover edition to be followed by a softcover edition. Proceeds will help benefit the Friends of the Valley Center Library.

The history of Valley Center is an interesting piece of Americana. The settlers were basically farmers who capitalized on the Homestead Act of 1862 to claim up to 160 acres of land for a nominal filing fee. Many of these settlers were immigrants from foreign lands while others were emigrants relocating in the newly opened western United States. One common denominator was that they were all striving for a decent existence on land of their own.

This little, out-of-the-way valley had never been part of a Spanish land grant and provided the homesteaders the means to establish their own land holdings. Many settlers were forced to abandon their claims due to harsh weather conditions which included either drought or floods. Others not only maintained their claims, but were able to amass large ranches or farms for their descendants. Today there are few descendants of the early settlers living in the valley, but the lure of the valley remains the same. It still provides a peaceful setting with that small back-country flavor.

ACKNOWLEDGMENTS

This work could not have been completed without the guidance and assistance of numerous people. First, to the archivists and library staff who assisted in my research at the Valley Center Library, Escondido Pioneer Room, Escondido Public Library, Carlsbad City Library, San Diego Library California Room, San Diego Historical Society Research Archives, Family History Center at the Church of the Latter-Day Saints in San Diego, and the National Archives in Laguna Niguel. My gratitude also goes to the staff members of the San Diego County Surveyor's Office, Assessor's Office, and Recorder's Office, for their hours of patience and photocopying.

Finally, to all of my friends and family who not only encouraged me to undertake this project, but assisted in proof-reading, computer technology, and moral support when necessary, the greatest of which came from my husband, Gray. My love and appreciation to all.

Funding for this museum edition was provided by the Wells Fargo Foundation of California, and a grant from the Community Projects Fund of San Diego County Supervisor Bill Horn.

CHAPTER ONE

INTRODUCTION

Valley Center, California, a small rural community originally known as Bear Valley, is located inland in northern San Diego County, California. It is not incorporated and does not have a formal town council. The community was never planned; it developed as large tracts of land that were single-family farms or ranches. The road system was not planned either but developed as a means of travel between farms or ranches, with the roads usually named after the families.

The main business district consists of about two dozen buildings within a half-mile stretch and the main industry has always been agriculture. The majority of privately owned parcels of land consist of two acres or more, many with horses or other domestic animals corralled in the front yards. A water system was installed in 1953 and a sewer system is planned for the future.

The population as of 1997 is approximately 20,000 people and high school students are still transported to Escondido because the community does not have their own high school. These reasons, however, are part of the charm of this back-roads community — it is still rural and devoid of the hustle-and-bustle of big city life.

A formal account of the history of Valley Center has never been compiled, although two books and one manuscript have been written by descendants of early settlers. These accounts were printed, but not published. The first personal account was written in 1925 by John Lincoln Kelly[1] whose family lived outside the current study area. The second personal memoir was written in 1953 by Abel M. Davis,[2] a son of one of the first settlers in the valley. The third personal account was written in the 1970s by Clyde S. James,[3] whose family homesteaded land in the mid-1860s. One unpublished master's thesis has been written,[4] but the boundaries fall outside the current study area. Additional accounts written were also checked regarding the history of San Pasqual,[5] San Luis Rey valley,[6] Palomar Mountain,[7] and Escondido.[8]

Research for the current study included viewing primary documents such as census records, school records, county directories, land deeds, survey maps, birth, death, and marriage records, wills, tax records, voter registration registers, individual family records, photo albums, and descendants of early settlers personal accounts recorded on audio tapes. Newspaper accounts were also examined for information on obituaries, marriages, births, or any interesting stories regarding the residents.

Official government agency sources consulted include the National Archives and Records Administration in Laguna Niguel, San Diego County Assessor's office, San Diego County Recorder's office, and San Diego County Surveyor's office.   Public archival material researched include San Diego Historical Society Archives, Church of the Latter-Day Saints (LDS) Family History Center, San Diego County Public libraries in San Diego, Escondido, and Valley Center, Pioneer Room in Escondido, California Room in San Diego, and Carlsbad Library.

Recorded archaeological site locations were checked with the clearing houses at the South Coastal Information Center (SCIC) at San Diego State University, and the San Diego Museum of Man. Computer-generated genealogical programs were useful in collecting family information regarding the early settlers of Valley Center. Two compact-discs programs used include *International Genealogical Index,©*[9] registered to the LDS church, and a privately owned program, *Family Tree Maker©.*[10]

Valley Center is located approximately 45 miles northeast of San Diego, 10 miles northeast of Escondido and 20 miles east of the Pacific Ocean coastline. The area considered Valley Center consists of more than 200 square miles and extends north-to-south from the San Luis Rey River to the city of Escondido and east-to-west from Palomar Mountain to Interstate 15 (Figure 1). This area includes Townships 9, 10, and 11 South, Ranges 1 East, 1 West, and 2 West, of the San Bernardino Base Meridian (Figure 2).   Included within the Valley Center area are the historic ranchos of Pauma, Cuca or El Potrero, and Guejito. Rancho Guejito is the only historic land grant intact today, for the others have been divided and developed for housing tracts or industrial purposes. The Indian reservations of Pala, Pauma, La Jolla, and Rincon are also within this area.   Topography includes mesas, valleys, and mountains with elevations ranging from 300 to over 3,000 feet above sea level.   Due to the vast area as described, it became necessary to focus this study within 40 square miles centered around the cultural and business district of Valley Center.   Included in the study area are portions of Townships 10 and 11 South, and Ranges 1 and 2 West (see Figure 2). Unfortunately, this concentration omits several

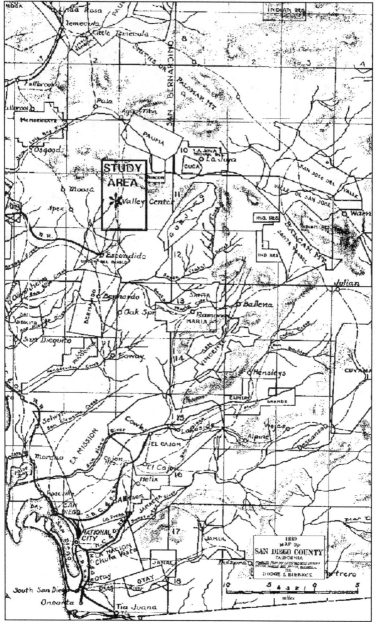

Figure 1. Regional Map Showing Location of Valley Center.

Figure 2. Study Area.

pioneering families from this study area usually found in discussions of early Valley Center residents. Biographical information of the early settlers within the study area is presented chronologically to the year 1900 in the following chapters.

The history of Valley Center is an important subject in that the community was founded in one of the few portions of California not included in historic Spanish land grants.[11] The Treaty of Guadalupe Hidalgo, signed February 2, 1848, ended the war with Mexico over the legal ownership of California, Texas, New Mexico, and Arizona by setting the boundary line between the United States and Mexico. The treaty also guaranteed Mexican citizens the right to become U.S. citizens and maintain land holdings already established.[12]

Several large land tracts, or *ranchos* surrounding Valley Center had been granted during the Mexican Era (1841-48). These include *Pauma*,[13] *Cuca*,[14] *Guejito*,[15] *Rincón del Diablo*,[16] *Bernardo*,[17] *San Marcos*,[18] *Buena Vista*,[19] *Guajome*,[20] and *Monserrate*.[21] Northern inland San Diego County remained U.S. government property until the Homestead Act of 1862 proclaimed the land as 'public domain' to settlers who would improve and homestead the land with their families. Each person was allowed to claim up to 160 acres of public land for a nominal fee of $10, provided that improvements to the land were made after the legal claim was filed with the county land assessor's office. A house was to be built, land either cultivated or used for grazing, and the person filing the claim was to reside on the land for at least five years.[22] Many early settlers claimed land and then later abandoned that claim for another parcel of land.

A pre-emption claim could also be issued to those settlers on unappropriated public land by way of utilizing the Pre-emption Act of September 4, 1841.[23] Under this act, a single adult over the legal age of 21, the head of a family, or a widow could settle on land and make improvements before filing a Declaration of Intent with the local land office. This allowed the person filing to later purchase the land at a minimum price without competition. This act was repealed in 1891 at repeated requests of the Commissioner of the General Land Office based on abuse of the law and fraudulent entries.[24] Timber and mineral claims were also granted.[25]

The original Native American occupants of the land were forced to reside on lands federally provided as reservations even though their ancestors had lived on the land for generations.[26] Ironically, some of the homesteaders were forced to give up portions of their land claims for the establishment of these reservations.

The Valley Center area attracted people for reasons other than just "free" land and the mild climate. The area consists of a broad, fairly flat, rocky mesa with a high water table from water draining from the surrounding hillsides providing good soil for agriculture. After the removal of the granite rocks, farming was not only suitable and profitable for many settlers, it also provided ample grazing land for livestock.

Table 1 lists some of the wildlife inhabiting the valley today. This includes both migratory and non-migratory birds,[27] mammals,[28] reptiles and amphibians.[29] Not all animals are indigenous; several species are introduced.

*Table 1. **Wildlife in Valley Center***

Birds:	Mammals:
Canadian geese (*Branta canadensis*)	deer mouse (*Peromyscus maniculatus*)
swallow (*Hirúndo pyrrhonóta*)	
oriole (*Ícterus cucullátus*)	harvest mouse (*Reithrodontomys megalotis*)
mallard (*Ánas platyrhýnchos*)	
gnatcatcher(*Polióptila melanúra*)	pocket mouse (*Perognathus fallax*)
towhee (*Pípilo erythrophthálmus*)	
blackbird (*Agelaíus phoeniceus*)	jumping mouse (*Zapus trinotatus*)
scrub jay (*Aphelócoma coeruléscens*)	woodrat (*Neotoma fuscipes*)
mourning dove (*Zenáida macroúra*)	pocket gopher (*Thomomys bottae*)
quail (*Callipépla califórnica*)	ground squirrel (*Spermophilus beecheyi*)
roadrunner (*Geocóccyx californiánus*)	
crow (*Córvus brachyrhýnchos*)	vole (*Microtus californicus*)
raven (*Córvus córax*)	brush rabbit (*Sylvilagus bachmanii*)
red-tailed hawk (*Búteo jamaicénsis*)	
red-shouldered hawk (*Búteo lineátus*)	cottontail rabbit (*Sylvilagus audobonii*)
owl (*Búbo virginiánus*)	
turkey vulture (*Cathártes áura*)	jackrabbit (*Lepus californicus*)
finch (*Carpódacus mexicánus*)	raccoon (*Procyon lotor*)
skunk (*Mephitis mephitis*)	opossom (*Didelphis virginiana*)
bushtit (*Psaltríparus minumus*)	fox (*Urocyon cinereoargenteus*)
hummingbird (*Calýpte ánna*)	mountain lion (*Felis concolor*)
sparrow (*Pásser montánus*)	coyote (*Canis latrans*)
meadowlark (*Sturnélla mágna*)	bobcat (*Lynx rufus*)
	mule deer (*Odocoileus hemionus*)
Reptiles and Amphibians:	
rattlesnake (*Crotalus horridus*)	side-blotched lizard (*Uta stanburiana*)
gopher snake (*Pituophis melanoleucus*)	
king snake (*Lampropeltis getulus*)	horned lizard (*Phrynosoma douglassi*)
frogs (*Scaphiopus hammondi*)	whiptail lizard (*Cnemidophorus tigris*)
pond turtle (*Clemmys marmorata*)	
skink (*Eumeces skiltonianus*)	alligator lizard (*Gerrhonotus multicarinatus*)

According to early settlers, the wildlife also included the grizzly bear (*Ursus arctos*) and black bear (*Ursus americanus*), but these animals are no longer in the area. Older residents recall tales of wolves (*Canus lupus*) in the area. Due to over-culling, the population of wildlife is considerably less today than when the settlers entered the valley. It was important to the farmers and ranchers of the area to keep predatory animals at a minimum for the sake of profit, and they would often kill a predatory animal whether it was threatening or not. Many times, bounties were placed on the carcasses or hides of certain animals, including rabbits and quail, even though they are not considered predatory. Rabbits and quail cause considerable destruction to crops and were occasionally 'rounded up' by the thousands. There are many accounts of these activities throughout the years in the newspaper files.

The story of how Valley Center got its name of 'Bear Valley' originated with one of the last grizzly bears found in the county.[30] The family of moved to the area and settled on government land after the Civil War. They built a cabin made of oak posts and willow poles. The sides of the cabin were made of tules woven together and topped with a thatched roof of tules. Mr. Lovett sold wood from his homestead in San Diego and would occasionally make trips into town which took several days. The story as told by one of residents living on the original homestead follows:[31]

> The father was on one of his wood hauling trips to San Diego; the mother was washing in front of the cabin close to the brook; the two children were playing in the manger built along side of the cabin. A third child had been born by now and was in a basket beside the mother when she heard a noise and saw an immense bear charging down upon her from the hill side. She grabbed the baby in the basket and climbed up a ladder to a loft above the one room of the cabin. The other two children crouched down in the manger and the bear did not see them. The mother fired off her husband's Army musket and scared the bear away. He went up the canyon about two hundred yards away and caught and killed one of their yearling calves, under the leaning oak tree which you can see in the picture on our Bear Valley Peach label. After eating what he wanted, he wandered away and the mother came down from the loft and went up the canyon, where a Indian named Florencio was cutting wood and asked him if he would climb the tree and kill the bear when he came back to finish his meal.

> The Indian had no gun, so she loaned him her husband's Army musket. They loaded it with everything they could find and sure enough the bear did come back and the Indian shot him, but did not kill him at once. The bear tried to get the Indian out of the tree, but as a grizzly bear cannot climb, he did not succeed. After he found he could not get him, he wandered away and the Indian came down and went further up the canyon and got two white men who had guns to go with him to finish the bear. They tracked him to another canyon, where they found him desperately wounded and finished him.

> About this time the father returned from his San Diego trip. He took his team and dragged the bear down to where it could be loaded into the wagon and they drove over to Col. Maxcy's, about eight miles away, where the bear was weighed on his cattle scales. It

weighed about 2200 pounds and was said to be the largest grizzly bear ever killed in California, or for that matter, any other place.

The bear was a great cattle killer and various cattlemen, including Col. Maxey [sic], who had a large ranch of several thousand acres and hundreds of cattle, had offered rewards aggregating about three hundred dollars for his destruction. The only one who ever paid, however, was Col. Macey [sic] who paid the Indian fifty dollars in gold.

The geology of the area as described in the United States Department of Agriculture Soil Survey[32] includes gentle to steep slopes (2-75% incline) at elevations of 200 to 3,500 feet with granitics, gabbro, tonalite, metavolcanics, and metasedimentary rocks. Rock outcrops or boulders cover approximately 10 percent of the land surface. The soils consist mainly of moderately to well-drained, sandy, or silty loams suitable for growing citrus and avocados, flowers, or field crops such as grains. Natural vegetation within the valley environment consists of several species of oak, sycamore, and willow trees in the riparian areas as well as along the valley floor. Chaparral with grasses and shrubs on the open areas provide natural habitation for many small animals. Rainfall averages fall between 12 to 20 inches. The annual mean air temperature is 59° to 64° F. The valley provides a frost-free season of 240-340 days, allowing a long growing season for agricultural purposes.[33]

PREHISTORIC OR PRE-CONTACT PERIOD

The historic period of Valley Center cannot be told without first discussing the prehistoric period. San Diego County's prehistoric, or pre-European contact, Native American occupation includes two distinct major cultural time frames: Early and Late periods.[34] The Early, or Archaic Period, generally falls within the dates of 9,000 to 1,300 years ago. The Late Prehistoric Period extends from 1,300 years ago to the time of European contact. The Historic Period extends from European contact (A.D. 1769) to the present.[35]

Early twentieth-century anthropologists believed the Early Period inhabitants of San Diego County were big game hunters. This theory is based on archaeological remains. Those indigenous people are now better described as a hunting and gathering society who depended on the availability of natural resources. They appear to have had a relatively diverse and non-specialized economy and moved from coastal to inland areas.[36] The artifacts associated with the early inhabitants generally include crudely-shaped metavolcanic tools which originally gave researchers the big game hunting hypothesis. Radiocarbon dates from these early sites have been reported as early as 9,030±350 years BP (Before Present).[37]

The Native American inhabitants living in the area of Valley Center are known as the *Luiseño*.[38] They were given that name by the Spanish because they lived near the Mission San Luis Rey and its outpost, the mission at Pala.[39] Their name for themselves simply meant 'people', as many Native American tribes or bands name themselves. Originally called the *San Luiseños*, it has been shortened to Luiseños and adopted by the band as their designation.[40] As illustrated on Figure 3, the cultural territory of the Luiseño extended along the coast from north of San Juan Capistrano to the mouth of Agua Hedionda Lagoon, then inland through what we now call San Marcos, and Escondido, east through Rancho Guejito into the Cahuilla Valley, north through Temecula, and from there west to the ocean near San Juan Capistrano.[41] The Luiseño are considered the most southwesterly tribe of the Shoshonean linguistic family in the United States. They are believed to have migrated into this area from the east.[42]

Many early ethnographers and anthropologists studied the descendants of the local prehistoric people, but the first to do so was Philip Stedman Sparkman. He was an anthropologist who operated a general store located at the intersection of present-day State Route 76 and Rincon Road, living near the Luiseño in the late 1800s and early 1900s. He studied the culture and language of these local people for more than twenty years and published several scholastic articles before his death. He was shot and killed at his home in Rincon on May 19, 1907.[43] Though many blamed a local Native American for the brutal murder, the killer was never caught. The accounts of the murder described in the local newspapers, *The Escondido Times* and *The Advocate*,[44] were based on interviews of Sparkman's neighbors. They described him as a quiet, peaceable man and insisted that the murderer could not have been a Native American. He was a friend to them and always treated them fairly at his store and, therefore, would not have been so brutally murdered.[45]

Several Luiseño plant and place names appeared in Mr. Sparkman's last manuscript, The Culture of the Luiseño Indians, published posthumously in 1908.[46] Some of those Luiseño place names included on Table 2 are also shown on Figure 3, A.L. Kroeber's map. Kroeber continued the study of the Luiseño begun by Sparkman and published numerous articles and books on the subject until his own death in 1960.[47]

The Valley Center area attracted the native inhabitants for thousands of years as it provided a year-round supply of food and areas for food preparation. Evidence of acorn-grinding mortar holes and grain-processing 'slicks' can still be seen on many of the large granitic boulders in the area. Many of these milling sites are recorded in the national data base at the South Coastal Information Center (SCIC) at San Diego State University (SDSU).

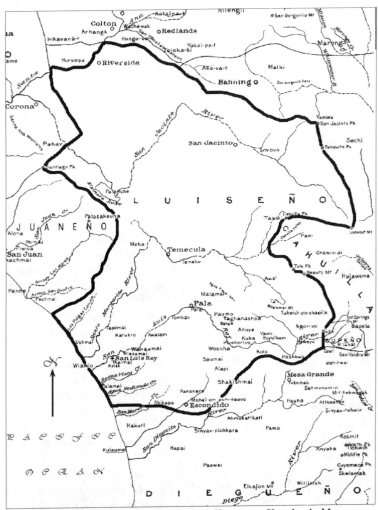

*Figure 3. Luiseño Cultural Area Shown on Kroeber's Map
(Plate 57, 1925).*

The SCIC and the San Diego Museum of Man provided a records search of the archaeological sites within the study area. This search revealed more than 200 recorded sites as a result of more than 40 archaeological studies. These studies include: Advance Planning & Research Associates 1978, 1979,[48] American Pacific Environmental Consultants, Inc. 1979,[49] Brown 1993,[50] Bull 1977,[51] Carrico 1975, 1976, 1978,[52] Chace 1979, 1979, 1984, 1988,[53] Chace and Collins 1986, 1987,[54] Chace and Hightower 1979,[55] Fink 1973, 1974,[56] Foster

Table 2. Luiseño Place Names[57]

Paauw	Palomar Mountain
Wikyo	highest peak on Palomar Mountain
Takwish poshapila	rocky peak east of *Wikyo*
Yamiwa	San Jacinto Mountain
Pepipwi	San Bernardino Mountain
Kolo	mountain nearly opposite where Escondido creek meets the San Luis Rey River
Kuka	old Potrero village site
Kupa	Agua Caliente
Temeko	Temecula
Pichaang	Pechanga
Keish	San Luis Rey
Alapi	San Pascual [sic]
Saumai	site of J.Q. Adams' store at Valley Center
Woshha	Rincon
Pala	Pala
Awa'	Aguanga
Ahuya	old village site above Rincon on road to Potrero
Tokamai	old village site on Palomar

Table 3. Luiseño Plant Names[58]

Kwila	Black Oak: favorite for acorns
Tovashal	White or Engelmann Oak: acorns not preferred; chewing gum from insect deposit
Wiashal	Live Oak: acorns for food
Avahut	Cottonwood: inner bark used for apron-like garment
Shakapish	Mushroom from cottonwood and willow trees
Pevesash	Bulrush, tule: young shoots eaten raw
Shoila	Juncus: used for baskets and mats
Panal	Yucca: head used for food, flowers boiled & eaten
Tokapish	Wild Hyacinth: bulb is eaten
Kahawut	Soap plant: root used for soap, seeds for food
Ataushanut	California poppy: leaves used for greens, flowers chewed with gum
Ela	Mesquite: beans ground into meal & used for food
Shoval	Sumac: berries ground for food, bark used for baskets, seed-fan for beating seeds off plants

1989,[59] Fulmer 1977, 1977,[60] Gallegos and Carrico 1985,[61] Gallegos et al. 1987,[62] Gallegos et al. 1992,[63] Hanna 1977,[64] Hanna and Bull 1978,[65] Hector 1988,[66] Heuett 1980,[67] Kyle and Gallegos 1992,[68] Kyle et al. 1996,[69] Laylander and Chace 1980,[70] Mooney 1993,[71] Napton and Greathouse 1984,[72] Peak and Associates, Inc. 1980,[73] Pettus and Fulmer

1978,[74] Rector et al. 1984,[75] Robbins-Wade and Whitehouse 1992,[76] Smith 1989,[77] Sutton 1978,[78] TMI 1988,[79] True et al. 1974,[80] Wade et al. 1990,[81] and Van Horn 1978.[82]

Many of the recorded sites are simple milling stations on granitic boulders scattered along the drainages throughout the valley. This patterning is somewhat predictable given that the drainages contain water, boulders for milling acorns, and a high population of oak trees and acorns. Chace grouped several clusters of sites together in his 1986[83] and 1987[84] reports in which he postulated the existence of prehistoric villages in these locations. Not surprisingly, these locations also fall within drainages. Sparkman noted several local Luiseño village site names and gathering places as well as the Luiseño name for some of the early settler's houses in his last publication, dated 1908. These locations also appear on Kroeber's map (see Table 2; Figure 3).[85]

Another dictionary of Luiseño grammar was published in 1926 in Italy.[86] Pablo Tac, a young Luiseño boy, was taken from the San Luis Rey Mission in 1832 by Father Antonio Peyri to study for the priesthood in Rome. While studying at the College of Propaganda Fidé, Pablo Tac compiled a grammar of his native language of Luiseño to the end of the letter 'C'. He died in 1841 at the age of 19 before completing his work. After his death his work was mistakenly credited to 'Padre Jac' misread from his signature of 'P. Tac'.[87]

Many of the descendants of the Luiseño now live on federal reservations which were set up by Executive Orders dated 1875 and 1881 within Township 10 South, Ranges 1 West and 1 East. These include Pala, Rincon, Pauma, and La Jolla reservations.[88]

HISTORIC OR POST-CONTACT PERIOD

The lure of land in California had begun as early as the 1500s with European interest in the New World. Several explorers were sent to the western coast of North America to claim land under the name of the Spanish Crown. Old World tensions had escalated as a result of religious and political ideals to the point of almost continuous wars and bloodshed for millennia.[89] The need for expansion was paramount and the New World provided the necessary space. The competition had begun between several countries to dominate the land and send their citizens to colonize this seemingly vast wasteland. Unfortunately for the native inhabitants of the land, this meant the loss of not only their ancestral lands, but their cultural foundations and the acceptance of the new landholders cultures, often to the point of annihilation. An Indian Federation was set up after the turn of the century as a means of allowing some of the control of the Indians to be in their own hands. A story told by Adam Costillo,[90] the President of the La Jolla Reservation, on February 7, 1932, states:

> In the beginning our people were not well organized into tribes, but peacefully occupied all the area that is now Southern California. They were not able to offer any resistance to the occupancy of this land by the Padres. Because of this, soon after the Padres came, all of the Indians were virtually slaves. They were taught to leave their original mode of life by hunting and fishing, and to work in the fields and vineyards. They were taught to build houses, and cultivate the soil after the white man's fashion. They could not of course do this as well as the white man, for they were Indians, and it was as difficult for them to learn the white man's way, as it would have been for the white man to adopt the mode of life of the Indian.

The colonization of California began in San Diego in 1769 with the establishment of the Mission San Diego de Alcalá in what is now known as Mission Valley. Father Junípero Serra was assigned to establish missions at a distance of one-day's journey apart along the length of California. From these establishments, the priests and Franciscans could 'civilize' the native population while building the foundations of Spanish culture with free labor. Fritz Gutheim, a member of the Brookings Institute in Washington, D.C., submitted his report in the Bureau of Indian Affairs Fact-Finding Study of 1932:[91]

> Historical considerations which have determined the present conditions of these Indians demand that more weight be given to the fact that they are recently freed slaves than that they are recently 'civilized' Indians. The reign of the padres unquestionably left a marked impression for both good and evil on the people. It prepared them certainly for a place in that society. While they were slaves the Indians worked and learned: they were the laborers of Spanish colonial civilization: they irrigated the fields and cultivated the farms: they herded cattle and sheep: they built the missions: the curved tiles of ancient irrigation systems and of historic buildings were shaped on the bronzed thighs of peon women. Indians became skilled workers: carpenters, masons, wheelrights, blacksmiths, carters: they supplied the varied and mental services of a provincial society. But they learned to work only so long as there was an overseer. The net result of this experience was that the Indians ceased to be Indians; they became workers - but they were also slaves.

The natives were grouped around the missions in order to instruct them in the European ways of agriculture and industry as well as a means of control by the Padres and Franciscans. As a result of this new form of subsistence, livestock husbandry became an integral part of the culture and wealth of this New World.

The population of the Native Americans decreased steadily after contact with the Europeans, in part due to childhood illnesses introduced such as measles and mumps. Kroeber listed the population of the ancient Luiseño as between 3,000 to 4,000. By 1856, their number was down to more than 2,500; by 1870, it had decreased by almost half to 1,300; by 1885, only 1,150 people were counted according to the Indian Office; and by 1925, less than 500 were accounted for on the Federal Census.[92]

After 1841 when the Mexican government allowed land grant applications to foreigners, many wagon trains, as well as individual travelers, followed the trails to California.[93] The influx of settlers in California caused many boundary disputes. The American ideal of 'manifest destiny' increased these disputes until war finally erupted between the United States and Mexico.[94] The last battle fought occurred east of Escondido and south of Valley Center in San Pasqual Valley on December 6, 1846. General Stephen Watts Kearny and his troops traveled from Fort Yuma and encountered the *Californios* who were the descendants of the original Spanish colonists.

Felicita La Chappa, the daughter of the last hereditary chief of the San Pasqual Indians, recalled that fateful day as told to Elizabeth Judson Roberts:[95]

> Mexican soldiers riding beautiful horses came through our valley quite often and at last a company came and camped in our village. They took some of our huts as we crowded into those that were left for it was winter time. Early one rainy morning we saw soldiers that were not Mexicans come riding down the mountain side. They looked like ghosts coming through the mist and then the fighting began.
>
> The Indians fled in fear to the mountains on the north side of the valley from where they looked down and watched the battle. All day long they fought. We saw some Americans killed and knew they were in a bad way.
>
> That afternoon Pontho, my father, called his men together and asked them if they wished to help the Americanos in their trouble. The men said they did. When darkness was near Pontho sent a messenger to the Mexican chief telling him to trouble the Americans no more that night else the Indians would help the Americans. And the Mexican chief heeded the message and the Americans were left to bury their dead and to rest because of my father's message. The Americanos do not know of this but my people know of it.

The war in California ended with the signing of the Capitulation of Cahuenga on January 13, 1847, and the Treaty of Guadalupe Hidalgo, signed on February 2, 1848. These treaties ended the Mexican Era of control in the United States and started the rush for land in the western portion of the country.[96]

Many people arrived in California after the discovery of gold by James Marshall on January 24, 1848, at Sutter's Mill located in Coloma.[97] The Gold Rush of 1849 lured thousands of people in search of riches only to find thousands of people already here with the same objective. The population of California skyrocketed from more than 14,000 in 1848 to almost 100,000 by the end of 1849, excluding the Native American population.[98] The admission of California into the Union in 1850 and the available government land enticed many gold seekers to stop prospecting and begin farming with their families instead.

The journey to California was a difficult one at best. The settlers of Valley Center came from around the world after the Gold Rush and Civil War using various methods of travel which usually took months. Some immigrated from foreign lands and others emigrated from other portions of the United States. They traveled by foot, horseback, or ox-drawn wagons as single units or as part of a larger group in wagon trains, often encountering hostile Native American Indians, natural disasters, or illnesses. Many settlers sailed around Cape Horn, often in very treacherous seas. The settlers had various customs and faiths. Many were searching for a better environment in which to raise their families on land of their own and to enjoy life.

The newly formed southwestern portion of the United States provided just that for many. Resources such as water and wildlife were generally plentiful and easily attained. The weather was mild with little snow or cold temperatures, and the land was vast. By taking advantage of the government claims, a person could own enough land that they literally could not see their next-door neighbor, if they chose. Of course, this type of lifestyle caused extreme difficulties and hardships. Oftentimes, people did not survive or were forced to move back into 'civilization'. All who settled the land, even for a short time, left visible traces of their lives and it is those persons who became the backbone of this small agricultural community.

NOTES

[1] Kelly, John Lincoln. *Life on a San Diego County Ranch.* Unpublished, 1925.

[2] Davis, Abel. *Valley Center, California,* unpublished memoir, circa 1955.

[3] James, Clyde. *The Unpublished Memoirs of Clyde James,* circa 1970.

[4] Hirsch, Jill Louise. *Recreational Land Use Planning for Valley Center Parcel #1, San Diego, California.* Unpublished Master's thesis, Department of Geology, San Diego State University, San Diego, California, 1988.

[5] Peet, Mary Rockwood. *San Pasqual - A Crack in the Hills.* The Highland Press, Culver City, California, 1949.

[6] Hudson, Tom. *Three Paths along a River - The Heritage of the Valley of the San Luis Rey.* Desert-Southwest Publishers, Palm Desert, California, 1964.

[7] Wood, Catherine M. *Palomar: From Tepee to Telescope,* Frye and Smith, San Diego, California, 1937.

[8] McGrew, Alan B. *Hidden Valley Heritage: Escondido's First 100 Years.* Blue-Ribbon Centennial History Committee, Escondido, California, 1988.

[9] *International Genealogical Index©,* Church of the Latter-Day Saints, 1980, 1994.

[10] *Family Tree Maker©,* Blue Banner Division, Brøderbund Software, Inc., Fremont, California, 1995.

[11] Pourade, Richard F. *The History of San Diego, The Silver Dons,* Volume 3. Union Tribune Publishing Company, San Diego, California, 1963:64-73. Spanish land grants were given to soldiers of the Mexican Army as a reward or payment for their duty in the military. Other grants were given to persons who provided: proof of Mexican citizenship, a map of the area desired including land marks, would promise to construct a residence to occupy and include grazing stock on the land.

[12] Engstrand, Iris H.W. *Document Sets for California and the West in U.S. History.* D.C. Heath and Company, Lexington, Massachusetts, 1993:51-52.

[13] Pourade, *The History of San Diego, The Silver Dons.* 1963:66. *Pauma Rancho,* situated along the San Luis Rey River southeast of the Pala Mission, was granted to José Antonio Serrano in 1844 and consisted of more than 13,300 acres.

[14] *Ibid. Rancho Cuca or El Potrero,* located south of Palomar Mountain, was claimed by María Juana de los Angeles in 1845 and consisted of 2,174 acres.

[15] *Ibid.:* 67. *Rancho Guejito y Cañada de Palomía,* situated northeast of the town of Escondido and consisting of more than 13,200 acres, was granted to José María Orozco in 1845.

[16] *Ibid.:* 64-65. Juan Bautista Alvarado held *El Rincón del Diablo Rancho* which consisted of more than 12,600 acres adjoining *San Bernardo* on the north which is presently the site of the town of Escondido.

[17] *Ibid.:* 64. *Rancho San Bernardo* was claimed in 1842 by María Antonio Alvarado Snook, the daughter of Juan Bautista Alvarado and wife of Captain Joseph Snook who together held more than 17,700 acres which stretched from north of Lake Hodges south to Peñasquitos Creek along present-day Interstate 15.

[18] *Ibid.:* 66. *Los Vallecitos de San Marcos*, consisting of 8,877 acres west of *El Rincón del Diablo Rancho*, was originally granted to José María Alvarado in 1840. It later became the property of Lorenzo Soto and is now the town of San Marcos.

[19] *Ibid.* A Native American named Felipe was granted *Buena Vista Rancho* in 1845 and included 1,184 acres which is now the site of the town of Vista.

[20] *Ibid. Guajome Rancho* was granted to two Native Americans, Andrés and José Manuel from the San Luis Rey Mission in 1845. It was located east of the mission between the present towns of Vista and Bonsall and consisted of 2,219 acres. The rancho became the property of an American merchant from Los Angeles, Abel Stearns, who had married a daughter of Juan Bandini.

[21] *Ibid.:* 73. *Monserrate Rancho*, consisting of 13,322 acres and located south and east of Fallbrook, was granted to Ysidro María Alvarado.

[22] Robinson, W.W. *Land in California.* University of California Press, Berkeley, 1948:168.

[23] *Ibid.:* 167.

[24] *Ibid.*

[25] *Ibid.:* 170.

[26] *Ibid.:* 14, 20-22. Treaties such as the Act of September 30, 1850, were to effect a just settlement with the California Indians. Under these treaties which the U.S. government never honored, the Indians were to relinquish their ancestral land but maintain the right to use and occupy certain areas. New land was purchased for the establishment of reservations and the native people were moved onto those new lands, oftentimes forcibly. They were promised clothing, supplies, tools, livestock, as well as the service of agents, teachers, and carpenters. This opened additional prime land for the infiltrating emigrants to 'settle'.

[27] Robbins, Chandler S., Bertel Bruun, and Herbert S. Zim. *Birds of North America, A Guide to Field Identification*, Golden Press, New York, Western Publishing Company, Inc., Racine, Wisconsin, 1983.

[28] Jameson, E.W., Jr., and Hans J. Peeters. *California Mammals, A California Natural History Guide*, University of California Press, Berkeley, California, 1988.

[29] Stebbins, Robert C. *California Amphibians and Reptiles, California Natural History Guide: 31.* University of California Press, Berkeley, California, 1972.

[30] Friends of the Valley Center Library. *Once Upon a Time in Valley Center.* Unpublished booklet, 1992: 7-8.

[31] Haskell, Edward Prince. Unpublished account written in 1984, located in the San Diego County Library, Valley Center Branch, Local History files.

[32] United States Department of Agriculture, Soil Conservation Service and Forest Service. *Soil Survey*, San Diego Area, California, 1971:9-14.

[33] *Ibid.*

[34] Gallegos, Dennis R. A Review and Synthesis of Environmental and Cultural Material for the Batiquitos Lagoon Region. In *San Dieguito-La Jolla: Chronology and Controversy.* San Diego Archaeological Society, San Diego, California, 1987:*23-34.*

[35] *Ibid.*

[36] *Ibid.*

[37] Warren, Claude N. Cultural Tradition and Ecological Adaptation on the Southern California Coast. In Archaic Prehistory in the Western United States, C. Irwin-Williams, ed., *Eastern New Mexico University Contributions in Anthropology*, 1(3), 1968:1-14; James R. Moriarty, III. Cultural Phase Divisions Suggested by Typological Change, Coordinated with Stratigraphically Controlled Radiocarbon Dating at San Diego. *Anthropological Journal of Canada*, 7(3), 1966:1-18.

[38] Sparkman, Philip Stedman. The Culture of the Luiseño Indians. *University of California Publications in American Archaeology and Ethnology* 8(4). Berkeley, California, 1908:187-234.

[39] *Ibid.* In the Luiseño language, *paala* means 'water'. This word is also found in *An Introduction to the Luiseño Language*, by Villiana Hyde, Malki Museum Press, Morongo Indian Reservation, Banning, California, 1971:226, 236. The Pala Valley was named *Valle de Pala,* a combination of Spanish and Luiseño, by Father Peyri in the early 1800s: Hudson, Tom, *Three Paths along a River*, 1964:213. William Duncan Strong states that the old site from which the mission Pala got it name was a spring located on the hill about two miles northeast of present-day Pala. William Duncan Strong, Aboriginal Society in Southern California. In *University of California Publications in American Archaeology and Ethnology*, Vol. 26, ed. By A.L. Kroeber and R.H. Lowie, 1929. Reprinted by Kraus Reprint Company, Millwood, New York, 1976:284.

[40] Sparkman, The Culture of the Luiseño Indians, 1908.

[41] *Ibid.*

[42] Kroeber, A.L. *Handbook of the Indians of California.* Dover Publications, Inc., New York, 1976: 648-88.

[43] *The Escondido Times*, May 24, 1907:7; *The Advocate*, May 24, 1907, p. 1. Sparkman was reported as being an Englishman approximately 50 years old with no relatives in the United States. The local authorities believed that his death involved robbery. It was common knowledge that Sparkman had been selling large quantities of wheat recently and had made a deposit of $1,500 about six weeks prior to the murder. Whether Sparkman had surprised someone upon entering his house or the person had been invited into the store, was never determined. The facts state that a book was open on a table and the lights were still burning on the morning following the murder. Sparkman's body was found outside the store with two bullet wounds, his throat cut, and his pockets rifled. There was evidence of a struggle and blood inside the store, suggesting that Sparkman was first shot inside the building and was shot a second time upon his attempted escape. His throat was slashed after being shot and was the immediate cause of death.

[44] *Ibid.*

[45] *Ibid.*

[46] Sparkman, The Culture of the Luiseño Indians, 1908.

[47] Hudson, *Three Paths along a River*:41, 1964.

[48] Advance Planning & Research Associates. Metzner Lot Split TPM 13592, Log #77-8-228 and Vuksic Lot Split TPM 13618, Log #77-8-232. Unpublished report on file at the South Coastal Information Center (SCIC), San Diego State University (SDSU), San Diego, California, 1978.

Ibid. Schulleri Lot Split Archaeological and Biological Survey TPM 15202, EAD Log #78-8-277, Valley Center, California. Unpublished report on file at SCIC, SDSU, San Diego, California, 1979.

[49] American Pacific Environmental Consultants, Inc. Archaeological Investigation on Choumas Lot Split Valley Center, California. Unpublished report on file at SCIC, SDSU, San Diego, California, 1979.

[50] Brown, Joan. Archaeological Testing and Significance Assessment of Three Prehistoric Sites Located in Valley Center, San Diego County, California. Unpublished report on file at SCIC, SDSU, San Diego, California, 1993.

[51] Bull, Charles S. An Archaeological Surface Reconnaissance of the Stone Property. Unpublished report on file at SCIC, SDSU, San Diego, California, 1977.

[52] Carrico, Richard. Archaeological Survey of the Proposed Valley Center Commercial Development. Unpublished report on file at SCIC, SDSU, San Diego, California, 1975.

Ibid. Archaeological Survey of the Daley Ranch North of Escondido, San Diego County. Unpublished report on file at SCIC, SDSU, San Diego, California, 1976.

Ibid. Phase I Archaeological Investigation at Rancho Viejo, Escondido, California. Unpublished report on file at SCIC, SDSU, San Diego, California, 1978.

[53] Chace, Paul G. An Archaeological Survey of the Leads Property, Near Valley Center, County of San Diego. Unpublished report on file at SCIC, SDSU, San Diego, California, 1979.

Ibid. The Archaeology of the Sulsberger Property, Valley Center. Unpublished report on file at SCIC, SDSU, San Diego, California, 1979.

Ibid. A Cultural Resources Survey for the Central Valley Center Sewer SWCB Project No. C-06-1567. Unpublished report on file at SCIC, SDSU, San Diego, California, 1984.

Ibid. Archaeological Survey of T.P.M. 19072, County of San Diego. Unpublished report on file at SCIC, SDSU, San Diego, California, 1988.

[54] Chace, Paul G., and Donna Collins. Addendum, A Cultural Resources Survey for the Central Valley Center Sewer. Unpublished report on file at SCIC, SDSU, San Diego, California, 1986.

Ibid. 1987 Addendum, A Cultural Resources Survey for the Central Valley Center Sewer. Unpublished report on file at SCIC, SDSU, San Diego, California, 1987.

[55] Chace, Paul G., and Janet Hightower. An Archaeological Survey of the Atwood Property Near Valley Center, California. Unpublished report on file at SCIC, SDSU, San Diego, California, 1979.

[56] Fink, Gary R. Archaeological Reconnaissance of Couser Canyon Road. Unpublished report on file at SCIC, SDSU, San Diego, California, 1973.

Ibid. Archaeological Survey for the Proposed Realignment of Valley Center Road, Valley Center, California. Unpublished report on file at SCIC, SDSU, San Diego, California, 1974.

[57] Sparkman, The Culture of the Luiseño Indians. 1908.

[58] *Ibid.*

[59] Foster, Daniel. Valley Center Forest Fire Station, San Diego County Sewer System Improvements. Unpublished report on file at SCIC, SDSU, San Diego, California, 1989.

[60] Fulmer, Scott. Archaeological Reconnaissance of the Bond, Campbell, King, and Sharp Lot Splits in Valley Center, California. Unpublished report on file at SCIC, SDSU, San Diego, California, 1977.

Ibid. DEBS Proposed Lot Split TRM 13719 Log #77-8-272 Valley Center, California. Unpublished report on file at SCIC, SDSU, San Diego, California, 1977.

[61] Gallegos, Dennis R., and Richard Carrico. Cultural Resource Survey of Woody Orchards. Unpublished report on file at SCIC, SDSU, San Diego, California, 1985.

[62] Gallegos, Dennis R., Carolyn Kyle, and Richard Carrico. Test and Evaluation Program for Archaeological Site SDI-7209, Valley Center, California. Unpublished report on file at SCIC, SDSU, San Diego, California, 1987.

[63] Gallegos, Dennis R., Ivan Strudwick, and Roxana Phillips. Historical/Archaeological Test Report for Daley Ranch, Escondido, California. Unpublished report on file at SCIC, SDSU, San Diego, California, 1992.

[64] Hanna, David, Jr., An Archaeological Reconnaissance Near Valley Center San Diego County, California. Unpublished report on file at SCIC, SDSU, San Diego, California, 1977.

[65] Hanna, David, Jr., and Charles Bull. Archaeological Survey Report of the Haviland Parcel. Unpublished report on file at SCIC, SDSU, San Diego, California, 1978.

[66] Hector, Susan. Revised Cultural Resources Survey of 54-inch Raw Water Pipeline Alignment. Unpublished report on file at SCIC, SDSU, San Diego, California, 1988.

[67] Heuett, Mary Lou. Archaeological Reconnaissance and Significance Test for the Thomas Lot Split, Valley Center, San Diego County, California. Unpublished report on file at SCIC, SDSU, San Diego, California, 1980.

[68] Kyle, Carolyn and Dennis R Gallegos. Historical/Archaeological Survey Report for the Proposed Valley Center Sewage and Water Reclamation Facilities - Valley Center, California. Unpublished report on file at SCIC, SDSU, San Diego, California, 1992.

[69] Kyle, Carolyn E., Roxana L. Phillips, and Dennis R. Gallegos. Cultural Resource Evaluation of Four Sites For The Valley Center Road Widening Project, County of San Diego, California. Unpublished report on file at SCIC, SDSU, San Diego, California, 1996.

[70] Laylander, Don, and Paul G. Chace. An Archaeological Assessment of the Kapernick Property Near Valley Center, County of San Diego. Unpublished report on file at SCIC, SDSU, San Diego, California, 1980.

[71] Mooney, Brian F. Draft EIR for the Valley Center Country Estates (TM5039RPL). Unpublished report on file at SCIC, SDSU, San Diego, California, 1993.

[72] Napton, L. Kyle, and E.A. Greathouse. Cultural Resource Investigations, San Pasqual Indian Reservation, California. Unpublished report on file at SCIC, SDSU, San Diego, California, 1984.

[73] Peak and Associates, Inc. Cultural Resources Assessment of AT&T's Proposed San Bernardino to San Diego Fiber Optic Cable, San Bernardino, Riverside and San Diego Counties, California. Unpublished report on file at SCIC, SDSU, San Diego, California, 1990.

[74] Pettus, Roy E., and Scott Fulmer. Archaeological Testing and Data Recovery at SDI-752: Mitigation of Adverse Impacts from the Proposed Metzner Lot Split TPM 13592. Unpublished report on file at SCIC, SDSU, San Diego, California, 1978.

[75] Rector, Carol H., Pat Welch, and Judyth E. Reed. Cultural Resources Inventory for the 1984 and Part of 1985 California Metropolitan Project Area Public Lands Sale Program. Unpublished report on file at SCIC, SDSU, San Diego, California, 1984.

[76] Robbins-Wade, Mary, and John L. Whitehouse. Cultural Resources Survey for the Valley Center (South Segment) Reconstruction (Activity No. 3C1007) Valley Center, San Diego County, California. Unpublished report on file at SCIC, SDSU, San Diego, California, 1992.

[77] Smith, Brian F. An Archaeological Survey and A Cultural Resource Evaluation at the Duncan/Crews Development Subdivision Project. Unpublished report on file at SCIC, SDSU, San Diego, California, 1989.

[78] Sutton, Mark Q. An Archeological Survey of the Talbert Property Near Valley Center, County of San Diego T.P.M. #14991. Unpublished report on file at SCIC, SDSU, San Diego, California, 1978.

[79] TMI Environmental Services. Phase II Test and Evaluation Program for Archaeological Site SDI-7209. Unpublished report on file at SCIC, SDSU, San Diego, California, 1988.

[80] True, D.L, C.W. Meighan, and Harvey Crew. Archaeological Investigations at Molpa, San Diego County, California. Unpublished report on file at SCIC, SDSU, San Diego, California, 1974.

[81] Wade, Sue A., Stephen R. Van Wormer, and Dayle M. Cheever. *An Archaeological Testing Program for Twelve Sites Within Woods Valley Ranch Project Area, Valley Center, California.* Unpublished report on file at SCIC, SDSU, San Diego, California, 1990.

[82] Van Horn, David M. Archaeological Survey Petlewski Lot Split, Valley Center. Unpublished report on file at SCIC, SDSU, San Diego, California, 1978.

[83] Chace, Paul G., and Donna Collins. Addendum, A Cultural Resources Survey for the Central Valley Center Sewer. Unpublished report on file at SCIC, SDSU, San Diego, California, 1986: 18-20.

[84] Chace, Paul G., and Donna Collins. 1987 Addendum, A Cultural Resources Survey for the Central Valley Center Sewer: 7. Unpublished report on file at SCIC, SDSU, San Diego, California, 1987.

[85] Sparkman, The Culture of the Luiseño Indians. 1908.

[86] Hudson, *Three Paths along a River,* 1964: 40-41. Tac's work was originally published in *L'Archiginnasio, Bulletino della Biblioteca, Communale di Bologna*, Italy, 1926. A dictionary translated from Luiseño into Spanish also appeared in *Proceedings of the International Congress of Americanists,* 1930.

[87] *Ibid.*

[88] United States Geological Survey (USGS) Plat Maps: Township 10 South, Range 1 West, San Bernardino Meridian (SBM), 1886. Notes on this plat map

state: "By Executive Order dated March 2nd, 1881, Sections 26 and 35 of this township were withdrawn from sale and set apart as a reservation for the permanent use and occupancy of the Mission Indians of California provided that this withdrawl shall not affect any existing valid adverse rights of any party." Township 10 South, Range 1 East, SBM, 1886, notes state: "1st By Executive Order dated December 27th, 1975, Sections 10, 23, 25, 26, 30, 31, 32, 33, 34, 35, 36 and fractional Sections 17, 18, 19, 20, 21, 22, 27, 28 and 29 of this Township were withdrawn from sale and set apart as the Potrero Reservation including Rincon, Gapich and La Joya for the permanent use and occupancy of the Mission Indians in Lower California. 2nd By Executive Order of May 3rd, 1877, Sections 16 and 36 of this Township were restored to the public domain."

[89] Ringrose, David. Introduction, From Lope de Vega to San Diego, The Backgrounds of Spanish Colonization in the Californias. *The Journal of San Diego History*, 24(1):1-4, San Diego Historical Society, San Diego, California, Winter 1978.

[90] Bureau of Indian Affairs. *Fact Finding Study of Social and Economic Conditions of Indians of San Diego County, California and Reports from Specialists in Allied Fields*, 1932: 52.

[91] Gutheim, Fritz, Brookings Institute, Washington, D.C. Report on Some Aspects of the Condition of the Mission Indians. In Bureau of Indian Affairs *Fact Finding Study of Social and Economic Conditions of Indians of San Diego County, California and Reports from Specialists in Allied Fields*, 1932: 88.

[92] Kroeber, *Handbook of the Indians of California*, 1976: 649.

[93] Engstrand, *Document Sets*, 1993:51-52.

[94] *Ibid.*

[95] Peet, *San Pasqual*, 1949: 88-92.

[96] *Ibid.*

[97] Engstrand, *Document Sets*, 1993:65-66.

[98] *Ibid.*

CHAPTER TWO

BEAR VALLEY 1860-1879

The settlers of Bear Valley who arrived during the years of 1860-1879 found little except a high valley situated in the back country of San Diego County. There were no towns within close proximity, and the trip into San Diego was an all-day affair by wagon, buggy, or horseback over very rough trails, for a road system had not been established.

Valley Center was not easy to find, for it was off the normal travel route from San Diego to San Bernardino and fairly difficult for a traveler to just 'stumble' upon.

Valley Center[1]

Do not laugh at Valley Center,
It sits just where God has meant her,
Like a tiny outflung star
On the road to Palomar.
Splendid neighbors, kindly folk,
They sit back and laugh and joke,
Do not fret and fume and stew
As their neighbors southward do.

When you enter Valley Center,
Do not laugh, it's where God meant her,
Planning, dreaming of the day,
When the world shall pass its way.
Journeying to Palomar,
Looking for a long-lost star,
Tiny, shining Valley Center,
Sleeping just where God has meant her.

Anonymous

A few Native American brush houses could be found in certain places in the valley, but for the most part, it was large, open space. Those first European settlers had the pick of the richest, most fertile locations with water easily available for crops and livestock. If Native Americans lived on the desired land, they were sometimes allowed to remain, at least for awhile, or forced to vacate.

The only businesses in the valley during the decades of 1860-79 were those trades the pioneers brought with them. There were blacksmiths, clergy, merchants, farmers, and ranchers. Most of the women who arrived in the valley were wives or daughters of the pioneering men. They tended their household duties, which included all cooking, cleaning, washing, sewing, and most importantly, caring for the children. There were no schools until after 1876, so any training the children received came from day-to-day living.

Families had little need for money. The goal was to provide sustenance for the family, and if anything was left over, it became profit. As a direct result of the Homestead Act of 1862, settlers who arrived in the valley with little in their pockets were able to build great fortunes for their descendants. Many of the early families originated from the same areas in the east, traveled across the plains of America as members of wagon trains and settled first in northern California before coming to San Diego County. Families intermarried, either prior to leaving their homelands or after arriving in California, thereby weaving the history of the valley.

Land included in the newly formed western United States was surveyed after 1850 by teams from the United States Geological Surveyor's (USGS) Office. Early maps of the area are not available at the San Diego County Surveyor's Office because they were incorporated into the subsequent surveys during the 1870s following the Civil War.[2] Though the maps show dates of surveys taking place in 1853 or 1854, these had been undertaken to establish the boundary lines of the townships and ranges, and not the specific land holdings of individuals. Confirmation of parcels claimed, therefore, by individuals could not be accurately determined until the surveys completed after 1875 divided the sections into 40-acre parcels in order to map the exact location of the land claimed by the settlers under the Homestead Act of 1862.

When the actual claim was made, the exact section, quarter-section, and quarter-quarter-section location was needed by the land office to determine the legitimacy of the homestead claim. Although many settlers had been living in Bear Valley in the 1860s, official documents were not compiled until after 1870. In order to ascertain the settlers' locations, it was necessary to combine the two decades for this discussion. Other types of documents such as census records, voter registration records, tax records, newspaper articles, and county directories were researched for references of early settlers.

Given that the history of Valley Center revolves around the pioneers who settled there, the families of those settlers were researched to provide a description of the chronological history.

Originally illustrated by Abel Davis,[3] a map of the location of the Valley Center pioneers who settled prior to 1900 is included as Figure 4. Although Adam's illustration is fairly accurate, a composite of contemporary USGS topographic maps[4] is included as Figure 5 to provide the exact locations of the early homestead claims. This figure illustrates the mapped location of the 31 pioneering families' land claims during the years 1860-79 discussed in this section.

The United States Census of 1860 was not divided into separate communities within San Diego County. It simply listed everyone as being in the San Diego Township. The houses and families were given consecutive numbers in the order visited by the enumerator. Individuals were listed under those dwellings and family numbers if this was their usual "...place of abode on the first day of June, 1860."[5] Each listing showed the individual's age, sex, color, profession, occupation, or trade of each person, male or female, whether the person was over 15 years of age, the value of their real or personal estate, place of birth, married or if the person attended school that year, persons over 20 years of age who could not read and write, whether the person was "...deaf and dumb, blind, insane, idiotic, pauper, or a convict."[6] No individuals known to have been in the Bear Valley area are listed in this census.

There are no San Diego county directories published for the decades 1860-79 to determine whether a family lived in the area; therefore, official records such as government survey maps, voter registration registers, or newspaper articles were used to determine regional occupancy during this period.

The 1870 United States Census[7] is divided into districts since no towns existed in the area at that time. Temecula, San Pascual Valley Reservation, San Pascual and Pala districts represented the northern portion of San Diego County. No known families who lived in the Valley Center study area are listed under either the Temecula or San Pascual Valley Reservation districts. Families known to have lived in the Valley Center area are listed within the San Pascual and Pala districts in 1870. These include:

John Q. Adams	James Davis	James Lovett
John T. Adams	Joseph Fleishman	Robert Price
John Antes	Nancy Hedden	Samuel Striclin [sic]
Robert Daily [sic]	Benejah Holcomb	

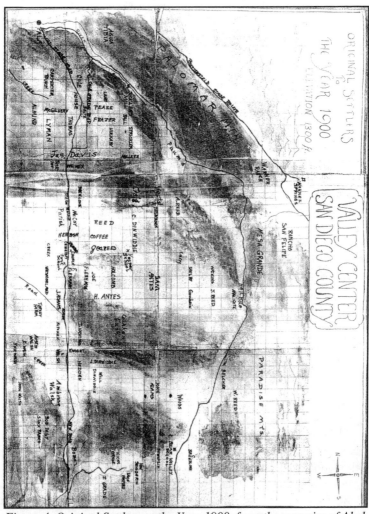

Figure 4. Original Settlers to the Year 1900, from the memoirs of Abel Davis, ca. 1955.

The census includes all persons of families who lived in the same place or abode on the first day June, 1870. Powy [sic], San Diego County, California, was the post office listed for San Pascual and Pala districts.

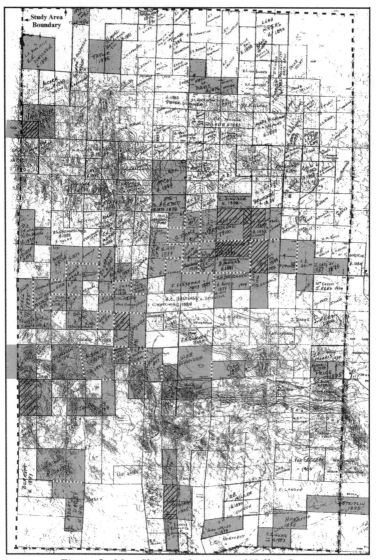

*Figure 5. Map Showing Location of Valley Center
Pioneers, 1860-79.*

<u>John T. Adams</u> is listed on the census sheet as a 53-year old, white male farm laborer, with $500 value real estate and $200 value personal estate, born in Ireland, with both parents of foreign birth.[8]

Listed in the same household is <u>John Q. Adams</u>, 21-year old born in New York, white male farm laborer, claiming no personal or real estate.[9]

John Thomas Adams became a naturalized citizen in New York in October 1848.[10] He is listed in San Diego County Great Register of Voters as being sworn in on August 24, 1871. Adams studied for a professional career as a young man and traveled to the Bermuda Islands. He taught school there while employed by the British government. In Bermuda he met his wife, Anna Morton, born on the island in 1816. Together they had ten children, one of whom was John Quincy Adams. John T. Adams later settled in America and became involved in railroad life as a civil engineer. His wife remained in Salem, Marion County, Illinois.[11]

<u>John Quincy Adams</u> arrived in San Diego on December 14, 1869, and claimed government land in Valley Center a few days later.[12] The Homestead Register in Los Angeles listed claim #226 filed on February 11, 1876, for 40 acres in the southwest quarter of the northwest quarter of Section 21, Township 11 South, Range 1 West. The filing fees paid included $5, plus $1.25 commissions for each 20 acres.[13] This parcel had been claimed in 1875 by Robert Price, and by Edmond Jones just the week before John Adams filed his claim. It is located north of Woods Valley Road, and is surrounded by the San Pasqual Indian Reservation (see Figure 5).

John Q. Adams came to San Diego by way of Los Angeles after he and his father had worked in the mines near White Pine, Nevada. He had been a passenger on the first west-bound train going to Elko, Nevada.[14] John Quincy Adams registered to vote in San Diego for the first time when he was 22 years old.[15] He listed his birthplace as New York, and his occupation as a farmer in San Pasqual. Records show his birthdate as March 20, 1849, in Westchester County, New York.[16]

John Q. Adams soon became an active resident of Bear Valley. He began a mercantile business in 1884 which became one of the focal points in the valley for many years. Figure 6 shows the Valley Center Store, date unknown, and the building today as the Corral Liquor Store. This store became the first Valley Center post office sanctioned by the U.S. Government in 1901. Adams stated the name of the post office as Bear Valley, but the commission was denied until the name was changed. Another post office in California already used that name, and since only one post office could have a certain name within the state, the latest applicant had to be renamed. At this time the name of Bear

Figure 6. Top Photo: Valley Center Store, ca. 1906;
Bottom Photo: Corral Liquor Store, ca. 1997.

Valley became simply 'Valley', and later 'Center' was added.[17] Figure 7 is a copy of the original document dated July 6, 1874. It is signed by his father, John T. Adams. Adams was commissioned Post Master in 1901 by President Theodore Roosevelt.[18]

John Q. Adams married <u>Annie E. Hoyt</u> in San Diego on September 4, 1877.[19] Annie was born in Indiana in 1852.[20] They had

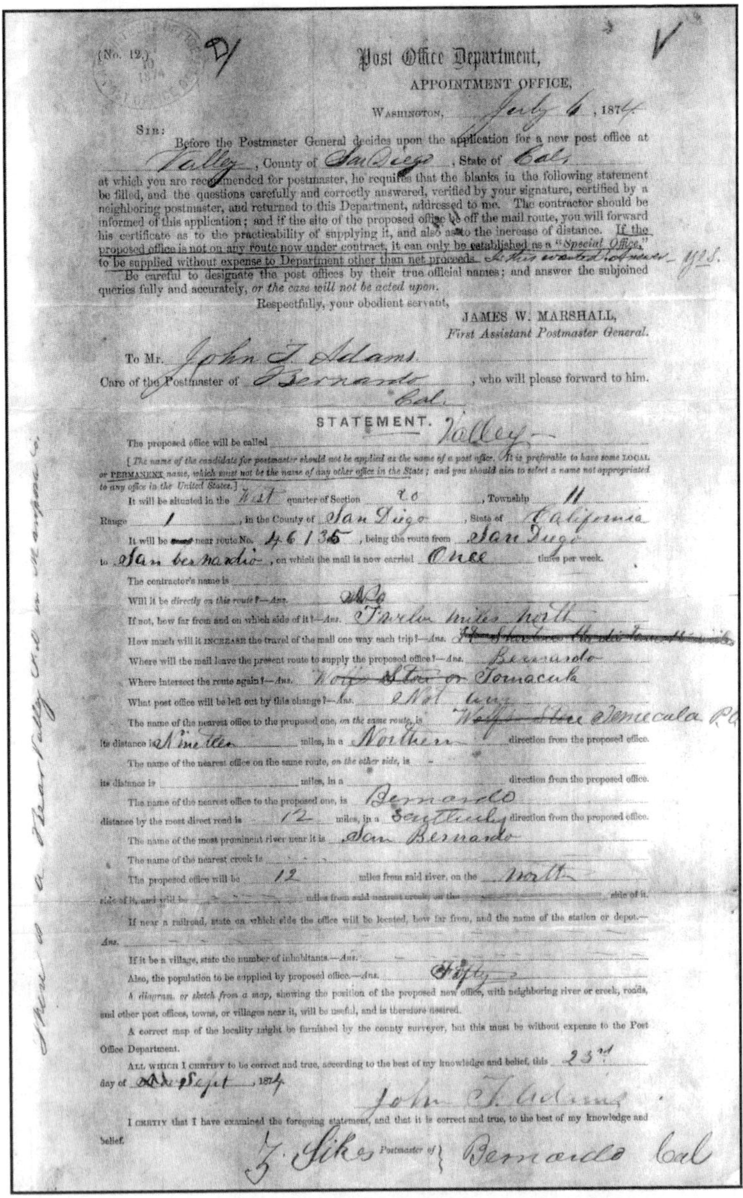

(No. 12.)

D/ V

Post Office Department,

APPOINTMENT OFFICE,

WASHINGTON, July 6, 1874

SIR:

Before the Postmaster General decides upon the application for a new post office at Valley, County of San Diego, State of Cal, at which you are recommended for postmaster, he requires that the blanks in the following statement be filled, and the questions carefully and correctly answered, verified by your signature, certified by a neighboring postmaster, and returned to this Department, addressed to me. The contractor should be informed of this application; and if the site of the proposed office be off the mail route, you will forward his certificate as to the practicability of supplying it, and also as to the increase of distance. If the proposed office is not on any route now under contract, it can only be established as a "Special Office," to be supplied without expense to Department other than net proceeds.

Be careful to designate the post offices by their true official names; and answer the subjoined queries fully and accurately, *or the case will not be acted upon.*

Respectfully, your obedient servant,

JAMES W. MARSHALL,
First Assistant Postmaster General.

To Mr. John T. Adams

Care of the Postmaster of Bernardo Cal, who will please forward to him.

STATEMENT.

The proposed office will be called Valley

[*The name of the candidate for postmaster should not be applied as the name of a post office. It is preferable to have some* LOCAL *or* PERMANENT *name, which must not be the name of any other office in the State; and you should aim to select a name not appropriated to any office in the United States.*]

It will be situated in the West quarter of Section 20, Township 11

Range 1, in the County of San Diego, State of California

It will be near route No. 46135, being the route from San Diego

to San Bernardio, on which the mail is now carried Once times per week.

The contractor's name is

Will it be *directly on this route?*—*Ans.* No

If not, how far from and on which side of it?—*Ans.* Twelve miles North

How much will it INCREASE the travel of the mail one way each trip?—*Ans.*

Where will the mail leave the present route to supply the proposed office?—*Ans.* Bernardo

Where intersect the route again?—*Ans.* ~~Wolfs Store~~ or Temacula

What post office will be left out by this change?—*Ans.* Not any

The name of the nearest office to the proposed one, *on the same route,* is ~~Wolfs Store~~ Temecula P.O.

its distance is Nineteen miles, in a Northern direction from the proposed office.

The name of the nearest office on the same route, *on the other side,* is

its distance is miles, in a direction from the proposed office.

The name of the nearest office to the proposed one, is Bernardo

distance by the most direct road is 12 miles, in a Southerly direction from the proposed office.

The name of the most prominent river near it is San Bernardo

The name of the nearest creek is

The proposed office will be 12 miles from said river, on the North

side of it, and will be miles from said nearest creek, on the side of it.

If near a railroad, state on which side the office will be located, how far from, and the name of the station or depot.—*Ans.*

If it be a village, state the number of inhabitants.—*Ans.*

Also, the population to be supplied by proposed office.—*Ans.* Fifty

A diagram, or sketch from a map, showing the position of the proposed new office, with neighboring river or creek, roads, and other post offices, towns, or villages near it, will be useful, and is therefore desired.

A correct map of the locality might be furnished by the county surveyor, but this must be without expense to the Post Office Department.

ALL WHICH I CERTIFY to be correct and true, according to the best of my knowledge and belief, this 23rd day of Sept 1874.

John T. Adams

I CERTIFY that I have examined the foregoing statement, and that it is correct and true, to the best of my knowledge and belief.

Z. Sikes Postmaster of Bernardo Cal

Figure 7. First Post Office Application, 1874.

three children: Blanche, born September 14, 1880, in Valley Center; B.E. Adams, no birthdate known; and William H. Adams, born in Valley Center in October 1885.[21] Unfortunately Mr. Adams' wife, Annie, died on February 2, 1899, after an illness.[22] His daughter, Blanche, committed suicide in Freeman, Missouri, in December 1905, after several years of ill health.[23] His son, William, committed suicide on May 26, 1907, at the age of 19 years.[24] Mr. Adams' other son, B.E. Adams, married <u>Annie B. Melhuish</u> of Valley Center and resided there for several years.[25]

After selling his original land claim to W.H.H. Dinwiddie, John Adams filed another homestead claim for 160 acres in Valley Center. Adams filed claim #3373 on June 10, 1887, for the southwest quarter of the southeast quarter, the east half of the southwest quarter, and the northeast quarter of the northwest quarter of Section 12, Township 11 South, Range 2 West, total fees paid included a $10 filing fee and $6 commissions.[26] This parcel had been claimed in 1885 by J.S. German, and was later purchased by W.I. Mundell. It is located on the west side of Valley Center Road at the bend toward Cole Grade Road (see Figure 5).

Soon after filing this second claim, J.Q. Adams planted corn, peach, apple, and nectarine trees, and established his mercantile business.[27] The store location was called *Saumai* by the local Luiseño Indians (see Figure 3, Chapter One, and Figure 4, this chapter).[28] Adams served the community as Justice of the Peace and county clerk for several years between 1894 and 1897.[29]

John Q. Adams later married <u>Louisa J. Coffee</u>, the widow of Thomas Coffee, on March 1, 1900, in San Diego. He sold all of his holdings in the valley and moved to La Jolla in 1907.[30]

The 1900 U.S. census for Bear Valley Township lists the family of J.Q. Adams as: J.Q., born March 1849, in New York, father born in Scotland, mother born in the West Indies, occupation merchant and farmer. His wife, <u>Louisa J.</u>, is listed as born June 1830, in Missouri, both parents born in Tennessee, mother of two children, one of whom was living at the time. Adams' daughter, <u>Anna B.</u>, is listed as born March 1881, in California, both parents born in Missouri. His son, Will H., is listed as born October 1888, in California.[31] Blanche is listed under her husband, <u>L.L. Hill's</u> household. Her son's name is listed as <u>Reginald</u>, born October 1899.[32]

In *The History of California*, Guinn states that John Adams was a man of strong convictions, independent in his opinions, and a believer in Socialism, even though he had formerly supported the Republican Party.[33] John Q. Adams and his father were two of the early pioneers to enter the area known as Valley Center. Others were soon to follow. An interesting reference to another person named John Q. Adams was found in the San Diego County Coroner's reports. It lists his death on December 11, 1896, in San Diego as a result of exposure.

Other early settlers were <u>John Henry Antes</u> and his brother, <u>Samuel G. Antes</u>. John is listed on the 1870 U.S. census of San Pascual and Pala Districts as living in dwelling number 71 with another early settler, Benajah Holcomb. John is listed as a 32-year old, white male farmer, U.S. citizen born in Pennsylvania, with $1000 real estate value, and $230 personal estate value.[34]

John Henry Antes registered to vote in San Diego County and was sworn in on August 26, 1871. He stated his age as 34 years old, born in Pennsylvania, and a farmer in San Pasqual.[35] John filed homestead claim #454 on March 14, 1879, for 120 acres located in the north half of the northwest quarter and the southwest quarter of the northwest quarter of Section 17, Township 11 South, Range 1 West. Fees paid totaled $10 plus $4.50, under the Act of March 3, 1877.[36] This parcel is located south of Valley Center Road east of Cole Grade Road (see Figure 5). J.H. Breedlove purchased this parcel in 1900.

John H. Antes is listed on the 1880 U.S. census as living in dwelling number 197. He is listed as a single, white male, age 43, farmer, born in Pennsylvania, both parents born in Pennsylvania.[37] Bernardo Despaso is listed as living in the same household as John Antes. Bernardo is listed as a single, Indian male, 15-year old farm laborer, who cannot read or write. Bernardo and both of his parents are listed as being born in California.[38]

John's ranch was located east of Joe Fleshman's (see Figure 4). Abel Davis states Antes built an adobe house with roof timbers hewn from tall alders grown along the San Luis Rey River and roofed with shingles split from red cedars grown on Palomar (Smith's) Mountain.[39] Davis referred to John Antes as being quite the sportsman. Apparently he liked to drive fast horses, and bet heavily on horse races. John also attended all fiestas.[40]

John Antes married his brother Samuel's daughter, Ada C. Antes, on March 23, 1882, in Valley Center. Ada was 22 years old at the time, and John was 45.[41] No children from this union are known.

Samuel G. Antes is not listed in the 1870 census record with his brother, but appears in the San Diego County Great Voter Register as being sworn in on May 31, 1875. Samuel stated his age as 47 years, born in Pennsylvania, and a farmer in Bear Valley.[42]

The 1875 USGS Plat Map of Township 11 South, Range 1 West, San Bernardino Meridian, shows "S. Antes House" in the southeast quarter of Section 8. Samuel filed homestead claim #211 on July 10, 1876, for 160 acres located in the west half of the northeast quarter of Section 17, and the west half of the southeast quarter of Section 8, Township 11 South, Range 1 West. Fees totaled $10 plus $6 at $1.25 per 20 acres.[43] "S. Antes" is shown in Section 8 on the map of Old Survey No. 24, dated September 1877. This parcel is located south of Vesper Road and east of Cole Grade Road (see Figure 5).[44]

Samuel and his wife, María, had three children: Ada C., born in California in 1860, who married her uncle John H. Antes; Ruby D., born in California in 1870, who married John Doane; and <u>Willie</u>, born in California in 1878.[45] According to the *Escondido Times,* April 20, 1893, Willie attended college in San Diego.

Samuel is listed in the 1897 *Directory of San Diego City and County* as a farmer. He also kept records of the rainfall in the valley for several years. Sam was appointed as a delegate of the roads in Bear Valley along with Sam Striplin.[46] Abel Davis described Sam Antes as a retired Carmelite preacher who raised stock and farmed all of his 640 acres.[47] Samuel died on March 21, 1899, and is buried in the Valley Center Cemetery.[48]

The 1900 U.S. census lists Ruby D. and her mother, María A., living in the household of John Doane, Ruby's husband. Ruby's birth is listed as February 1870, she was 30 years old, married five years; and María A. is listed as a 63-year old widow, born in Michigan in December 1836, with both parents born in New York.[49]

Possible ancestors of Samuel and John Antes were found in the *International Genealogical Index,* from the Church of the Latter-Day Saints. The father is listed as John Henry Antes, the mother as Ann Elizabeth Shoemaker, married December 11, 1789, living in Nippenose, Lycoming, Pennsylvania. Eleven children are listed including one "John" and one "Samuel" with birthdates from 1791 to 1818. Although these obviously cannot be the Samuel and John Antes from Valley Center, they could be ancestors.

<u>Alveron S. Beard</u> registered to vote in San Diego on August 26, 1878, stating his age at the time as 58, born in North Carolina, and his occupation as a farmer in Bear Valley. He registered again on June 14, 1880, at which time his age was 60, with all other information the same.[50]

A.S. Beard served as a Justice of the Peace in 1883-84 according to the *Pacific Coast Directory.*[51] He also served as the community postmaster for several years.[52] No homestead claim or further information regarding Mr. Beard or his family was found during research for this study.

Another early land claimant is <u>Sarah J. Blevins</u> who is listed in the Homestead Register. She filed claim #487 on June 30, 1879, for 80 acres described as the west half of the southeast quarter of Section 13, Township 11 South, Range 2 West, San Bernardino Base Meridian. Fees totaled $5 plus $3 commissions at $1.25 per 20 acres under the Act of June 8, 1872.[53] The parcel is located west of Valley Center Road, approximately one-quarter mile south of Lilac Road (see Figure 5).

Her name does not appear on any census record, county directory, or USGS map, and no further personal information is available. A portion of the acreage claimed had been previously claimed in 1876 by Joel C. Hedden and abandoned.[54] This practice was fairly common due to the low cost of filing and the availability of land.

Another early settler who made several claims in Valley Center and surrounding areas was <u>Oliver H. Borden</u>. He was not listed on the 1870 census as living in the Bear Valley area, although he later purchased 15 acres in 1898 from one of the first ranches started by the Walsh family.[55] Oliver also bought the ranch of pioneer Columbus B. Dinwiddie located in Section 8, Township 11 South, Range 1 West. This parcel is bisected by Vesper Road today (see Figure 5).[56]

Oliver was sworn in to vote in San Diego on July 15, 1875, and listed his residence as San Luis Rey, his birthplace as Missouri, with no age listed.[57] In 1880, he again signed the register of voters, but stated his occupation as a farmer in San Marcos and his birthplace as Kentucky in 1821.[58] The 1900 census of Bear Valley Township also states his birthdate as 1821, and his birthplace as Kentucky.[59] Mr. Borden did not have any young children listed in the local schools.

The Borden family history lists <u>Oliver Harrison Borden</u> as having been born the eighteenth child of Thomas and Lucy Borden on January 16, 1821, with no location listed. He married <u>Minerva Jane Wright</u> and they had five children: <u>Mary Ann</u> , <u>Harrison Wright</u>, <u>Jefferson Scott</u>, <u>Ellen</u>, and <u>William Lester</u>.

O.H. Borden moved his family to California in late 1869 or early 1870 and settled on a government claim of 640 acres in Santa Ana. After farming that land for a few years, he sold the property for $2.50 an acre and moved in 1874 to 400 acres of land near Batiquitos Lagoon. He built a concrete, two-story house on the north side of the slough on the stage road in an area now known as Ponto. The family later moved to the San Luis Rey area where Minnie died on July 22, 1890. O.H. Borden died on May 10, 1906, in La Mesa at the age of 85 years. They were both buried in the old cemetery south of the Mission San Luis Rey.

<u>Mary Ann Borden</u> was born in Indiana on April 17, 1847, and died in 1874, shortly after the birth of her twins. She had married William Field in 1867 and had two sons in Missouri: John Markle (Mark), born 1868, and <u>William Oliver (Ollie) Field</u>, born 1869. Mary Ann moved to California in the early 1870s to be with her parents who lived in Anaheim at the time and brought her youngest son with her. She later married <u>David J. Watson</u> in 1871 and had three additional children: <u>Lewis</u>, <u>Minnie</u> and <u>Nealy Watson</u> (twins).

O.H. and Minnie Borden's second child, <u>Harrison Wright Borden</u>, was born in 1848 in Indiana and died in 1918 in Anaheim, California. Wright married <u>Elizabeth Bush</u> on November 17, 1870, in a triple wedding during which his brother, Jefferson, married <u>Pauline Bush</u>, and their sister, Ellen, married <u>Jacob (Jake) Watson</u>. Wright and Elizabeth's nine children are <u>John Charles</u>, <u>William Oliver</u>, <u>Lulu Frances</u>, <u>Robert Lee</u>, <u>Elizabeth May</u>, <u>David Wright</u>, <u>Alfred Harrrison</u>, <u>Edward Hamilton</u>, and <u>Lois Millicent</u>.

<u>Jefferson Scott Borden</u>, the third child of O.H. and Minnie, was born November (or September) 13, 1852 in Indiana. He was 17 years old when the family moved to California where he married <u>Pauline J. Bush</u> in 1870 in Anaheim. They had four children, one of whom lived to adulthood. <u>Mary Jane Borden</u> was born December 26, 1872. Mary married <u>John Shoemaker</u> and had four children. Jefferson and Pauline divorced and he married <u>Mittie M. Moore</u> in Valley Center in 1881. They had four children: <u>A.C. (Bert) Borden</u> who married <u>Jean C. Young</u>, <u>Frank Borden</u> who died in childhood, <u>Clara Borden</u> who married <u>Lawrence Walsh</u> in 1905, and <u>Olive May Borden</u> who married <u>Lee Peebles</u>.

Jefferson Borden did not file a claim on property in the valley, but purchased another early settler's ranch. Reference to "Shelby's House" is shown on the 1875 plat map in the southwest quarter of Section 9, Township 11 South, Range 1 West. Reference to "J. Shelby" also shows in Section 10 on the Old Survey 24 map, dated September 1877. The 1900 plat map of Township 11 South, Range 1 West, shows "J. Shelby's fence" in Section 9.

J.S. Borden is not listed on the 1870 census, but registered to vote in San Diego on August 11, 1880. He stated he was a farmer in Hope, born in Idaho, 1853.[60] J.S. Borden is listed on the 1900 U.S. census for Bear Valley Township. His birthdate is listed as April 1852, born in Indiana, married 19 years, his parents born in Kentucky, and his occupation as blacksmith and farmer. His wife is listed as either <u>M.M.</u>, or Mimi [the name is smudged], born May 1861, in Texas, father born in Georgia, mother born in Texas, mother of six children, four of whom were living at the time. Their children were all born in California and are listed as: <u>Albert</u>, born July 1885; <u>Clara</u>, born June 1886; <u>Olive M.</u>, born May 1888; and one more daughter whose name cannot be read.[61]

J.S. Borden became a noted citizen of the community and member of the Alliance Business Association, Valley Center District Number Six.[62] He is listed on the school census of 1891 as having two male children enrolled and living in Section 13, Township 11 South, Range 2 West. His daughter, Clara, married Lawrence Walsh, a grandson of Valley Center pioneer <u>Walter Walsh</u>.[63] Clara had one son, <u>Everett Scott Walsh</u>, born in 1906 in La Mesa. She died in 1935.

<u>Ellen J. Borden</u>, O.H. and Minnie Borden's fourth child, was 15 when the family moved to California from Indiana. Ellen was born in 1856 and died in 1915. She married <u>Jacob Watson</u> in 1870 and they had five children: <u>Laura</u>, <u>Clara</u>, <u>Flora May</u>, <u>Roy</u>, and <u>Percy</u>. Ellen and Jake are both buried in the old San Luis Rey cemetery next to Ellen's parents.

<u>William Webster Borden</u> was the fifth and youngest child of O.H. and Minnie Borden. He was born in 1858 in Carrolton, Missouri. He was eleven years old when the family moved to California. He married <u>Minnie Lillian Kelly</u> in 1881 and they had four children: <u>Charles Garfield</u>, <u>Carroll Elmer</u>, <u>Bertha Ellen</u>, <u>E. Raymond (Sammy</u>), <u>Genevieve Lillian</u>. W.W. Borden published a small local newspaper, *The Plain Truth* for several years during the 1880s.

One pioneer who lived on his land prior to filing the homestead petition was <u>Daniel E. Bowman</u>. Reference to "D.E. Bowman's House" is shown in the northeast quarter of the 1875 government plat map of Section 31, Township 11 South, Range 1 West. He filed claim #361 for 160 acres on May 4, 1878. Bowman paid a $10 filing fee and $6 commissions under the Act of March 3, 1877. The legal claim included the east half of the southwest quarter of Section 30, the northeast quarter of the northwest quarter, and the northwest quarter of the northeast quarter of Section 31.[64] This parcel is located on both sides of Valley Center Road along the grade east of the Daley Ranch (see Figure 5).

Daniel E. Bowman was born in Berlin, Canada, in 1839, a child of John B. and Lydia E. Erb Bowman, both born in Pennsylvania.[65] Daniel listed his birthdate as June 1839, widowed, married 35 years on the 1900 census.[66] Mr. Bowman stated his birthdate as 1842 on his voter registration dated July 19, 1881, at which time he became a naturalized citizen of the United States in the Superior Court of San Diego.[67] Daniel's birthdate is also stated as 1842 on the 1880 census.[68]

Daniel worked as a teacher near his hometown until he moved to Lawrence, Kansas in 1869. He came to the west coast in 1874 and began an apiary in Valley Center. At one time he stated he had 700 bee colonies established.[69] He also raised soap root and corn on his ranch.[70] While D.E. Bowman maintained his bee colonies, he also became interested in mining operations in the area from 1886 until 1898.[71]

D.E. Bowman remained a bachelor until December 11, 1905, when he married <u>Jean C. Strong</u>, a widow in the area.[72] The Bowmans had no children, although a <u>David Bowman</u> is listed as an apiarist in Valley Center in the 1897 *Directory of San Diego City and County*.

D.E. Bowman was a valuable asset to the small community of Valley Center and a member of the Methodist Episcopal Church of Escondido.[73]

Two brothers who each became well respected residents of Valley Center in the 1870s were <u>Columbus</u> and <u>William Breedlove</u>. Their families acquired large parcels of land through homestead claims and personal acquisitions, turning the land into profitable ranches.

William, the older brother, was born in Alabama in 1818. He is listed in the 1880 U.S. census as a 62-year-old, white male farmer, living in dwelling number 190 with his wife, <u>Susan</u>, age 62, and son, <u>Doctor</u>, age 22. His father is listed as born in Tennessee and his mother born Alabama. Susan was born in Tennessee and her parents both born in Georgia. Their son is listed as born in Missouri.[74]

There are several discrepancies regarding William and Susan Breedlove in J.M. Guinn's, *The History of California.* Listed in the discussion of their son, <u>John H. Breedlove</u>, Susan is said to have died while crossing the plains from Missouri to California, with no date given.[75] In the discussion of their son, <u>Doctor M. Breedlove</u>, however, it is stated that Susan died on the family farm in Missouri and the age of 73 years.[76] Given that Susan's name appears on the 1880 census in California, she obviously did not die while traveling across the plains. The Valley Center Cemetery records show that Susan Breedlove died on September 26, 1888, and is interred at the cemetery.

The two discussions do, however, agree on the death of William. He died on the family farm in 1892 at the age of 74 after living in the Valley Center area for several years.[77] A family history transcribed from an interview with Waldo Breedlove in 1958 states that William returned to the family farm in Missouri after his wife's death in 1888 and remarried a yound girl of 16 (he was 85 years at the time).[78]

Another inconsistency regards the birthplace of William Breedlove. Guinn states that William was born in Kentucky.[79] He also reports that Susan was born and raised in Kentucky. In the discussion of D.M., however, the birthplaces are listed as Tennessee for William with no reference as to Susan's. One other discrepancy in Guinn regards the number of children born to William and Susan Breedlove. One account states the couple had six children, and another states that seven children were born.[80]

Although William and Susan did not live in Valley Center for very long, their children remained and became very successful. Their oldest child, <u>Ransom D. Breedlove</u>, became a successful rancher in his own right. Ransom was born in Missouri in 1844 according to the San Diego County Voter Registration Index of 1880-87. He stated he was a farmer in Bear Valley. Ransom never filed a homestead claim, but he did rent out the Sutter ranch in 1894 located outside of the study area in the eastern portion of the valley.[81] He was also voted as a Valley Center school trustee in 1894.[82]

The second-born child of William and Susan Breedlove was John Henry Breedlove. He was born in Webster County, Missouri on December 26, 1846. John left the home farm in 1864 at the age of 18 for the mines in Montana. He returned to the farm in 1874 and stayed for two years after trying his luck in Kansas and Texas.[83]

While in Missouri, John married Edith A. Rogers in 1875. They had two sons and two daughters.[84] The family is listed in the 1880 census in Bear Valley, dwelling number 193. John is listed as a white male farmer, 33 years of age. Edith is listed as a white female, 26-year old housekeeper, born in Missouri with both of her parents born in Tennessee. John and Edith's son, Elmer R., is listed as a 4-year old, born in Missouri. A daughter, Lilian [sic], is listed as a two-year old, born in California.[85] Elmer Roy, or Roy, as he was known, attended the University of Southern California.[86] Lillian Breedlove Sheldon is listed in the Valley Center Cemetery records as born in November, 1878, and died in June, 1961. Two other children were listed by Guinn. Grace, born in California in 1888, is listed in the Valley Center Cemetery records as having died in 1979. Abel Davis states that she later went to school and became a teacher in the Los Angeles area.[87] Carl, the youngest son of John Henry and Edith A. Rogers Breedlove, is listed with no birthdate given.[88]

John H. Breedlove came to San Diego County in 1878 and took up homestead claim #364 in Sections 23 and 24, Township 11 South, Range 1 West, which is outside the study area.[89] He abandoned that claim after five years and bought Henry Antes ranch located in Section 17, in the same township and range (see Figures 4 and 5).[90] In 1888, the *Escondido Times* reported that John was growing pears, almonds, quince, and grapes, as well as growing all of the hay and grain used on his farm.[91] He also started a dairy on his farm, reportedly milking from fifty to seventy-five milk cows per day.[92] He served as a Vista school trustee in 1894.[93]

The 1900 U.S. census lists the family of J.H. Breedlove on page 207. The census lists John as born in 1848, and his age at the time as 51. Edith's birthdate is listed as May 1854, married 25 years, mother of four children, all living at that time. R.E. [Roy Elmer] is listed as being 24 years old, born March 1876, occupation Salvation Army. Lillian was 22 years old, born in October 1877, occupation bookkeeper. Grace E., 12 years old, was born in February 1888. Carl V., 10 years old, is listed as born in February 1890.[94]

John Henry Breedlove died in Imperial Valley on July 17, 1908, the result of apoplexy, or stroke, at 61 years of age. It was believed that the extreme heat of the desert was a factor in his sudden death. J.H. had sold all of his holdings in Valley Center and moved to Imperial Valley a few months before his death. He had wanted to start a dairy in that community with his son Roy. J.H. Breedlove is buried in the Valley Center Cemetery.[95]

The third child of William and Susan Breedlove, <u>Harriet</u>, married a Valley Center pioneer, William H.H. Dinwiddie. Harriet is listed as W.H.H Dinwiddie's wife and mother of five sons, living in dwelling number 186, page 20 of the 1880 U.S. census record. She is listed as a 29-year old, white female, born in Missouri. Her father is listed as born in Missouri and her mother was born in Tennessee.[96]

The fourth child, born in 1850 to William and Susan Breedlove, was <u>William O. Breedlove</u>. He was sworn in to vote in San Diego on May 24, 1888, at which time he stated he was 38 years old, born in Missouri, and a farmer in Bear Valley.[97] It is not known whether he left shortly thereafter, as no further information regarding him was found during research for this study.

William and Susan Breedlove's second daughter, <u>Artelia C.</u>, married Valley Center pioneer, <u>William F.C. James</u>, who homesteaded land outside of this study area. Artelia is listed in dwelling number 189 on the 1880 U.S. census record. She is listed as a white female, 26 years old, housekeeper and wife, born in Missouri, with her father born in Alabama and her mother born in Tennessee. The oldest of her three sons is listed as four years old.[98] The 1900 U.S. census of Bear Valley Township lists Mr. and Mrs. James as married for 26 years, placing their wedding date at 1874.[99] Valley Center Cemetery records show that Mrs. James was born in February 1854, and she died in April, 1932. An unpublished book written by her son, Clyde James, corroborates those dates.[100]

<u>Doctor Marion Breedlove</u> was the fourth son and sixth child of William and Susan Breedlove. The origin of his unusual name was not discussed. He was always referred to as D.M. or "Doc". J.M. Guinn states that D.M was born in Webster County, Missouri, on February 26, 1859. At the age of 22, he left his home state and set up a homestead claim in the Valley Center area known as Paradise Mountain.[101]

Claim #498 was filed on July 31, 1879. The 120-acre claim was located in Sections 23 and 24, Township 11 South, Range 1 West. He later claimed an additional 40 acres adjacent to his original homestead claim, making a total of 160 acres. These sections fall outside of the current study area.

D.M Breedlove married <u>Laura Eleanor Harrison</u> in Bear Valley on December 5, 1883. Laura was the daughter of Nathan and Ellen

Burt Harrison, and was born in Illinois in 1860. According to Guinn, D.M and Laura had five children: <u>Edward</u>, <u>Waldo</u>, <u>Inez</u>, <u>Harry</u>, and <u>Myrtle</u>.[102] Although birthdates for the children were not given, the school census in 1891 shows one male in school and one child less than five years old at home. By 1893, the school census showed one male in school and three children less than five years at home. A report from the Bear Valley School for the month of February, 1894, listed Ed Breedlove as being in the second grade.[103] The 1895 census listed two male children in school and two children less than five years old at home. By the year 1900, the school census listed three males and one female in school, with one child at home less than five years old.[104]

D.M. Breedlove proved very instrumental in settling Valley Center. He served for several years as the constable of the community and on January 18, 1888, he became a target for some 'squatters' on land belonging to L.P. Stone in Moosa Canyon.

Constable Breedlove had to serve an eviction notice to the persons living there, but when he tried to serve those papers, he was shot in the face and hit on the head. A "shoot-out" ensued, and when the fight was over, several people had been shot. One young rancher, Stockman Reed, was killed, as were some of the squatters. The incident became known as the "Moosa Canyon Tragedy."[105]

An Order of Adjudication of Insolvency was filed in the Superior Court of San Diego on May 27, 1891, under the name of Doctor Marion Breedlove. All personal and real estate were to be given over to the sheriff of the county as ordered by the Superior Court of San Diego County. D.M. remained in the area, as he was mentioned in later newspaper articles as working on his ranch and hunting bear.[106]

The fifth son, and seventh child born to William and Susan Breedlove, was <u>Charles W. Breedlove</u>. Charles registered to vote and was sworn in on August 2, 1888. He is listed as having been born in California in 1861. He listed his occupation as farmer, and residence in San Diego Ward #4.

Charles filed homestead claim #3357 on June 2, 1887, for 160 acres located in Section 34, Township 11 South, Range 1 West. This claim falls outside of the current study area.

In 1893, Charles hauled wood from Palomar Mountain used to repair the Pala mill, which served the Pauma Valley.[107] His name also appeared several times in 1894 reporting his new buggy and the happy prospects for the local young women.[108]

<u>Columbus Breedlove</u>, William's brother, was born in Tennessee in 1825. Columbus followed his brother to Valley Center after the Civil War. He registered to vote on September 4, 1877, as a transfer from Yolo County, California. He stated at that time that he was 52 years

old, born in Tennessee, his occupation was farmer, and his residence was Bear Valley.

Columbus and his family appear in the 1880 Bear Valley Township census as residing in dwelling number 185. Columbus is listed as a white male farmer, 54 years old, born in Tennessee, whose father was born in Tennessee, and his mother in Alabama. Columbus' wife is listed as <u>Jane</u>, a white female, 56 years old, housekeeper, born in Tennessee, as were both of her parents.[109]

The children of Columbus and Jane Breedlove are listed as all being born in California. They include: <u>William</u>, 19 years of age, attending school; <u>Rebecca</u>, 16 years of age, at home; and <u>Josephine</u>, 11 years old.[110]

William Breedlove filed homestead claim #2657 on March 2, 1886, for an 80-acre parcel located in Section 25, Township 11 South, Range 1 West.[111] This claim falls outside of the current study area. The family history reports that William and his father, Columbus, died in the desert near Coyote Wells while on a trip looking for a mine in 1890.[112] Rebecca Breedlove married Valley Center pioneer Robert Daley in 1881, and Josephine married Frederick Fleshman.[113]

The Breedlove family was known for their dairy business in the valley. Their ranches provided excellent grazing for their cattle. The family members were all respected and provided valuable services to the community for many years.

<u>John Peter Christensen</u>, an early pioneer, immigrated from Denmark and filed a Declaration of Intention in the Superior Court of San Diego on May 30, 1873.[114] He settled in Bear Valley and on May 27, 1879, filed homestead claim #479 for 120 acres at a total cost of $14.50 under the Act of May 27, 1878. The legal description of the property is the east half of the southwest quarter and the southeast quarter of the northwest quarter of Section 31, Township 11 South, Range 1 West.[115] This parcel is bisected by Valley Center Road along the grade into Escondido, just north of the junction of Lake Wohlford Road (see Figure 5).

John registered to vote on May 22, 1875, and stated his birthplace as Denmark in 1830. His occupation is listed as a mason and his residence as Bear Valley.[116] His name appears on the 1880 U.S. census as John P. Christenson, living in dwelling number 179 with his wife, <u>Hannah A</u>. He is listed as a white male farmer, age 53, born in Denmark, with both parents also born there. Hannah is described as a white female housekeeper, age 35, born in Ireland with both parents' birthplace listed as Ireland.[117]

Two children appear as John's stepsons living in the same household. They are <u>Howard R</u>. and <u>Oscar D. Marshall</u>, ages 12 and 7, respectively. Howard was born in Iowa and Oscar was born in California.[118] In 1891, the Valley Center School census listed three males and one female attending the school during that year in the Christensen family. The same data was listed in 1893. By 1895, there were two male children attending school, and only one male attending the Valley Center School in 1896. Even though little information is available for the Christensen family, they were pioneer settlers in Valley Center and contributed to the area history by being some of the first settlers in the valley.

Benjamin J. Cook is another pioneer settler in Valley Center. He was born in Dublin, Ireland in September, 1827. He came to the United States as an infant with his parents.

Benjamin arrived in California in 1860 after traveling across the plains in a covered wagon from Iowa. The wagon train included 60 wagons with a destination of Marysville, in northern California. Benjamin moved on to Virginia City and Washoe after arriving, and remained in that area for eight years before coming to San Diego in 1869. He settled in Valley Center in 1871. A house, listed only as "Cook's House," is shown in the northwest quarter of Section 20, Township 11 South, Range 1 West, on the 1875 U.S. plat map. This property is located north of Woods Valley Road, approximately one mile from Valley Center Road (see Figure 5).

Mr. Cook's name does not appear on the 1880 U.S. census of the Bear Valley Township. He filed a Declaration of Intention in the Superior Court of San Diego County on November 15, 1883, and became a naturalized citizen on that day.[119]

Benjamin was a wheelwright by trade. He was a member of the Methodist Episcopal Church of Escondido and had one son and one daughter. Benjamin died on October 29, 1887, and is buried in the Oak Hill Cemetery in Escondido.[120]

William Cook was also a pioneer settler of the small community of Valley Center. It is not known if William Cook is a relative of Benjamin Cook, for research proved inconclusive. William was a farmer on Smith's Mountain for a time, where he operated a hotel. In the Valley Center School census of 1895, Mr. Cook listed his residence as Section 13, Township 11 South, Range 2 West. He was awarded the mail route from Valley Center to San Diego, according to Abel Davis.[121] Although William Cook may not have acquired great land holdings, he was a very integral part of the history of the valley.

One immigrant to the valley, Robert Daley, arrived as a young man from England with little personal wealth, and through a life of hard work, was able to build a valuable asset to both the community and his family for generations to come. Including the original homestead land of 160 acres claimed in 1876 for the standard $10 filing fee, Daley had acquired more than 1,880 acres by the time of his death in 1916. His sons were able to increase the family acreage to more than 3,000 acres over the years.

Robert settled in a valley north of Escondido at the southern edge of Valley Center. He built a log cabin in the southern end of the valley early in 1869. It was located in Section 35, Township 11 South, Range 1 West and is shown on the 1875 plat map. By 1875, he had built a wooden frame house of pine boards and a redwood barn approximately one-half mile north of the original cabin. The redwood barn was still in use in 1983 when an evaluation survey was completed.[122]

A pre-emption claim was made in 1875 for 160 acres surrounding the original cabin site in Section 35.[123] Another 160 acres was homesteaded around the new house site in Section 26 (see Figure 5). Robert later acquired 640 acres through a school lands claim and another 640 acres by a "lieu land" grant. Farming and ranching were his primary occupation, although he also hauled freight.[124]

Robert Daley is listed on the 1860 U.S. census as a 29-year old, white male farm laborer, with real estate valued at $400 and personal estate valued at $100, born in Massachusetts, and a citizen of the United States.[125] When he registered to vote on August 9, 1872, however, he stated that he was a 28 year old teamster in San Diego, and a naturalized citizen originally from England.[126] His obituary, printed in the *Daily Times Advocate* on August 4, 1916, states his birthdate as October 16, 1842, in London, England.[127]

Robert Daley at age 37 married Valley Center resident, Rebecca A. Breedlove, age 17, on February 1, 1881. They had four children: Mary Ann, born 1883, who married Lester D. Rockwood of San Pasqual; George R., born 1885, who married Jeanette Moss; Bryant Howard, later known as Howard, born in 1886, who married Mabel Foster; and one daughter who died in infancy.[128] The Daley children attended school in Escondido from 1891 until 1898; Mary Ann and Howard graduating the eighth grade, and George stopping after the sixth grade.[129]

In the late 1890s, Robert began a family dairy, or creamery, called the Fern Valley Dairy. They had 30 cows from which the cream was separated from the milk in order to produce butter. The butter was taken by wagon into Escondido and then shipped by stage to San Diego. The dairy was later leased out and continued in business for many years even after the Daley family had moved from the ranch.

Robert died on July 31, 1916, at the age of 74 years following an operation at the Agnew Sanitarium in San Diego. He is buried at the

Oak Hill Cemetery beside his brother, <u>James</u>, who had died a few years before.[130]

George had left the dairy in 1909 to begin his own business. He took with him five teams of horses and three wagons to begin a road contracting business in San Diego. Howard left the dairy in 1916 after his father's death to help George build the rapidly growing business. Together they became one of the largest heavy construction firms in San Diego County and by the early 1920s, they were one of the first to convert to Caterpillar tractors and other heavy mechanized construction equipment.[131]

The brothers continued the construction business until Howard retired in 1952 and returned to the family ranch. He died there in 1962. His sons, <u>Donald</u> and <u>Lawrence</u>, continued the family construction business. George died at the Jamul ranch in 1957.[132]

The very enterprising family of Robert Daley proved not only an important part of the Valley Center history, but also for San Diego County; first through the foresight and hard work of the father, and then on through subsequent generations.

One of the earliest pioneers to settle down on homesteaded land in Valley Center was <u>James Davis</u>. In a book written by his son, <u>Abel</u>, it is stated that James first came to this section of the southwest as a member of General Stephen Watts Kearny's army.[133]   He was a survivor in the Battle of San Pasqual fought in December, 1946, which was the last battle of the War in California. Twenty-two American soldiers died in that battle and were buried on the battlefield. The bodies were later moved to Old Town San Diego, and then moved again to their final resting place in the Fort Rosecrans National Cemetery on Point Loma.[134]

After the war ended and California became a state in the Union in 1850, a survey team was enlisted to map this newly acquired portion of the United States. Colonel James Davis was hired as part of that team from 1852-57 as the map maker, or cartographer.[135]

The survey team established the San Bernardino Base Line, running east to west, and the San Bernardino Base Meridian, running north to south. It is from these base lines that all land is divided into townships, ranges, sections, quarter sections, and quarter-quarter sections. These land measurements are still in use today, although few landowners claim more than a few acres.

Abel Davis states that the James Davis family arrived in Valley Center in 1862 as settlers on government land.[136]   Although there is no legal record of this, the family is listed on the 1870 U.S. census record as living in dwelling number 73. James is listed as a 34-year old, white male farmer born in Ireland. He claimed $800 worth of real estate and

$500 worth personal estate. Both parents are listed as foreign-born, and James is listed as a citizen of the U.S. His wife, <u>Sarah</u>, is listed as an 18-year old housekeeper, born in Texas. One child is listed under the name <u>James</u>, age 1 year, born in California.[137]

A person named <u>George Davis</u> is also listed as living in the household of James. It is not known if he is a relative of James. He is listed as a 35-year old, white male farm laborer born in Pennsylvania.[138]

The James Davis family also appears on the 1880 U.S. census in dwelling number 210. James is listed as a 50-year old farmer, and his wife, Sarah A., is listed as a 27-year old housekeeper. Their children are listed as being born in California. This includes: <u>James</u>, white male, 12-year old son attending school; <u>Anthony</u>, white male, 10-year old son attending school; <u>Abel</u>, white male, eight-year old son; <u>Mary</u>, white female daughter, age six; <u>Frederick</u>, white male, two-year old son; and <u>Martha M.</u>, white female baby, seven months old.[139] According to Abel Davis, there were two other children in the family. <u>Matthew</u>, no birthdate given, and <u>Mabel Rainbow</u>, adopted by the parents as a young girl, with no birth information given.[140]

James Davis became a naturalized citizen of the United States on November 25, 1874, in the Superior Court of San Diego County.[141] He filed homestead claim #247 on April 22, 1876, for 160 acres. The legal description reads: the north half of the northeast quarter of Section 31, the northwest quarter of the northwest quarter of Section 32, and the southwest quarter of the southeast quarter of Section 30, Township 10 South, Range 1 West.[142] The property is located on the east side of Cole Grade Road at Hilldale Road. According to the map drawn by Abel Davis (presented in this chapter as Figure 4), the original homestead would have also extended across the road to the west side of Cole Grade Road (see Figure 5).

On September 30, 1976, Davis filed claim #341 for the additional 169.25 acres of land. This included the north half of the northwest quarter of Section 31, the southwest quarter of the southwest quarter of Section 30, and the southeast quarter of the southeast quarter of Section 25, Township 10 South, Range 1 West.[143]

The Davis homestead consisted of an adobe house, milk house, and a smoke house at the bottom of the creek. A flat area in front of the house was a swamp covered with tules, willows, and wire grasses. A flowing spring near the house kept a small reservoir filled to over-flowing which irrigated the family garden and orchard of pear trees. When the family first settled on the land, and for several years afterwards, a small group of Native Americans lived around the spring in brush houses made of tules. They had a grist mill located in the rocks above the spring where they would grind the corn and wheat they grew.[144]

Figure 8. The James Davis Adobe Ruins, ca. 1950.
Photo Courtesy of Gail and Ron Lamb

James Davis died at home on December 20, 1893. He had been ill with influenza, which was also called La Grippe, or Spanish flu at the time. His estate was listed under a Notice to Creditors in the *Escondido Times* dated January 29, 1894. Another article in June of the same year listed the property sold.[145]

Frederick died from pneumonia on May 4, 1896; Anthony died on December, 17, 1897, leaving a wife and two sons; and Mary died June 19, 1898, leaving a husband, son, and daughter.[146] Martha reportedly died in a fire as a child, although no official records confirmed this information. They are all buried in the Valley Center Cemetery. Records show that influenza was the cause of many deaths in the area at that time.

By 1900, the only Davis family members listed in the census were Abel and Matthew. They were living with their sister-in-law's new husband, the Reverend C.S. Perry and his family. Abel married the Reverend's daughter, Emma S. Perry in 1901 and together they had five children: E.T., birthdate unknown, who later married Hugh Abbott; another daughter whose name was listed in Abel's obituary simply as Mrs. Cloid Farley; Miriam A., birthdate unknown, who later married William M. Jones; Sidney L., birthdate unknown; and R. Perry, birthdate unknown, who later became a doctor.[147]

Mabel became a nurse during World War I and served under General John Joseph Pershing and General George Smith Patton in

France. She never married and died in 1945. She is buried in the National Cemetery in southern California.[148]

The eldest child, James, studied blacksmithing and machine shop as an apprentice. He later traveled to Guatemala to work on the construction of the railroad across the Isthmus of Panama. He also worked in Albuquerque, Needles, San Bernardino, and Los Angeles. Matthew, the youngest child, worked in the Los Angeles City Maintenance Department.[149]

The family of James Davis may have been the first pioneering family to settle in Valley Center. There is no information to dispute the claim, but there is also no confirmation. What cannot be disputed, is the fact these early settlers gave the valley part of its early history whether they were the first emigrating family to settle or not.

William Henry Harrison Dinwiddie and his brother, Columbus Barton Dinwiddie were also part of the valley's history. The two brothers each homesteaded acreage in Valley Center in the 1870s and through the years were able to purchase large tracts of land adjacent to their original holdings. They each had large families who intermarried into other pioneering families of the area, thereby weaving the family tree of Valley Center.

Columbus and William were sons of John Dinwiddie born in Washington County, Missouri. They arrived in the Sacramento area of California with their family in the early 1850s. In their journey across the plains, the family encountered Indians who stole most of the stock the family was taking to California. Upon arrival in this state, the family settled on a farm near Sacramento. Their father died on that farm at eighty-seven years of age, and their mother died later at the age of ninety-seven.[150]

Columbus was the eldest brother, born in 1835. The 1880 U.S. census lists Columbus B, as a white male farmer, 45 years of age, born in Missouri, with father born in Kentucky and mother born in Tennessee. His wife, Silence, is listed as a white female housekeeper, 37 years old, born in Illinois, with both parents born in Virginia. The nine children listed were all born in California. This includes: John A., a 20-year old farm laborer; Mary E., 18-year old daughter living at home; Edwin D., 14-year old son attending school; Sarah F., 11-year old daughter attending school; Henry F., a nine-year old student; James W., six years old; May, eight years old; Arthur, four years old; and Robert, one year old.[151]

A search in the *International Genealogical Index,* Church of the Latter-Day Saints,[152] lists Columbus and Silence Dinwiddie as being married in Knights Landing, Yolo County, California, on February 11, 1858. One child, Lucy May, is listed as being born in Knights

Landing, Sutter County, California, on May 16, 1872. A search of the Brøderbund Family Tree Maker© CD Census Index,[153] lists Columbus B. as residing in Utah in 1850 and in California in 1870. Silence is listed as residing in California in 1870.

Columbus filed homestead claim #658 on November 19, 1880. It consisted of 160 acres located in the south half of the southwest quarter of Section 5, the north half of the northwest quarter of Section 8, Township 11 South, Range 1 West.[154] Although a legal claim was not filed prior to 1880, the family was living on the property. "C. Dinwiddie" appears in Section 8 on the surveyor's map in 1877.[155] This property today is bisected by Fruitvale Road, approximately one-half mile east of Cole Grade Road (see Figure 5).

A second claim was filed in 1882 for 160 acres in the northeast quarter of Section 8. This second claim also included the originally claimed acreage.[156] This parcel today is bordered by Fruitvale Road on the north and Vesper Road on the southern boundary, approximately one mile east of Cole Grade Road (see Figure 5).

According to Abel Davis, "Columbus raised a large family and kept adding to his small adobe house until it became a veritable hacienda." Columbus sold his acreage to O.H. Borden, and left the area, with no reference as to a date by Davis.[157] Columbus and family do not appear on the Bear Valley Township, 1900 U.S. census, although several of his children remained in the area for several years.

Edwin D. Dinwiddie filed homestead claim #4087 on March 30, 1888. The claim appears outside of the current study area in Section 26, Township 10 South, Range 2 West.[158] Edwin is listed on the 1900 U.S. census as a single head of the household, a farm laborer, 34 years old, born January 1866, in California.[159]

Henry F. Dinwiddie is listed on the 1895 Valley Center School census as living in Section 18, Township 11 South, Range 1 West, with one child less than five years old. In 1896 and 1897, he is listed in the same location with two children less than five years old.

Although Columbus left the area, as did many of his children, his brother remained in Valley Center and operated a family dairy business until 1912, at which time W.H.H. sold his land in Valley Center and moved with two of his sons to Utah to homestead another government claim. He died in Utah on October 19, 1916.[160] While living in the Valley Center district, W.H.H. served as a Justice of the Peace and Deputy County Clerk.[161] He also served as school trustee for several years.[162]

William Henry Harrison Dinwiddie, generally referred to as W.H.H.,[163] appears on the 1870 U.S. census of San Pascual and Pala Districts. He is listed as living with his family in dwelling number 186. W.H.H. is listed as 38 years old, a white male farmer, born in Missouri, father born in Kentucky, mother born in Tennessee. His wife, Harriet, is listed as 29 years old, a white female housekeeper, born in Missouri, father born in Missouri, and mother born in Tennessee.

W.H.H. and Harriet's five sons are all listed as born in California. This includes: John, 12 years old, attending school; William, nine years old, also attending school; George, seven; Thomas, five; and Lawrence, two years old.[164]

W.H.H Dinwiddie filed homestead claim #240 on April 1, 1876. The claim included 160 acres located in Section 19, Township 11 South, Range 1 West. The legal description is the southwest quarter of the northwest quarter, the northeast quarter of the southwest quarter, and the north half of the southeast quarter. Today this property is located east of Valley Center Road on Woods Valley Road (see Figure 5).

W.H.H., like many other early settlers, lived on the unsurveyed government land for several years before filing a legal claim. The 1875 U.S. plat map shows "Dinwiddie's House" in the northwest quarter of Section 19, Township 11 South, Range 1 West. Before leaving the area in 1912 and selling his land holdings, W.H.H. acquired more than three thousand acres, of which approximately 600 acres were in Valley Center.[165] He successfully practiced dry-farming by raising peaches, apples, apricots, grapes, and pears.[166]

W.H.H. served the community for several years in many different capacities. He served as Justice of the Peace and school trustee for several years.[167] He also provided a valuable service by his operation of a dairy and creamery, a business in which he was helped by his sons. The family also raised their own grain for feeding the livestock on their property.[168]

The W.H.H. Dinwiddie family is listed on the 1900 U.S. census of Bear Valley Township, as living in dwelling number 99. W.H.H is listed as 60 years old, married 35 years, born 1840 in Missouri, father born in Missouri, and mother born in Scotland. His wife, Harriet M., is listed as 49 years old, married 35 years, born 1850 in Missouri, as were both parents.

Their sons are listed as: George, 27 years old, born March 1873, foreman of the creamery; Thomas, 24 years old, born October 1875, farm laborer; L.W., 22 years old, born 1877, farm laborer; and their youngest son, Abel B., 17 years old, born September 1882, listed as a farm laborer.[169]

William H.H. Dinwiddie sold his land in 1912 and moved to Nada, Utah, to establish a claim of government land with three of his sons, whom a newspaper article named as Will, Lloyd, and Bert. W.H.H. died while in Utah on October 19, 1916. He was 80 years old and had suffered from an illness for several weeks.[170] Two of his sons, George H. and J.T.(Tom), remained in the Valley Center area.[171]

John F. Dinwiddie is listed in the 1897 *Directory of San Diego City and County*. He is also listed on the 1900 U.S. census as living in dwelling number 100 with his family. Listed are: J.H., a 32-year old white male farmer, born October 1867, married seven years; his wife, Minnie, listed as a white female, 22 years old, born August 1877 in Kansas, father born in Illinois, mother born in Missouri; son, John, seven years old, born February 1893, in California; daughter, Maude, four years old, born November 1895; and daughter, __lie [name partially unreadable], two years old, born April 1898.[172]

William C. Dinwiddie is listed in the 1893-94 *Directory of San Diego City, Coronado, and National City*. He is also listed on the 1895 school census record as having two children less than five years old. The 1899 and 1900 Valley Center School records list two female children in school with two other children less than five years of age at home. The residence of the family is listed on the school census as Section 21, Township 11 South, Range 1 West, which corresponds to the parcel marked on the 1900 U.S. plat map in Section 21.

The family is also listed in dwelling number 38 on the 1900 U.S. census of Bear Valley Township. William is listed as a 30-year old farmer, born May 1870, married eleven years. His wife, Anne L., is listed as 26 years old, born December 1873, in Missouri, married eleven years, mother of four children, all of whom were living at the time, her father born in Tennessee, and mother born in Missouri. William and Anne's four children are all listed as born in California. They are: Viola, nine years old, born August 1890; Laura, seven years old, born December 1892; Maggie, five years old, born April 1895; and Charles, two years old, born March 1898.[173]

The families of Columbus and William H.H. Dinwiddie arrived in the Valley Center area at a time when land was virtually free. Through years of hard work and determination, both families and their descendants benefited and became part of the history of the community.

Francis and Joseph Fleshman were another set of brothers who came to the Valley Center area in the 1870s to claim government land to homestead. They were German immigrants who came to the United States as children with their parents. The children were citizens through their father's naturalization.[174]

The family name was originally spelled "Fleishman" on several documents, and as "Fleshman" on later references. Guinn lists Francis as Frederick under the original spelling of the surname. All documents researched for this study stated his given name as Francis or Frank, including voter registration and census records. Guinn does not give any information concerning Joseph or their father's history.[175]

The brothers registered to vote in San Diego County on June 14, 1880. Francis stated his age as 51, a farmer in Bear Valley, born in Hesse Darmstadt, and a citizen by right of his father's naturalization. Joseph stated the same information except that his age was given as 46 years.[176]

Francis was the first Fleshman brother to register a homestead claim. On December 24, 1875, he filed claim #207 for 166.30 acres located in Bear Valley. The legal description is Lots 2, 3, and 4, and the northeast quarter of the southwest quarter of Section 7, Township 11 South, Range 1 West, San Bernardino Base Meridian. Fees paid included a $10 filing fee and $6 commissions, with the price per acre listed as $1.25. Excess receipt #427 was given in the amount of $7.87.[177] Abel Davis states that Frank first filed a claim in 1864 for land around a rocky ridge which separated the southern portion of the valley from the middle portion extending across the road.[178] Today the property is on both sides of Valley Center Road, bordered on the west by Miller Road and the east by Cole Grade Road (see Figure 5).

Although Joseph did not register a legal claim prior to 1875, his name appears as "Fleshman's House" on the 1875 U.S. plat map in the northeast quarter of Section 18, Township 11 South, Range 1 West. His name also appears on Old [road] Survey 24, dated September 1877, in Section 18 as "J. Fleishman", and his brother's in Section 7 as "F. Fleishman".[179] Abel Davis states that the brothers' land adjoined each others extending across Valley Center Road. Davis also notes that the present-day Community Church stands on what was Joe Fleshman's land.[180]

Joseph first registered to vote in San Diego County on August 31, 1869, and again on December 31. He listed his age as 33 years at the time.[181] He filed claim #603 on June 16, 1880, for 80 acres. The legal description is the west half of the southeast quarter of Section 7, Township 11 South, Range 1 West.[182]

Joseph Fleishman is listed on the 1870 U.S. census of San Pascual and Pala Townships as living in dwelling number 72. He is listed as a 35-year old farm laborer with $500 worth real estate and $400 worth of personal estate. He stated he was born in California and is listed as a citizen of the U.S.[183] The 1880 census lists Joseph living in dwelling number 204 as a single, white male farmer, 46 years old, with himself and his parents born in Hesse Darmstadt.[184] Joseph is listed as retired on the 1900 U.S. census living in the household of his nephew, William. His age at the time was 67, born in 1832 in Illinois, as were both of his parents.[185]

Francis is not listed on the 1870 U.S. census. The 1880 census lists his family as living in dwelling 198. Francis is listed as a white male farmer, 51 years old, born in Hesse Darmstadt, as were his parents. His wife, Rebecca, is listed as a white female housekeeper, born in Ohio, her father and mother born in Pennsylvania.

Their children listed are: Joseph J., a single white male farm laborer, 26 years old, born in Iowa, who married Maggie Tweed and had seven children; Minnie, a single, 18-year old, white female living at home, born in California, who married E.F. Brady and had four children; Frederick, single 16-year old farm laborer, attending school, born in California, who married Josie Breedlove and moved to Los Angeles; William S., 12 years old, attending school, born in California, who married Martha Watkins in 1894 and had two children, was constable in Bear Valley in 1894; and Dolly D., nine years old, attending school, born in California, who died at the age of 17 years and is buried in the Valley Center Cemetery.[186]

According to Guinn, an older child, John, was living in his home state of Iowa, and a younger child, Edna, resided in Glenellen, Sonoma County in 1907.[187] Edna is also buried in the Valley Center Cemetery according to the cemetery records. No birth or death date is recorded.

In *The History of California* published in 1907, Guinn states in the biography of Frederick that he was born on February 11, 1829. His family immigrated to America in 1840 and settled in Pennsylvania for four years, then moved to Iowa in 1843. Francis married Rebecca Helmrick in 1850. She was born November 15, 1835, in Ohio.

Francis left Iowa in 1854 to join a wagon train traveling to California. He traveled with the train for a few weeks, then set off on foot. He walked to Colfax, in Placer County where he farmed for a short time. He then turned his attention to mining in northern California where his wife and family joined him in 1860.[188]

In November 1875, Francis settled in Valley Center and filed his homestead claim. His wife and family joined him in San Diego County in 1876. Through his years of hard work, Francis obtained 240 acres of land on which he practiced general farming until his death.[189] Francis is listed in the Valley Center Cemetery records, with no death or birthdate given, although, Guinn states that Rebecca was a widow living on the family farm in 1907.[190]

William S. Fleshman is listed on the 1900 U.S. census living in dwelling number 113 with his family and his Uncle Joseph. William is listed as a white male farmer, age 30, born August 1869, in California, married seven years. His wife, Martha, is listed as a white female, 27 years old, born February 1873, in California, married seven years, mother of two living children. Their son, Earnest, is listed as six years old, born February 1894; and daughter, Eula, is listed as four years old, born in January 1896.[191] William's mother, Rebecca is listed as head of household number 114, 64 years old, born in 1834 in Iowa, as were her parents.[192]

According to Abel Davis, William helped Sam Striplin haul wood and lumber down the steep grades in the area by controlling the wheelhorse, or the horse closest to the wheel, and managing the wagon brake with a rope.[193]

Guinn referenced <u>Elizabeth Fleshman</u> marrying <u>Herman Jacoby</u> of Valley Center and having three children. The family relationship between Joseph, Francis, and Elizabeth Fleshman, born 1854, is not known, as no record of Elizabeth was found other than Guinn's.[194] Elizabeth Jacoby died in 1896 according to Valley Center Cemetery records and is buried in the community cemetery.

The Jacoby family members are also early pioneers of Valley Center. A map published circa 1915, shows a 40-acre parcel in the northeast quarter of Section 24, Township 11 South, Range 2 West. This land had been a portion of J. Hedden's claim in 1876. The family is not listed on the Bear Valley census records prior to 1900.

<u>Donald Gray</u> filed homestead claim #476 on May 5, 1879. Mr. Gray claimed 40 acres located in the northeast quarter of the southwest quarter of Section 13, Township 11 South, Range 2 West. Total fees paid at the time of filing included a $5 filing fee, and $1.50 commissions at $1.25 per acre. Excess receipt #720 was issued at that time.[195] Today this property is located west of Valley Center Road, south of Betsworth Road (see Figure 5).

No further information was found regarding Donald Gray during research for this study. His name does not appear on the 1880 U.S. census records of the Bear Valley Township, nor in the county directories.

<u>Nancy Hedden</u> has the distinction of being the first settler to file a homestead claim listed in the Los Angeles County Land Office for land in Bear Valley. She filed claim #185 on December 3, 1875, for 82.59 acres located in Lots 2 and 3, Section 19, Township 11 South, Range 1 West. The total fees paid included a $5 filing fee and $3 commissions at $1.25 per acre. Excess receipt #422 was issued in the amount of $3.24. This claim, amended on February 1, 1877, included an additional 80 acres located in the southeast quarter of the northeast quarter and the northeast quarter of the southeast quarter, Section 24. An additional fee of $5 filing fee and $3 commissions was paid at the time. A comment to the entry stated: "See Comm. letter "C" December 14, 1876."[196]

Although the claim was made under Nancy Hedden's name, her son, <u>George</u>, is referred to as the owner of the property. No homestead record substantiating this claim could be located during research for this study. However, the 1875 U.S. Government plat map of Township 11 South, Range 1 West, shows "G. Hedden's House" west of Section 19 and in the northeast quarter of Section 24, Township 11 South, Range 2 West of the 1876 plat map. Today, this property is located on the east and west sides of the intersection of Woods Valley Road and Valley Center Road, with Banbury Drive threading through the western parcel (see Figure 5).

George raised English walnuts and almonds on his farm.[197] According to Abel Davis, George used all the claims allowed one person and settled on most of the level land at the south entrance to the valley. Valley Center Road was the western boundary of his property. George built two large adobe houses on the southwest corner where a flowing spring furnished water for both his household and his livestock. He established a small reservoir to water his orchard and garden. George also erected a small frame building near the intersection of Valley Center Road and Woods Valley Road which was later used as a general store by Mr. Foster.[198]

J.M Guinn states that George was born on October 21, 1835, in Madison County, Illinois, near the city of Alton. He moved from his home state in 1859 when his father, J. Hedden, decided to try his luck at farming in California. His father died in the Sierras after becoming ill while in the plains. His mother, <u>Nancy Moore Hedden</u>, continued on the journey with their children and settled in the Sacramento valley for approximately ten years before settling in Valley Center in 1869.[199]

George's brother, <u>Joel C. Hedden</u>, filed homestead claims for several different parcels in the Valley Center area over a period of fifteen years. The first claim, #250, filed on April 24, 1876, consisted of 160 acres located in Sections 24 and 13, Township 11 South, Range 2 West.[200] This parcel is located west of Valley Center Road with Old Road bordering the property on the north (see Figure 5).

The second claim was filed by Joel Hedden in the San Diego County Land Office on August 25, 1885. It consisted of 80 acres located in the west half of the southeast quarter of Section 6, Township 9 South, Range 3 West, SBM. The homestead claim, legally abandoned on October 26, 1885, was also filed in the San Diego County Land Office. The abandonment consisted of the west half of the southeast quarter of Section 5 and the north half of the southeast quarter of Section 6.[201] This parcel is located outside of the current study area.

Joel C. Hedden's third homestead claim, #5904, was filed on April 13, 1891, for 160 acres located in the northeast quarter of Section 23,

Township 11 South, Range 2 West.[202] This parcel is located approximately one mile west of Valley Center Road, and abuts the northern boundary of the Daley Ranch and adjoins his nephew, Albert Striplin's land to the east (see Figure 5). The school census for 1895 and 1896, lists the residence of J.C. Hedden as Sections 23 and 24, and maps published after the turn of the century show J.C. Hedden as the owner, even though Joel died in 1896.

Nancy Hedden is the only person in her immediate family listed in the 1870 U.S. census for San Pascual and Pala Townships. Nancy is listed as "lives with Striclin" [sic], her daughter and husband. Her age is given as 56 years and her birthplace as Illinois.[203] Mrs. Hedden is listed on the 1880 U.S. census for Bear Valley Township living with her son, George, in dwelling number 207. Nancy is listed as a white widowed female housekeeper, age 66 years, born in Illinois, parents both born in North Carolina. George is listed as a single white male farmer, 45 years of age, born in Illinois, father born in Kentucky.[204]

Joel Calvin Hedden is listed on the 1880 U.S. census as living in dwelling number 183 with his family. Joel is listed as a 37-year old, married, white male farmer and apiarist, born in Illinois, father born in Kentucky and mother born in Illinois. Joel's wife, Luvica J., is listed as 22 years old, housekeeper, born in Missouri, both parents born in Tennessee. Their daughter, Frances J., is listed as five years old, born in California. Their second daughter, Sarah Lulu, is listed as four years old, born in California.[205]

George is listed as retired and living with his nephew, Charles Lefevre, in dwelling number 102 on the 1900 U.S. census for Bear Valley.[206] According to Guinn, George sold his land to W.H.H Dinwiddie in 1902.[207] Joel died in 1896 and his mother, Nancy, died in 1898. They are both buried in the Valley Center Cemetery. The Hedden family proved to be an integral part of the early history of Valley Center through their foresight, dedication, and hard work.

George Herbst did not raise a large family or begin a successful business in Valley Center as did other settlers. He was a kind, hard working man who was always there to help anyone in need.[208] His property has become an integral part of Valley Center as the location of the first church and the community cemetery. George died on June 25, 1883, only seven years after filing his claim and is buried in the Valley Center Cemetery. Although no record of a family was located during the research for this study, a William Herbst is listed as marrying Emily F. Smith in Escondido, no date given.[209]

George filed homestead claim #186 on December 7, 1875, for 122.92 acres of land located in Section 6 and Section 7 of Township 11 South, Range 1 West. The legal description includes the south half of the southwest quarter of Section 6 and the northeast quarter of the northwest quarter of Section 7. The total fees paid at that time included a $10 filing fee and $6 commissions at $1.25 per acre.[210]

According to Abel Davis, George Herbst filed his claim in 1866. This could not be corroborated during the research for this study. Davis also states that after George's death, the property was sold to Dr. J.H. Clark by Reverend Sherrard who had been named as administrator of the estate.[211] Today, this property contains an adobe house built on Miller Road by Reverend Sherrard in the early 1880s which has the distinction of being the oldest remaining residence in Valley Center. The legal description of the Herbst property, however, does not include this parcel (see Figure 5).

The 1875 U.S. plat map of Township 11 South, Range 1 West, shows "G. Herbert's House" in the western portion of Section 6. The 1876 U.S. plat map of Township 11 South, Range 2 West, shows "G. Herberts House" in the southeast portion of the southeast quarter of Section 1. The 1877 Old Survey 24 map shows "G. Herbst" in Section 7.

George Herbst registered to vote in San Diego on June 14, 1880. He stated his age as 50 years, born in Kentucky, occupation farmer in Bear Valley.[212] The 1880 U.S. census lists Mr. Herbst as living alone in dwelling number 203. He is listed as a single, white male farmer, 50 years old, born in Kentucky, father born in Prussia, mother born in New York.[213] Although George Herbst lived in Valley Center for a relatively short time, his influence has left a significant mark in the history.

John J. Hicks filed homestead claim #1341 on September 4, 1883, for 80 acres located in the southern end of the valley where Lake Wohlford is today. The legal description is the southeast quarter of the southeast quarter of Section 32, and the southwest quarter of the southwest quarter of Section 33, Township 11 South, Range 1 West. Fees collected at the time of filing included a $5 filing fee and $3 commissions of $1.25 per acre.[214] Although Mr. Hicks did not file a legal claim until 1883, "Hick's House" is shown on the 1875 U.S. plat map of Township 11 South, Range 1 West, in the southwest quarter of Section 33. This location is now under water in Lake Wohlford (see Figure 5).

John and his family are listed as living in dwelling number 180 on the 1880 U.S. census. John is listed as a married, white male farmer, 53 years old, born in New York, as were his parents. His wife, Ellen, is listed as a 50-year old, white female housekeeper, born in Ohio, father born in New Jersey, mother born in Pennsylvania.[215]

John and Ellen's son, <u>Fred A</u>., is listed as a 14-year old student, born in Michigan, father born in New York, and mother born in New York as well. <u>Laura E. Harrison</u> is listed as John's stepdaughter, living with them. She is listed as a 20-year old, white female, at home, born in Illinois, father born in England, and mother born in Ohio. Laura married D.M. Breedlove in 1883 and had five children. Apparently, both John and Ellen were married previously, as they each had a child with a different spouse.[216]

Also living with the Hicks family at the time is <u>Frank B. Good</u>. He is listed as 28 years old, occupation farm laborer, born in Indiana, father and mother born in Ohio.[217]

The Hicks family moved to the Bernardo area after selling their land in Bear Valley in 1888 to the State of California for the purpose of constructing the first water system into the newly founded town of Escondido. The water system, known as the San Luis Rey Flume, directed water from the river and stored it in Lake Wohlford for the purpose of irrigating fields and providing water to the new town and its residents.[218]

<u>Benajah E. Holcomb</u> is listed on the 1870 U.S. census of San Pascual and Pala Districts as living in dwelling number 71 with John Antes. Benajah is listed as a 23-year old male farmer, with $1000 worth of real estate and $430 value in personal estate, born in Connecticut, and a citizen of the U.S.[219] Benajah registered to vote in San Diego County on July 31, 1872. He stated his age as 25, born in Connecticut, and a farmer in San Pascual.[220]

The biographical profile of Benajah written in 1907 by Guinn, states that Ben enlisted to fight during the Civil War in Company I, First Connecticut Heavy Artillery. After the war, in poor health, Ben came to California. He lived in Mariposa County for a short time before he moved south to San Diego County and settled on government land in Valley Center.[221]

Benajah filed homestead claim #805 on August 8, 1881, for 160 acres of land. The legal description is the east half of the southwest quarter, the southwest quarter of the southwest quarter of Section 8, and the southeast quarter of the southeast quarter of Section 7, Township 11 South, Range 1 West. Total fees paid included a $10 filing fee and $6 paid in commissions at $1.25 per acre.[222] The land today is located south of Valley Center Road and Vesper Road (see Figure 5).

Benajah is not listed on the 1880 U.S. census of Bear Valley Township, but his wife, <u>Nancy</u>, is listed with two of the couple's daughters living in dwelling number 208. Nancy is listed as a married, white female housekeeper, 25 years old, born in Illinois, father born in

Connecticut, mother born in Illinois. Her eldest daughter, <u>Clara</u>, is listed as two years old, born in Illinois. Nancy's youngest daughter, <u>Bertha</u>, is listed as one year old, born in California. Also listed as living in the Holcomb household is <u>Aparieia Garcia</u>, listed as a 15-year old Indian, attending school, born in California, father born in Mexico, and mother born in California.[223]

Nancy died at the family ranch in the late 1890s. According to the Valley Center Cemetery records, Mrs. N.C. Holcomb died on June 22, 1897, and is buried in the community cemetery. Guinn stated in *The History of California* that Nancy died in 1895.

B.E. Holcomb is listed on the 1900 U.S. census of Bear Valley Township. He is listed in dwelling number 72 with four of his children. Ben is listed as a 53-year old widowed farmer, born September 1846, in Connecticut. The children were all born in California. They are: <u>Roy</u>, 19 years old, born November 1880, a single, white farm laborer; <u>Ray</u>, 16-year old son, born February 1884, attending school; <u>Walter B.</u>, 15 years old, born May 1885, attending school; and the youngest child is listed as <u>Mattie P.</u>, four years old, born August 1895.

Guinn listed B.E. and Nancy Holcomb's seven children as: <u>Clara</u>, who married G.H. Shelby; <u>Bertha</u>, who married Edward Hunter of Randsburg; <u>Nettie</u>, wife of C.M. James; <u>Myrtle</u>, <u>Ray</u>, married Elizabeth May Borden, <u>Roy</u>, who were living on the family farm at the time; and <u>Walter</u>, who was living in San Diego.[224]

<u>Walter Buell Holcomb</u> married <u>Hattie Lewis Clark</u> on April 24, 1906.[225] They had two children. He died in 1918 after contacting the Spanish flu, or influenza, while on the job as a San Diego police officer. His brother, Ray, was also a San Diego police officer.[226]

Benajah E. Holcomb died on April 2, 1903, and is buried in the Valley Center Cemetery. He had lived in the Valley Center area for more than thirty years as a rancher and operated a dairy business. His son, Roy Elmer, married <u>Allie Risdon</u> in 1905 and took over the family farm after Benajah's death.

The 1876 U.S. plat map for Township 11 South, Range 2 West, shows "Johnson's House" in the southeast quarter of Section 23. No information was recovered during research for this study to provide an identity of the family living there at the time of the survey. One article from the *Escondido Times*, dated March 9, 1893, states that a baby girl was born on March 6, 1893, to <u>Mr. and Mrs. Johnson</u>.[227]

<u>Edmond L. Jones</u> filed homestead claim #226 on February 7, 1876, for 40 acres legally described as the southwest quarter of the northeast quarter of Section 21, Township 11 South, Range 1 West. He

paid a total of $6.50 filing fees and commissions.[228] The same parcel of land had been included in a claim filed by Mr. Price in 1875. It was also claimed by J.Q. Adams just four days after the Jones claim was filed (see Figure 5). A house is shown as "Price's House" on the 1875 U.S. plat map in Section 21.

Edmond Jones is not listed on the 1870, 1880, or 1900 U.S. census records of Bear Valley. However, three children are listed in a newspaper article as attending the Bear Valley School in February 1894. These children are: Bessie, fifth grade; Ella, seventh grade; and Jennie, second grade.[229]

In 1894, Zeph Jones took over the D.M. Breedlove ranch and produced a good crop.[230] Zephaniah Jones is listed on the 1900 U.S. Bear Valley Township census as living in dwelling number 89 with his wife, Helen M. Zeph is listed as 51 years old, born in October 1856, in New York, with his parents also born in New York. Helen is listed as 43 years of age, born in March 1866, in California, father born in Massachusetts and mother in California. Zeph and Helen are listed as married 12 years with no children born to Helen.[231]

In 1905, Zeph Jones is cited in the *Escondido Times* as living in Vineyard, a small community located to the south of Valley Center on the boundary of the Guejito ranch.[232]

There are several persons with the surname Jones listed in the Valley Center Cemetery records. This includes: Jennie Jones, unknown birthdate, died May 17, 1894; John Ellsworth Jones, born October 28, 1883, died January 16, 1970; Mrs. Josephine Jones, born September 23, 1883, died November 4, 1973; Mrs. Trudy Jones, birth and death dates unknown; and Verne Arthur Jones, born December 19, 1889, died January 31, 1964.

Augustus Caesar Kitching was one of the early settlers in the valley who did not file on his land until after 1875 although he is listed as a farmer in the San Luis Rey and Agua Caliente areas on his voter registration application on July 30, 1869. He stated his age as 23, born in Texas.[233] He later registered to vote on April 6, 1880, stating at that time he was a farmer in Bear Valley.[234]

On June 3, 1876, Augustus filed homestead claim #261. He claimed 160 acres located in the south half of the northeast quarter, the northwest quarter of the northeast quarter, and the southeast quarter of the northwest quarter of Section 13, Township 11 South, Range 2 West. Total fees paid include $10 filing fee and $6 commissions at $1.25 per acre.[235] This location corroborates the reference to "Hitchening's House" in the northeast quarter of Section 13 of the 1876 U.S. plat map of Township 11 South, Range 2 West. Today this property is located at the junction of Valley Center Road and Lilac Road (see Figure 5).

The Kitching family is not listed on the 1870 U.S. census of the San Pascual and Pala Townships. They are listed on the 1880 census, however, as living in dwelling 209. Augustus C. is listed as a 33-year old white male farmer, married, born in Texas, father born in Georgia, and mother born in Mississippi. His wife, Amelia A., is listed as 33 years old, married, housekeeper, born in Arkansas, and her parents both born in Alabama.

Their eldest son, David C., is listed as 11 years old, attending school, born in California, as were all of the children. The eldest daughter, Jemima E., is listed as nine years old; Sarah Anne, seven years old; John M., five years old; and the youngest son, Julius K., is listed as two years old.

There are discrepancies regarding the spelling of the family surname, as well as the wife's and children's given names. As stated previously, the house was cited as belonging to "Hitchening" on the 1876 plat map. Guinn states in his biography of Mrs. P.E. Kitching, that she was the wife of A.C. Kitching. She was born in southern Arkansas to parents James M. and Sarah Black Griffin, raised in Texas for seventeen years, where she married A.C. Kitching, a native of Texas. She came to California in 1886 with her parents who settled first in Campo and then in San Luis Rey. Her father died on the ranch in 1901. Guinn states further that the children's names are: Jeremiah, Charles, Roy, and Sadie. In 1907, Mrs. P.E. Kitching was living on the 117-acre ranch on which she concentrated on raising stock and grains.[236]

According to Abel Davis, the family name was Kitchen [sic], and the children's given names were Dave, Sally, and Minn, also known as "Toad."[237] The father had built a frame and adobe house on his land. The frame front of the house was to be used as a store in which were sold the first groceries and clothing. Davis also stated that records indicated that Kitchen [sic] had settled on the land in 1865. No records confirming this statement were found during the research for this study.

A.C. Kitching filed another homestead claim in San Diego County on September 10, 1889. The claim consisted of 176.59 acres described as Lots 1 and 2, the north half of the southwest quarter and the southwest quarter of the southeast quarter of Section 35, Township 10 South, Range 4 West. This location is outside of the current study area.

William Loos is shown on the plat maps to have lived in Section 26 of Township 10 South, Range 2 West, in 1876, 1890, and 1898. The name written on the plat maps is "Lewis" on the early maps, yet it is written as "Loose" in 1913. Although his name appears in the same area for 25 years, no homestead claim was recovered during the research for this study in either San Diego County records or Los Angeles County records at the National Archives in Laguna Niguel.

William Loos' naturalization registration was located in the Superior Court of San Diego County records, filed on July 20, 1898.[238] William immigrated from Germany. According to the 1900 U.S. census for Bear Valley Township, William Loos entered the United States in 1884, had lived in the U.S. for 16 years, and was not naturalized.[239] He is listed in dwelling number 53, birthdate December 1869, a single, white male farmer, born in Germany, as were both of his parents.[240]

Either separate persons with a name of Lewis, Loos, or Loose, have lived on the same parcel of land, or perhaps a family member was there in the 1870s. The William Loos listed in the 1900 U.S. census cannot be the same person who lived in Section 26 in 1876, because if the information is correct, William Loos did not come to the U.S. until 1884, and he would have been only seven years old in 1876. Newspaper articles in the area could not corroborate information regarding William Loos.

The family of James Lovett is listed in dwelling number 47 of the 1870 U.S. census of San Pasqual and Pala Districts. James is listed as a 36-year old, born in Alabama, white male farm laborer, with $500 real estate value and $100 personal estate value. The categories "Born within the year and Married within the year" are both check-marked, which was probably a mistake by the enumerator. James' wife is listed as Ada, 26-year old, white female born in Hanover, with both parents listed as foreign-born. Children listed are: Frank, 10 years old, born in Texas; Katy J., eight years old, born in Texas; Ada E., five years old, born in Yuma; and Emelia, two years old, born in California.

The Lovett family is discussed in Chapter One for the naming of Bear Valley. According to the story, their family arrived from Fort Yuma with a few dollars in their pockets and settled on a government claim. The father had traveled to San Diego to sell wood and while he was gone, a large grizzly bear came near the family cabin. The mother was outside of the cabin washing clothes at the time with a young baby in a basket beside her. Two older children were playing in the manger nearby. The mother scared the bear off when she fired a rifle and missed him. The bear was later killed and was reportedly the largest bear from the area, possibly even the State of California.[241]

Figure 9. The James Lovett Family Adobe, ca. 1947.
Photo Reproduced from The California Rancher.

The family of James Lovett is not listed on subsequent U.S. census records, and a homestead claim was not found during research for this study.

John McCoy was an early settler who did not stay in Valley Center. He filed homestead claim #1977 for 167.79 acres on December 23, 1884. The legal description reads the north half of the southwest quarter and the south half of the northwest quarter of Section 6, Township 11 South, Range 1 West. The total fees paid included a $10 filing fee and $6 commissions at $1.25 per acre. Excess receipt #1381 was given for the amount of $9.74.[242] This property today is bordered on the west by Miller Road, approximately one-half mile north of the Valley Center Cemetery (see Figure 5).

According to Abel Davis, John filed on land east of Valley Center Road in 1878. McCoy was a bachelor who later sold his property and moved back East. At the time of the sale, he deeded three acres to the Methodist Episcopal church for camp meetings.[243] John McCoy was not listed on the 1870, 1880, or 1900 U.S. census records or in the San Diego County directories. Although John lived in the valley for a short time, he will be remembered for his generosity.

Robert Price was another short-term resident of Valley Center. He is listed as residing in dwelling number 75 on the 1870 U.S. census of San Pascual and Pala Districts. He is listed as a U.S. Citizen, 34 years old, white male farm laborer, born in Ireland, with both parents listed as foreign-born. Also listed living in the household is James Brown, a 43-year old white male farm laborer, born in Austin, with parents both listed as foreign-born.

The 1875 U.S. plat map of Township 11 South, Range 1 West, shows "Price's House" in the northeast quarter of Section 21. Subsequent maps and homestead deeds list the property as belonging to J.Q. Adams in 1876, and J. Jones, in 1876. This property is located north of Woods Valley Road and is surrounded on three sides by the San Pasqual Indian Reservation (see Figure 5).

Jennings Thompson Shelby was a blacksmith by trade who came into Valley Center with his family in the late 1860s or early 1870s. According to Abel Davis, J.T. and family filed a homestead claim on their land in 1866. Research could not confirm this date. The 1875 U.S. plat map of Township 11 South, Range 1 West, shows "Shelby's House" in the southwest quarter of Section 9. Old Survey 24, surveyed in September 1877, shows "J. Shelby" in Section 10. The 1900 U.S. plat map shows "J. Shelby's fence" in Section 9.[244] No homestead claim was found in San Diego or Los Angeles County during the research for this study. According to Nellie Shelby, daughter of Clara and Henry Shelby, she was born on what was known as the Thompson ranch, which later became known as the Cooper ranch located off of Cole Grade Road.[245] This property today is located west of Paradise Valley Road and south of State Route 79, approximately two miles east of the junction of Valley Center Road and Cole Grade Road (see Figure 5).

The family of J.T. Shelby is not listed on the 1870 or 1880 U.S. census of the Bear Valley Township. The 1900 U.S. census lists the family in dwelling number 35. J.T. is listed as 76 years old, born in December 1823, widowed, born in Illinois, both parents born in North Carolina, occupation blacksmith, renter of his property. His son, Henry, is listed as a white male, 33 years old, born February 1867, in California, father born in Illinois, mother born in Indiana, married two years, occupation farm laborer. Henry's wife is listed as Clara, a white female, 23 years old, born November 1877, in California, father born in New Jersey, mother born in Illinois. Their daughter, Nellie, is listed as an infant, born in January 1900, in California. Another granddaughter is listed in the J.T. Shelby household. Her name is Dora Crug, 12 years old, born in November 1887 [state of birth is unreadable], father and mother both born in California, attended school for eight months during the year.[246] A letter written by Nellie Shelby Chandler-Tomkin states that she had an adopted sister, and refers to her as Mrs. Jack Allen.[247]

Clara Holcomb Shelby later became the postmaster of Valley Center in 1909 when R.T. Baines retired.[248] Mrs. Shelby was also instrumental in founding the library in Valley Center when she petitioned the San Diego Free Library in 1916 for a branch to operate out of her store.[249]   The Valley Center Store was located on Valley Center Road and Lilac Road and is shown as Figure 10. According to Nellie, the family later moved to the building occupied today as "Corral Liquor." After Clara's death on April 19, 1923, Nellie took over the job of postmaster and grocery store operator with her husband, Fred Chandler, until 1943.[250] Nellie's father, George Henry Shelby, died on December 11, 1928 and is buried in the Valley Center Cemetery.[251]

Figure 10. Photograph of the Shelby Family, ca. 1916.
From left to right: G. Henry Shelby, Clara Shelby, George Rumfield,
and Nellie Shelby.

Nellie married <u>George Rumfield</u> in 1917 and had one daughter, <u>Georgette</u>, born in September 1918, in Tucson, Arizona. After Mr. Rumfield's death in 1919, Nellie returned to Valley Center and in January 1920, married <u>Fred Chandler</u>.   They had one daughter, <u>Novelle</u>, born before 1923 when the Chandlers took over the store and post office. The family later moved to Santa Cruz where Mr. Chandler died in 1965. Nellie then married A.J. Tomkin in 1971.[252]

<u>Hanna L. Shelby</u> married Valley Center pioneer, Ambrose Walsh in 1875. She is listed as his wife on the 1880 U.S. census of Bear Valley Township. Her birthdate is 1860 in California, her father was born in Illinois, and her mother's birthplace is not listed.[253]   It is possible Hanna is an elder sister of George Henry's, although there is no confirmation. A death date was not found, and she is not listed on the 1900 census. Ambrose Walsh is listed as a widower at that time.[254]

The Valley Center Cemetery records also list a <u>Mrs. Phyllis S. Shelby</u>. The birth and death dates are unknown as are any family relations.[255] No further information regarding Phyllis was found during research for this study.

Although no homestead or land records were found for J.T. Shelby, his family and their descendants contributed to the history of Valley Center.

Another family of early settlers of Valley Center is that of <u>Samuel Striplin</u>. Samuel is listed in dwelling number 69 of the 1870 U.S. census of San Pascual and Pala Districts. The surname is misspelled as "Striclin". Samuel is listed as a 42-year old farmer, with $1000 value real estate, $900 value personal estate, born in Tennessee, and a citizen of the U.S. His wife, <u>Priscilla</u> is listed as a 36-year old housekeeper born in Illinois. Children listed are: Aber [<u>Abel</u>], 16-year old male, born in Illinois; <u>Albert</u>, age 14, born in Illinois; <u>John</u>, age 11, born in Illinois; <u>Charles</u>, nine years old, born in California; <u>Nancy</u>, seven years old, born in California; and <u>Armis</u>, five-year old female born in California. Also listed in the Striplin residence is <u>Nancy Hedden</u>, a 56-year old female, born in Illinois. Nancy Hedden was Priscilla's mother.[256]

The family also appears in the 1880 U.S. census in dwelling number 181, with the correct surname spelling. Samuel is listed as 53 years old, married, born in Tennessee, parents both born in South Carolina, occupation farmer. His wife, Priscilla, is listed as 48 years old, occupation housekeeper, born in Illinois, father born in Kentucky, mother born in Illinois. Their children listed are: <u>Nancy</u>, 16-year old white female, born in California, occupation at home, attended school within that year. Their second daughter, <u>Ella</u>, is listed as a 14-year old, attending school, born in California. Samuel and Priscilla's son, <u>Gilbert</u>, is listed as eight years old, attending school, and born in California.[257]

Two boarders are listed living in the Striplin residence. They are: <u>Eduard A. Robinson</u>, a 23-year old white male farm laborer, born in Indiana, father born in Michigan, mother born in Indiana; and <u>Jason Deusmore</u>, 24 years old, occupation blacksmith, born in Wisconsin, father born in Pennsylvania, mother born in New York.[258]

The family is not listed on the 1900 U.S. census. According to Abel Davis, Samuel purchased the east end of the Davis ranch after James Davis' death in 1893.[259] Confirmation of this statement was not found during the research for this study. Homestead claim #553 was filed for 160 acres including the east half of the northwest quarter, the southwest quarter of the northwest quarter of Section 34, and the southeast quarter of the northeast quarter of Section 33, Township 11 South, Range 1 West, San Bernardino Meridian.[260]

Figure 11. The Samuel Striplin Family Adobe, ca. 1912.
Photo courtesy of Carl von Seggern

The Bear Valley School was built on the eastern portion of the Striplin ranch, possibly as early as 1976. The teachers of this small community school were usually housed with the Striplin family. The school continued with fewer and fewer students, until it finally closed in 1916, and later demolished.

Figure 12. The Bear Valley School House, ca. 1912.
Photo courtesy of Carl von Seggern

Sam raised rye, wheat, and barley, becoming a pioneer of agriculture. According to Davis, most of the other settlers raised livestock on their parcels and said that nothing could be grown in the soil of the valley.[261]

Striplin was a integral part of Valley Center history for not only his agriculture, but also for the fact that he worked with Will Wilhite to bring lumber down from the mill on Palomar to provide building materials for the fast growing towns of Escondido and San Diego.[262] Samuel was also appointed a delegate of the Bear Valley roads along with Samuel Antes in 1893.[263]

Sam and Priscilla Striplin later divorced and sold the homestead property to J.H. von Seggern. The saw mill was lost during bankruptcy proceedings.[264]

Samuel Striplin died on July 28, 1911, at the age of 84 years. The *Times Advocate* printed his obituary on August 4, 1911. The article stated that Samuel was born to Revolutionary parents. He emigrated to Illinois and left that state in 1859, at which time he was the captain of a wagon train crossing the plains to California. He is credited with saving the train when he threatened an Indian leader and told the braves to leave. According to the story, the next wagon train through the area was massacred. The Striplin wagon train arrived in the Sacramento Valley where Samuel and his family remained until 1868 when they moved to Bear Valley.[265]

Samuel registered to vote in San Diego on October 5, 1868, stating his age as 39, born in Tennessee, and his occupation was a farmer in San Diego.[266] His son, Albert J. Striplin registered to vote on April 14, 1879 at which time he stated his age as 22, born in Illinois, occupation farmer in Bear Valley.[267]

Albert filed homestead claim #5903 on April 13, 1891, for 160 acres in Township 11 South, Range 2 West. The legal description is the northwest quarter of Section 24.[268] He fulfilled all obligations and received a deed of ownership from the Los Angeles County Land Office on March 11, 1898. His witnesses were neighbors George Young, Ambrose Walsh, Charles Blackall, and John V. Walsh.[269] This property today is located approximately one-half mile west of the junction of Valley Center and Woods Valley roads (see Figure 5).

Samuel's son, Abel, claimed land in San Pasqual where he remained until 1893 and raised his family. In a letter written by one his adopted daughters, Opal Bemis, it is reported that Abel and his wife, Sarah, had three natural-born children, one of whom died in infancy. The two living children, Adrian and May, were away at school most of the time.

Abel and Sarah brought orphans to live with them and raised the children as their own. This included Earl, Elmer, Ella, Nita, Opal, and

Alice. The family were members in the Seventh-Day Adventists, and held church services for the community at their house in San Pasqual Valley. Opal refers to "Grandma Striplin, Uncle George Heddon [sic], and Uncle Joel Heddon [sic]", as being children of "Nancy Heddon [sic]" in her story. Research proved "Grandma" is Priscilla, wife of Samuel Striplin.

Opal also states that although the family lived in several different places in Valley Center, only Joel and Nancy Hedden are buried in the Valley Center Cemetery. She also recalls the San Francisco earthquake in 1906. Apparently, the shock waves were felt in Valley Center which caused knickknacks to fall off shelves. According to Opal, her father was responsible for naming the community "Valley Center" when he served as sheriff. This information was not confirmed during research for this study.[270]

Reverend Claude F. Thompson and his family were early settlers in Valley Center. Their names do not appear on the census records, nor on the land registries in San Diego or Los Angeles. The obituary of C.F. Thompson, printed in the *Daily Times Advocate*, states that C.F. moved to Valley Center when 14 years old. Claude served in the Civil War for almost four years with the 60th New York Regiment of the Union Army.[271] He was born in 1841 and married Ulba Anna Knowles. Ulba was a minister. She was born in 1857 and died on May 29, 1908. She is buried in the Valley Center Cemetery.[272]

Claude and Ulba had three children: Homer, James Theo, and Gertrude. Information regarding Homer is unknown. James Theo was born July 6, 1880, married Lelitha Garrett, and had two children. The family lived in Sections 29 and 30, Township 10 South, Range 1 West after the turn of the century. J.T. died October 27, 1964, and is buried in the Valley Center Cemetery. Gertrude married Mr. Bybee of Pasadena.[273]

Myrtle A. Thompson is also listed in the Valley Center Cemetery records. She was born in 1883 and died in 1959. No family relation was established, although she may have been a child of Homer, or possibly a fourth child of Ulba and Claude who was not mentioned in the obituary.

Claude's father, Charles F. Thompson, registered to vote in San Diego on July 11, 1872, at which time he stated his age as 43, born in New Jersey, occupation farmer, residence in San Pasqual.[274] The Thompson family contributed to the history of Valley Center as pioneers of the area.

George Tracy was a native Luiseño who did not claim a homestead, although "G. Tracy" is shown in Section 7 on the 1877 Old

Survey 24 map. The family is listed on the 1880 U.S. census of Bear Valley Township in dwelling number 192. George is listed as an Indian male, 32 years old, married, occupation farm laborer, born in California, father born in Vermont, mother born in California. His wife, Cornelia, is listed as an Indian female, 38 years of age, married, born in California, as were both of her parents. Their daughter, Ida, is listed as an Indian female, four years old, born in California.[275] Their son, Frank, is listed in the same census record as a farm laborer living with John D. German in dwelling number 182. Frank is listed as a white male, 19 years old, single, born in California, as were both of his parents.[276]

Given that the family did not own land, they simply moved around to various places throughout the years. George worked as a ranch hand whenever he could find the work. According to Abel Davis, George and Cornelia later separated and each became involved with other people. George was a servant working for María Sutter, a widow living on Palomar Mountain. George is listed on the 1900 U.S. census as 50 years old, born in 1850, and unmarried. Cornelia is not listed, although Davis states that she lived with Pete Weimer and had children by him. Research revealed Cornelia married Peter Wimmer, Jr., in 1889.[277]

A person named Ida Tracey was killed on April 26, 1898, in the Stingaree District of San Diego and is listed on the coroner's report records. The cause of death is recorded as gunshot wounds, and the perpetrator is listed as Jesse Daley.[278] Research did not conclusively prove this person to be the Ida Tracy from Valley Center.

Abraham J. Von Meter and his son, Isaac L. Von Meter did not file a homestead claim, but are listed on the U.S. Government plat map of 1875. "Van Meter's House" is shown in the southwest quarter of Section 35, Township 10 South, Range 2 West. The house location is also shown on the 1876 plat map in the northwest quarter of the northwest quarter of Section 2, Township 11 South, Range 2 West.

The surname is spelled on various documents as Von Meter, Von Metre, Van Meter, or Van Matre. Abraham registered to vote in San Diego on February 23, 1869. He stated his age as 46, born in Idaho, occupation farmer in San Luis Rey. Isaac registered on July 16, 1869, and stated his age as 24, born in Alaska, occupation farmer in San Luis Rey. Both entries were marked sworn, removed. They again registered in 1875. Abraham on June 9, 1875, stated his age as 52, with the additional information same as the first registration. Isaac registered on July 3, 1875, stating his age as 29, born in the U.S., occupation farmer in Bear Valley.[279]

No further information was found regarding the Von Meter family. They are not listed in the 1870, 1880, or 1900 U.S. census records for Bear Valley. Their name appears on the 1898 Official Map of San Diego County as "Von Meter Creek" (see Figure 2, Chapter One). Although there are no official land deeds or claims for the Von Meter family, their name remains as a permanent reminder of their presence in Valley Center.

The Walsh family also left their permanent mark on the community. Walter and his wife, Jane Holden Colby Walsh, arrived with their large family of 11 children in the late 1860s to early 1870s. They had traveled across the plains in 1854 in covered wagons drawn by oxen and originally settled near Sacramento in the San Ramon Valley, Contra Costa County, California.[280]

According to Guinn, the family moved to San Diego County in 1868 and settled in Mission Valley. On October 16, 1879, they came to Valley Center and began filing homestead claims for the government land.[281] There were few neighbors in the vicinity at the time of their arrival, and they settled on prime level land in the center of the valley.

Walter Walsh was born on the high seas enroute from Ireland to the U.S. with his parents in 1819. His family settled in Maine and began farming the land.[282] Walter married Jane Holden Colby in Moose River, Maine, circa 1840. The family is listed in the Moose River census record of 1850. Walter is listed as age 33, born in Ireland; Jane, age 26, born in Maine; son, James, age eight, born in Maine; son, Ambrose, age five, born in Maine; and Austin, age two months, born in Maine.[283]

Walter and his family left Maine and moved to Missouri to homestead land in 1851. While in Missouri, their children, Nicholas (1853) and Catherine (1854) were born. They left that homestead in 1854 to begin their journey across the United States plains.

Their last five children were born in Contra Costa County, California. Francis Phillip was born in 1856, Jerome in 1857, John Vincent in 1860, William S. in 1862, and the youngest, Anne Jane was born in 1864.

Walter Walsh, his wife, and two sons are listed on the 1880 U.S. census of Bear Valley. They are listed living in dwelling number 199. Walter is listed as a married white male, 61 years old, occupation farmer, born on the High Seas, with both parents born in Ireland. Jane is listed as a married white female, 59 years old, occupation keeping house, born in Maine, as were both of her parents.[284]

Their son, William S., is listed as a single white male, 18 years old, occupation farm laborer, born in California, father born on the

High Seas, mother born in Maine. John V. is listed as a 20-year old, single white male, occupation farm laborer, born in California.[285]

Walter died in 1887 and Jane died on the ranch in Valley Center in 1888.[286] They are buried in the Catholic cemetery in Escondido. Their son, Francis, died in San Diego in late 1879 or early 1880. His name was canceled and removed from the Register of Voters, on April 9, 1880, which listed him as 24 years old.[287] Their son, Walter's wife, Catherine A. Aherran Walsh, died January 12, 1881, and is listed on the Mortuary record as 24 years old at the time of death, born in Ireland, buried in the Catholic cemetery in Escondido.

Walter and Jane's son, Jerome, died in Bear Valley on December 21, 1884. The Mortuary Records of San Diego County list his age at the time of death as 27 years, born in California, single, buried in the Catholic cemetery.[288] A reference to their son, James, was located in the Walsh family file at the Valley Center Branch Library. The file stated that James was killed by Indians before 1900. No official record confirmed this information, although his name does not appear in the records after 1890. He is listed as living in the Banner area in 1889-90.[289]

Austin Walsh was the first in the Walsh family to file a homestead claim. He filed claim #329 on September 17, 1877, for 160 acres. The legal description listed is the southwest quarter of the southeast quarter and the north half of the southeast quarter of Section 11, and the northwest quarter of the southwest quarter of Section 12, Township 11 South, Range 2 West. Total fees paid included a $10 filing fee and $6 commissions at $1.25 per acre.[290]

Land to the south and southwest of Austin's claim was later claimed by his brothers. The land originally claimed by Austin today is the southern portion of the Hideaway Lake Resort north of Betsworth Road and west of Lilac Road (see Figure 5).

Austin and his brother, Jerome, are listed on the 1880 U.S. census of Bear Valley. They lived in dwelling number 201. Austin is listed as a 34-year old, single, white male farmer, born in Missouri, father born on the High Seas, and mother born in Maine.[291]

Austin married Nancy Carrie Merrill on May 3, 1884, in Merced, California. They had seven children, one of whom died as a young child. The children's names are: Alice G., Anna, Noval Augustine, Norman, Fannie, Merrill, and Paul W.[292]

Austin and his family are listed as living in dwelling 106 on the 1900 U.S. census of the Bear Valley Township. Austin is listed as "Augustine", 55 years old, married 16 years, born January 1845, in Missouri, father born in Missouri, mother born in Maine, occupation farmer on his own land. His wife, Nancy C., is listed as a 35-year old, white female, married 16 years, born April 1865, in California, parents born in Tennessee, mother of six children, five of whom were living at the time.[293]

Austin and Nancy's children were all born in California. Listed are: daughter, Alice G., 15 years old, born May 1885, attended school for nine months during the year; daughter, Anna C., 13 years old, born March 1887, attended school nine months during the year; son, Norman E., eight years old, born February 1892, attended school nine months during the year; daughter, Francis E., five years old, born October 1894; and son, James M., three years old, born May 1897.[294]

Austin's daughter, Anna, or Annie, married Mark Betsworth and they had one daughter, Gladys. Austin's wife, Nancy C., died in 1901 in Valley Center and is buried in the Catholic cemetery in Escondido.[295] Their son, James M., born on May 3, 1897, died in Valley Center on May 12, 1970, and is buried in the Valley Center Cemetery.[296]

Nicholas Walsh was the second member of the Walsh family to file a homestead claim in Valley Center. He filed claim #399 on October 4, 1878, for 120 acres. The legal description is the east half of the northwest quarter and the norhtwest quarter of the northeast quarter of Section 14, Township 11 South, Range 2 West, San Bernardino Base Meridian.[297]

Nicholas' land bordered his brothers properties: Francis to the east, Austin to the north and Jerome's to the east. His sister, Catherine, and her husband, Charles Blackall, owned land west and south. Nicholas' land was located on the south side of present-day Betsworth Road, approximately one mile west of Lilac Road (see Figure 5).

Nicholas had lived on the land prior to filing the legal papers. He stated on his voter registration in San Diego on October 2, 1874, that he was a farmer in Bear Valley.[298] The 1876 U.S. plat map of Township 11 South, Range 2 West, shows "N. Walsh's House" in the northwest quarter of Section 14. Nicholas retained ownership of this land and rented it out when he and his family later moved to northern California.

Nicholas and his brother, Francis P., are listed living in dwelling number 202 on the 1880 U.S. census of Bear Valley Township. Nicholas is listed as a 27-year old, single white male farmer, born in Missouri. Francis P. is listed as 24 years old, single white male farmer, born in California.[299]

Nicholas married Mary Ella Quinn and they had four sons, all born in California. This includes: Francis Xavier, born June 30, 1892; Jerome Monroe, born November 22, 1897; Nicholas Anthony, born June 22, 1900; and Norman, birthdate unknown.[300] The family is shown in Figure 13.

Figure 13. The Nicholas Walsh Family.
Left: Nicholas and Emma's Wedding Photo, ca. 1890.
Right: Nicholas, Francis, Jerome, Emma, and Nicholas, ca. 1910.

Jerome was the next Walsh family member to file a homestead claim in Valley Center. He filed claim #407 on October 18, 1878, for 80 acres. The legal description is the southwest quarter of the northeast quarter and the northwest quarter of the southeast quarter of Section 14, Township 11 South, Range 2 West. Total fees paid included a $5 filing fee and $3 commissions at $1.25 per acre.[301]

He later filed claim #1031 on May 27, 1882, for an additional 80 acres adjoining his original claim. The legal description of this parcel is northeast quarter of the southeast quarter of Section 14, and the northwest quarter of the southwest quarter of Section 13, Township 11 South, Range 2 West. Total fees paid included a $5 filing fee and $3 commissions at $1.25 per acre.[302]

Jerome's land adjoined his sister, Catherine's, to the west, brother Nicholas' to the northwest, and brother Francis' to the north. Three-quarters of the original claim was later claimed as a homestead by his sister-in-law's father, James M. Quinn, in 1890, which was later owned by his brother, John Vincent Walsh after the turn of the century. Today the land is located approximately one mile west of Valley Center Road and one-quarter mile south of Betsworth Road (see Figure 5).

According to Abel Davis, Jerome was the first European child to be born in Valley Center.[303] This statement cannot be true if Jerome was born in 1856. This would have been long before any settlers are reported to have lived in Valley Center. Also, the family did not move to San Diego County until 1868, according to Guinn.[304]

Jerome died in San Diego on December 21, 1884. He was 27 years, two months, and six days old at the time of his death. His brother, Nicholas, mentions Jerome in a letter written to his Aunt Nancy Ray Colby in Maine dated August 31, 1885. Nicholas states that Jerome was six feet, two inches tall and weighed 145 to 150 pounds when he was well. This suggests that Jerome died of some illness or health problem. Additional information regarding Jerome's death was not found during research for this study.

Francis Phillip Walsh filed the next claim in the family for 160 acres located in Sections 11, 12, and 14 in Township 11 South, Range 2 West. Claim #408 was filed on October 24, 1878, with total fees paid of $16. The legal description is the southeast quarter of the southeast quarter of Section 11, the northeast quarter of the northeast quarter of Section 14, and the southwest quarter of the southwest quarter of Section 12.[305]

This land today is bisected by Betsworth Road and includes Old Ranch Road, southeast of Hideaway Lake. It was surrounded on three sides by other holdings of the Walsh family. Austin's land was north and west, Nicholas' was west, and Jerome's was to the south (see Figure 5). H. Melhuish later purchased 20 acres of the land in Section 12 claimed by Francis at one time.

As previously mentioned, Francis died late 1879 or early 1880. In the letter his brother, Nicholas, wrote to their aunt in Maine, Francis was described as being six-feet tall and weighed 175 to 180 pounds before his death. No additional information regarding his death was found during research for this study.

Ambrose Walsh was the next family member who filed a homestead claim in Valley Center. He filed claim #494 on July 14, 1879, for 160 acres in Sections 13 and 24, Township 11 South, Range 2 West. Ambrose filed his claim under the Act of March 3, 1877, and May 27, 1878. The legal description is the north half of the northeast quarter of Section 24, and the east half of the southeast quarter of Section 13.

This property today is located west of Valley Center Road bordered on the north by Old Road (see Figure 5). This parcel was claimed by J. Hedden in 1876, purchased by Fred Chandler after the turn of the century, and a portion purchased by George Jacoby.

Although Ambrose did not file a legal claim until 1879 for the land on which he lived, he is cited as living there in 1876 on the U.S. plat map of Township 11 South, Range 2 West. "Walsh's House" is shown in the northeast quarter of Section 24.

Ambrose is listed on the 1880 U.S. census of Bear Valley Township living with his wife and children in dwelling 200. Ambrose is listed as a 34-year old, married, white male farmer, born in Missouri, father born on the High Seas, mother born in Maine. His wife, <u>Hanna L.</u>, is listed as a 20-year old, married, white female, occupation keeping house, born in California, father born in Illinois, mother's birthplace not listed. Their children listed are: son, <u>Lawrence A.</u>, three years old, born in California; and daughter, <u>Mary A.</u>, one year old, born in California.[306]

The 1900 U.S. census of Bear Valley Township lists the Ambrose Walsh family living in dwelling number 103. His wife is not listed, and Ambrose is listed as a widower. His age is 54, born in January 1845, in Missouri, father born in Missouri, and mother born in Maine. Lawrence is listed as a 21-year old farm laborer, single, white male, born April 1879, in California. Mary is listed as a 20-year old, single, white female, attending school, born April 1880, in California.[307] Photographs of Ambrose and his family are included as Figure 14. Ambrose's brother, <u>William S.</u>, is listed living with him and his family. William is listed as 38 years old, single, white male farm laborer, born February 1862, in California [parents birthplaces are unreadable].[308]

Figure 14. The Ambrose Walsh Family.
Left: Hannah and Ambrose Wedding Photo, ca. 1875.
Right: Lawrence, Ambrose, and Mary, ca. 1905.

Ambrose died of heart trouble on July 1, 1911, at his home in Valley Center where he had lived for 41 years. He is buried in the Catholic cemetery.[309] Lawrence A. Walsh married <u>Clara Borden</u> and they had one son, <u>Everett S. Walsh</u>, prior to the turn of the century. Lawrence had worked in a sugar factory in Chino before his marriage, and later became interested in the apiary industry.[310] Mary Agnes

Walsh married <u>Jack Helm</u> and they had three daughters: <u>Agnes</u>, <u>Rae</u>, and <u>Gertrude</u>. The family moved to the Los Angeles area where Mary died in 1940.[311]

John Vincent Walsh was the sixth family member to file a homestead claim in Valley Center. He filed claim #4379 on June 14, 1888, for 160 acres located in Sections 22 and 23, Township 11 South, Range 2 West. The legal description is the east half of the northeast quarter of Section 22, and the west half of the northwest quarter of Section 23.[312] Today this parcel is located approximately two miles west of Valley Center Road near Burnt Mountain (see Figure 5). A portion of this parcel was later purchased by J.V.'s brother-in-law's father, Maurice Reidy.

John V. Walsh is listed on the 1880 U.S. census for Bear Valley Township as living with his parents. He is listed as 20 years old, single, farm laborer, born in California.[313] John is listed living alone in dwelling 104 on the 1900 U.S. census for Bear Valley Township. He is listed as a single male, 42 years old, born 1858 (no month given), occupation farmer.[314]

John Vincent Walsh never married. He lived out his life on his ranch in Valley Center until his death on Sunday, November 4, 1917. He had been taken to St. Joseph's Hospital in San Diego for heart and kidney trouble. He was 58 years old at the time of his death. He is buried in the Catholic cemetery.

Walter J. Walsh was the seventh family member to file a homestead claim in Valley Center prior to 1900. He filed claim #4394 on June 25, 1888, for 160 acres located in Township 14 South, Range 1 West.[315] This parcel is located outside of this study area.

Walter J. registered to vote for the first time in San Diego on February 25, 1869. His age was 22 years, his birthplace was Maine, and he was a farmer in San Diego.[316] His second registration occurred on April 27, 1880. He stated his age at that time as 32 years, born in Maine, occupation farmer in the 4th Ward of San Diego.[317]

Walter J. Walsh married <u>Catherine A. Aherran</u> in the mid-1870s. Their firstborn son, <u>Charles Francis Walsh</u> was born in 1877 and their second son, <u>Robert J.</u>, was born in 1879.[318] Catherine died on January 12, 1881, in San Diego, cause of death unknown. She had been born in Ireland in 1857.[319]

Charles F. Walsh was an aviator. He was killed when he was 25 years old while performing for a crowd at the Trenton, New Jersey, State Fair in October 1912. His wife and two children attended the fair and witnessed the crash. Apparently, he was unable to bring the plane out of an almost vertical descent, and crashed into the ground, killing him instantly.[320]

Walsh family records show that Robert J. Walsh had one daughter, <u>Della</u>. There is no additional information regarding Robert's family.[321]

Walter and Jane Walsh's daughters, Catherine and Anne Jane (Jennie), each married men in the Valley Center area. Catherine, ten years older than Jennie, married <u>Charles Blackall</u> and had one daughter, <u>Agnes</u>. Birth information was not found, although Agnes is shown as a young girl in family photographs around the turn of the century, which suggests a birthdate in the 1890s. One such photograph is included as Figure 15.

Figure 15. From left to right: Ambrose Walsh, Millard Quinn, John Walsh, Austin Walsh, Lawrence Walsh, Charles Blackall, Catherine Walsh Blackall, and Agnes Blackall.

The Blackall family filed homestead claims in 1891 for land west and south of Nicholas Walsh's claim (see Figure 5). Catherine filed claim #5934 on April 24, 1891, for 160 acres. The legal description is the west half of the northwest quarter and the north half of the southwest quarter of Section 14, Township 11 South, Range 2 West. Her husband, Charles, filed claim #6001 on May 21, 1891, for an additional 160 acres adjoining the claim by Catherine. The legal description of this second claim is the east half of the northwest quarter and the east half of the southeast quarter of Section 15, Township 11 South, Range 2 West, San Bernardino Base Meridian.[322]

Charles Blackall registered to vote in San Diego on September 21, 1888. He stated his age as 32, born in Michigan, occupation farmer in Escondido.[323] He is listed in the 1893 through 1896 Valley Center School Census records as having one daughter registered in school during those years.[324] Charles is listed as a farmer living in Valley Center in the 1896 and 1897 San Diego County directories.[325]

There is no record of Walter Walsh, Sr., or William S. Walsh filing homestead claims in Valley Center prior to 1900. An article in the *Escondido Times,* dated October 19, 1898, stated that O.H. Borden had purchased the "old Walsh ranch", but did not mention which one.[326]

William S. is listed as a farmer in the 1897 *Directory of San Diego City and County* and on the Valley Center School census in 1898 as having two children less than five years old at home.[327] In 1900, he is listed as a single male living in his brother, Ambrose's, house. There is no mention of children or a wife.[328]

The youngest child of Walter and Jane Walsh, Anne Jane, married A. James Reidy, son of Maurice, Jr., and Julia McDermott Reidy. James was born in Illinois in 1853 according to his voter registration filed in 1879.[329] The Escondido School census of 1891 shows one female student registered in school, and three children less than five years old at home. The 1893 census shows two female students in school, and two children less than five years old at home.[330] The Reidy family lived in north Escondido which falls outside of the current study area.

John V. and Austin Walsh remained in Valley Center until after 1900, adding parcels to their holdings. Much of the land purchased had been homesteaded by family members. Today, there are no family descendants in the Valley Center area who remained on the family ranches.

John Wells did not remain in the Valley Center area after filing his homestead claim in 1878. His name does not appear on the 1870, 1880, or 1900 U.S. census records. Nor does his name appear in San Diego County directories as living in the Valley Center area. A search of the local newspaper index also failed to find additional information regarding this person.

John filed homestead claim #352 on February 25, 1878, for 160 acres under the Act of June 8, 1872. The legal description is the southwest quarter of the northeast quarter, the southeast quarter of the northwest quarter, and the north half of southwest quarter of Section 32, Township 11 South, Range 1 West, San Bernardino Base Meridian (see Figure 5).[331] This land was claimed by J.H. von Seggern after the turn of the century and is located northwest of Lake Wohlford.

William H. Willard lived in Valley Center on land where Old Castle Road and Lilac Road intersect today (see Figure 5). William filed homestead claim #506 on September 8, 1879, for 160.36 acres. The legal description is the south half of the southeast quarter of Section 34, the southwest quarter of the southwest quarter of Section 35, Township 10 South, Range 2 West, and the northwest quarter of the northwest quarter of Section 2, Township 11 South, Range 2 West. Excess receipt #725 was issued at the time of filing.[332]

W.H. Willard registered to vote in San Diego on July 26, 1879. He stated his age as 30 years, born in Wisconsin, occupation farmer in Bear Valley.[333] He again registered on August 30, 1880. William stated his age as 30, born in Wisconsin, occupation farmer in Bear Valley.[334]

John Allen Willard registered to vote on September 20, 1880. He stated his age as 41 years old, born in Wisconsin, occupation farmer in Bear Valley.[335] John A. Willard filed homestead claim #1243 on April 16, 1883, for land adjoining William's in Section 2, Township 11 South, Range 2 West.[336]

William H. is listed on the 1880 U.S. census living in the household of John D. German, dwelling number 182. He is listed as a married white male farmer, 30 years old, born in Wisconsin, father born in Missouri, mother born in Kansas.[337] William is also listed as living in Valley Center in the 1893-94 *Directory of San Diego City and County.*

John is not listed in the 1870 or 1880 U.S. census of Bear Valley Township. John A. Willard is listed in the 1900 U.S. census of Bear Valley Township living alone in dwelling number 48. He is listed as a 61-year old widower, born March 1839, in Wisconsin, father born in Missouri, mother born in Illinois, occupation farmer on rented land.[338]

J.P. Willard is listed in the 1891 Valley Center School census as having two male students enrolled during that year. W.P. Willard is listed in the 1893 and 1895 Valley Center School Census as having two male students enrolled during those years. There are two children listed as attending school in Escondido in 1894. Dora is listed in the fifth grade, and Alex is listed in the first grade.[339] The relationship between Willard family members could not be confirmed through data researched for this study.

The family of Goolsby Woods settled in Bear Valley during the late 1870s. Goolsby registered to vote in San Diego on April 24, 1879. He stated at that time his age as 54 years old, born in Missouri, occupation farmer in Bear Valley. He transferred his registration from Yolo County in northern California.[340]

Goolsby filed a homestead claim after living on the land for several years. On October 5, 1887, he filed claim #3616 for 40 acres of land in Valley Center. The legal description is the northeast quarter of the northeast quarter of Section 13, Township 11 South, Range 2 West. This land is located north of the intersection of Lilac Road and Valley Center Road on the east side of Valley Center Road. Goolsby operated a general store at this location as listed in the 1887-88 *Maxwell's Directory of San Diego City and County.*[341]

In 1897, the family is listed in the *Directory of San Diego City and County* living in Section 22 in Township 11 South, Range 1 West. It was on this ranch that Goolsby died on August 16, 1898, at the age of 73. He is buried in the Valley Center Cemetery. A valley located north of Bear Valley Ridge is named after the family. Woods Valley Road traveled to Woods Valley and the Woods family ranch. Portions surrounding this property later became part of the San Pasqual Indian Reservation. This parcel is outside of the current study area.

Goolsby married <u>Isabell L. Belshe</u>, a widow, in Missouri prior to migrating across the plains in a wagon drawn by oxen to California in 1849. The family settled first in Sonoma County and later in Yolo County where Goolsby engaged in mining. They sold the ranch in Yolo County and moved to Valley Center in San Diego County in 1878.[342]

The Woods family is listed on the 1880 U.S. census of Bear Valley Township living in dwelling number 189. Goolsby is listed as a married, white male, 55-year old farmer, born in Missouri, father born in Kentucky and mother born in Tennessee. Isabell is listed as 53 years old, keeping house, born in Kentucky, as were both of her parents.[343]

Their son, <u>Charles A.</u>, is listed as a single, 19-year old farm laborer, attending school and born in California, as were all of the children. <u>Joseph L.</u> is listed as 15 years old; <u>Henry W.</u>, 14 years old; <u>James M.</u>, 11 years old; and their only daughter, <u>Ida B.</u>, nine years old.[344]

The 1900 U.S. census of Bear Valley Township lists families of Charles A., James M., and Joseph L., living in separate households. Their mother, Isabell, is not listed and is assumed to have died prior to 1900.

<u>Charles Arthur Woods</u> is listed living in dwelling number 36 with his two sons in 1900. Charles is listed as a white male, 38 years old, born June 1862, in California, parents born in Kentucky, widowed, farmer who owns his land. His son, <u>James E.</u>, is listed as 13 years old, born September 1885, in California, attended school eight months during the year. Charles youngest son, <u>Perry V.</u>, is listed as 11 years old, born August 1888, in California, attended school eight months during the year.[345]

According to the Valley Center Cemetery records, Charles died in 1898 and is buried in the community cemetery. His birthdate is unknown. Mrs. Charles Woods is also buried in the cemetery with birth and death dates unknown.

James Woods is listed with his family living in dwelling 37 in 1900. James is listed as 33 years old, born June 1867, in California, both parents born in Kentucky, married eight years, occupation farmer on his own land. His wife, Anna C., is listed as 26 years old, born August 1873, in California, both parents born in Iowa.[346]

James and Anna's three children were all born in Valley Center. They are: Susan, seven years old, born August 1892, attended school eight months during the year; daughter, Orpha M., five years old, born October 1894; and their son, J.G., three years old, born May 1897.[347]

J.M. Guinn states that James M. Woods, born January 18, 1868, married Annie C. Jacoby on November 11, 1891. Annie was born in Burlington, Iowa, August 14, 1873, coming to California with her family in 1883. The couple had four children: Susie, Orpha, Ellis, and Inez. James began a dairy business which he sold milk and butter in Escondido. He also raised chickens which he also sold in town. He raised all grains and hay on his ranch to support his livestock.[348]

The Valley Center Cemetery records list J.M. Woods as born in 1867, died November 20, 1940, and buried in the community cemetery. The list also includes James Woods, unknown birthdate, died in 1905. Ellis G. Woods is listed as born on January 16, 1897, died on March 18, 1964.

Joseph L. Woods and family are listed on the 1900 census as living in dwelling number 40. Joseph is listed as 34 years old, married 15 years, born January 1865, in California, both parents born in Kentucky, occupation farmer on his own land. His wife's name is smudged, but appears to be Melie D. or Maxie D. She is listed as 33 years old, married 15 years, born October 1867, mother of seven children, all living at the time, born in Texas as were both of her parents.[349]

Their eldest son, William L., is listed as 15 years old, born in March 1885, in California, as were all of the children, attended school eight months during the year; daughter, Leah Isabel, listed as 13 years old, born April 1887, attended school eight months; Susan P., listed as 11 years old, born 1889 [no month given], attended school eight months; Pearl, nine years old, born 1890, attended school eight months; Hazel, seven years old, born 1893; Gertrude, five years old, born 1895; and youngest son, Leslie, three years old, born 1897.[350]

The Woods family is just one of many families whose lives are directly related to the history of Valley Center. Their determination and hard work at ranching and farming formed the basis for the community.

Although the members of these pioneering families did not make a large contribution to the history books of America, they definitely made an impact on the history of Valley Center as well as southern California. The fledgling community the families joined in the 1860s and 1870s has grown, but still has not changed dramatically. It is still the same in spirit.

During the decade 1880-89, more families settled on land in Valley Center. The majority of those families started on "free" government land which they homesteaded. The settlers received a deed to the property after five years of living on the land and making improvements such as building houses and other structures, farming, or raising livestock. From these beginnings, the community and people of Valley Center became intertwined in the making of history.

NOTES

[1] Anonymous. A Pioneer Teacher, Minnie Pease, San Diego, California. Unpublished manuscript on file Valley Center Branch Library Historical files.

[2] For example: the 1875 plat map of Township 11 South, Range 2 West, San Bernardino Base Meridian, was first surveyed in 1854 by J.E. Freeman; in 1858 by John C. Harris; in 1874 by William Minte, and M.G. Wheeler; and in 1875 by M.G. Wheeler. The maps were cited as of the last survey date.

[3] Davis, Abel. *Valley Center, California*, unpublished memoir, circa 1955.

[4] USGS Topographic Quadrangle maps: Pala 1968, photorevised 1988; Boucher Hill, 1948, photorevised 1988; Valley Center, 1968, photorevised 1975; and Rodriguez Mountain, 1948, photorevised 1988. Published by the United States Geological Survey, Denver Colorado.

[5] 1860 U.S. Census, San Diego County, California.

[6] *Ibid.*

[7] 1870 U.S. Census, Schedule 1, Inhabitants in San Pascual and Pala Districts, San Diego County, California.

[8] *Ibid.*, p. 520, entry 35, Dwelling 43.

[9] *Ibid.*, entry 36.

[10] One source, *The History of California* written by Guinn, J.M. 1907, page 860, states that John T. Adams was born in Scotland, not Ireland.

[11] *Ibid.* 860.

[12] Land records listed 40 acres claimed on February 11, 1876, by John Adams (claim #226), not the 160 acres stated by Guinn, J.M. page 860-861.

[13] Register of Receipts Issued by the Receiver of Public Monies at Los Angeles, California, for Lands Entered Under the Homestead Act, Vols. I and II, 1869-91, National Archives, Pacific Southwest Region, Laguna Niguel, California.

[14] Guinn, *The History of California*: 860.

[15] San Diego County Great Register of Voters, 1866-79. John Q. Adams, 22 years old, born New York, occupation farmer, San Pasqual, sworn May 7, 1872.

[16] 1880 U.S. Census, Schedule 1, Inhabitants in Bear Valley Township, San Diego County, California, p. 21, entry 26.

[17] "Valley Center system beat Pony Express", *San Diego Union*, February 14, 1987:11-2.

[18] *Ibid.*

[19] San Diego County Marriage Records, published in *Leaves and Saplings*, San Diego Genealogical Society Newsletter.

[20] Guinn, *The History of California*:680.

[21] *Ibid.*, 681.

[22] Valley Center Cemetery records.

[23] An article in the *Escondido Advocate*, December 8, 1905, page 3, stated that Blanche Hill, wife of L.L. Hill, had committed suicide with a revolver at her home in Freeman, Missouri. She and her husband had moved there in 1903 hoping it would improve Mrs. Hill's health. The couple was reported to have

one son. Blanche's body was interred in the Valley Center Cemetery next to her mother's grave according to cemetery records.

[24] An article in the *Escondido* Times, May 31, 1907, page 2 stated that William H. Adams, son of J.Q. Adams, was found dead of strychnine poisoning on the morning of May 27, 1907. He had been working on the ranch of J.V. Walsh and left a note in his pocket stating that he felt disappointment in love and had no reason to live. Valley Center Cemetery records show that William is buried near his mother and sister.

[25] Guinn, *The History of California*:681.

[26] Homestead Register, 1869-91.

[27] *Escondido Times*, September 27, 1888:3; *Maxwell's Directory of San Diego City and County*, 1887-88, George D. Maxwell, Publisher, San Diego, California.

[28] See Figure 3, Chapter One.

[29] *San Diego Union Tribune*, November 20, 1894; and the *Directory of San Diego City and County*, The Olmsted Company Printers, San Diego, California, 1897.

[30] *Ibid.*, 1907.

[31] 1900 U.S. Census, Schedule 1, Inhabitants in Bear Valley Township, San Diego County, California, p. 204, entries 95-98.

[32] *Ibid.*: entries 72-74.

[33] Guinn, *The History of California*: 861.

[34] 1870 U.S Census, p. 523, entry 30.

[35] Register of Voters, 1866-79.

[36] Homestead Register, 1869-91.

[37] 1880 U.S. Census, p. 21, entry 47.

[38] *Ibid.*, entry 48.

[39] Davis, *Valley Center*, circa 1955.

[40] *Ibid.*

[41] San Diego County Marriage records.

[42] Register of Voters, 1866-79.

[43] Homestead Register, 1869-91.

[44] San Diego Surveyor's Records Office, San Diego County Annex, San Diego, California.

[45] 1880 U.S. Census, p. 21, entries 29-33.

[46] *Escondido Times,* December 28, 1893:3.

[47] Davis, *Valley Center*, circa 1955.

[48] Valley Center Cemetery records.

[49] 1900 U.S. Census, p. 208, entries 12 and 14.

[50] Register of Voters, 1866-79; 1880-87.

[51] *Pacific Coast Directory of San Diego County,* 1883-84.

[52] *Maxwell's Directory of San Diego City and County,* 1887-88.

[53] Homestead Register, 1869-91.

[54] Claim #250 was recorded on April 24, 1876, by Joel C. Hedden which included the east half of the southeast quarter of Section 13, Township 11 South, Range 2 West, San Bernardino Meridian. Homestead Register, 1869-91.

[55] *Escondido Times*, October 19, 1898:8.

[56] Davis, *Valley Center,* circa 1955; U.S. Plat Map, 1885.

[57] Register of Voters, 1866-79.

[58] *Ibid.*

[59] 1900 U.S. Census, p. 204, entry 85.

[60] Register of Voters, 1866-79.

[61] 1900 U.S. Census, p. 204, entries 86-91.

[62] *Escondido Times*, June 4, 1891:3.

[63] Guinn, *The History of California*: 1162.

[64] Homestead Register, 1869-91.

[65] Guinn, *The History of California*: 1240, 1243; 1880 U.S. Census, page 20, entry 1.

[66] 1900 U.S. Census, p. 207, entry 29.

[67] Voter Registration, 1880-87.

[68] 1880 U.S. Census, p. 20, entry 1.

[69] Guinn, *The History of California*: 1240, 1243.

[70] *Escondido Times,* September 27, 1888:3.

[71] Guinn, *The History of California*: 1240, 1243.

[72] San Diego County marriage records.

[73] Guinn, *The History of California*: 1240, 1243.

[74] 1880 U.S. Census, p. 21, entries 14-16.

[75] Guinn, *The History of California*: 1088.

[76] *Ibid.*,1955.

[77] *Ibid.*, 1088, 1955.

[78] Interview of Waldo Breedlove, Sr. by Edgar F. Hastings, San Diego Historical Society, November 3, 1958.

[79] *Ibid.*,1955.

[80] *Ibid.*

[81] *Escondido Times*, January 11, 1894:3.

[82] *Ibid.*, June 7, 1894:3.

[83] Guinn, *The History of California*: 1088.

[84] *Ibid.*

[85] 1880 U.S. Census, p. 21, entries 22-25.

[86] Davis, *Valley Center,* circa 1955.

[87] *Ibid.*

[88] Guinn, *The History of California*: 1088.

[89] *Ibid.;* Homestead Register, 1869-91.

[90] Davis, *Valley Center,* circa 1955.

[91] *Escondido Times*, September 27, 1888:3.

[92] Guinn, *The History of California*: 1088.

[93] *Escondido Times*, June 7, 1894:3.

[94] 1900 U.S. Census, p. 207, entries 98-100; p. 208, entries 1-3.

[95] *Ibid.*, July 24, 1908:2; and *The Advocate*:1.

[96] 1880 U.S. Census, p. 20, entry 46.

[97] Register of Voters, 1866-79.

[98] 1880 U.S. Census, p. 21, entries 11-13.

[99] 1900 U.S. Census, p. 200, entry 18.

[100] Clyde S. James, unpublished memoir, circa 1975.

[101] Guinn, *The History of California*: 1088.

[102] *Ibid.*

[103] *Escondido Times*: February 22, 1894:2.

[104] Bear Valley and Valley Center School Census records, 1891-1900.

[105] *Valley Roadrunner*, May 22, 1986.
[106] *Escondido Times*, December 28, 1893:3; and March 15, 1894:3.
[107] *Ibid.*, December 28, 1893:3.
[108] *Ibid.*, March 1, 1894:3.
[109] 1880 U.S. Census, p. 21, entries 11-13.
[110] *Ibid.*; entries 41-43.
[111] Homestead Register, 1869-91.
[112] Interview of Waldo Breedlove, Sr. by Edgar F. Hastings, San Diego Historical Society, November 3, 1958.
[113] Davis, *Valley Center,* circa 1955.
[114] Index to Declaration of Intention, Superior Court of San Diego County, California, National Archives, Pacific Southwest, Laguna Niguel: Microfilm Reel M 1612, Roll No. 1.
[115] Homestead Register, 1869-91.
[116] Register of Voters, 1866-77.
[117] 1880 U.S. Census, p. 20, entries 8 and 9.
[118] *Ibid.,* entries 10 and 11.
[119] Declaration of Intention, (old) Vol. 2, Dec. #7; Naturalization records, Book 1-6.
[120] *Escondido Times,* November 3, 1887:3.
[121] Davis, *Valley Center,* circa 1955.
[122] Biographical information compiled by Stephen Van Wormer as part of the Cultural Resource Inventory and Evaluation of Rancho Escondido. Ms. on file at the South Coastal Information Center, San Diego State University, Archaeological Systems Management, 1983.
[123] Homestead claim #284, filed November 20, 1876 for 160 acres. Legal description: north half of the northeast quarter, the southeast quarter of the northeast quarter, and the northeast quarter of the southeast quarter, Section 35, Township 11 South, Range 2 West, Homestead Register, 1869-91.
[124] Archaeological Systems Management, 1983.
[125] 1870 U.S Census, p. 520, entry 27.
[126] Register of Voters, 1866-79.
[127] *Daily Times Advocate*, August 4, 1916:1.
[128] *Ibid.*; Archaeological Systems Management, 1983.
[129] *Ibid.*
[130] *Daily Times Advocate*, August 4, 1916:1; and *Escondido Times Advocate*, January 15, 1984: A-11.
[131] *Ibid.;* Archaeological Systems Management, 1983.
[132] *Ibid.*
[133] Davis, *Valley Center,* circa 1955.
[134] *Ibid.*
[135] *Ibid.*
[136] *Ibid.*
[137] 1870 U.S Census, p.523, entries 32-34.
[138] *Ibid.*, entry 35.
[139] 1880 U.S. Census, p. 23, entries 8-15.
[140] Davis, *Valley Center,* circa 1955.
[141] San Diego County Superior Court, 11-25-1874, Mn. Book, 5-144.
[142] Homestead Receipts, 1869-91.

[143] *Ibid.*

[144] Davis, *Valley Center,* circa 1955.

[145] *Escondido Times,* June 21, 1894:3.

[146] Davis, *Valley Center,* circa 1955.

[147] Fullerton, California, newspaper not referenced, "A.M. Davis Passes Away, Native of California", no date.

[148] Davis, *Valley Center,* circa 1955.

[149] *Ibid.*

[150] Guinn, *The History of California*: 2180-2181.

[151] 1880 U.S. Census, p. 22, entries 23-33.

[152] *International Genealogical Index,* Church of the Latter-Day Saints, © 1980, 1994.

[153] Brøderbund Family Tree Maker Deluxe Edition, Family Finder Index, Version 3, © 1994 Brøderbund Software, Inc.

[154] Homestead Receipts, 1869-91.

[155] Old Survey 24, San Diego County Surveyor's Office.

[156] Declaration of Homestead Book 3, p.164-165, November 21, 1882.

[157] Davis, *Valley Center,* circa 1955.

[158] Homestead Receipts, 1869-91.

[159] 1900 U.S. Census, p. 207, entry 87.

[160] *Escondido Times,* October 20, 1916:2.

[161] *The Directory of San Diego City and County,* 1887-88.

[162] *Escondido Times,* March 1, 1894:3.

[163] In an article in the *Escondido Times,* dated March 5, 1891, p. 2, it is stated that when a lawyer asked Justice Dinwiddie exactly what the "W.H.H." stood for, the judge replied, "William Henry Harrison Dinwiddie". The article further stated that the lawyer very quietly sat down.

[164] 1870 U.S. Census, p. 20, entries 45-50; and p. 21, entry 1.

[165] Guinn, *The History of California*: 2180-2181.

[166] *Escondido Times,* September 27, 1888:3.

[167] *Ibid.*, March 5, 1891:2; March 1, 1894:3; and June 7, 1894:3.

[168] Davis, *Valley Center,* circa 1955.

[169] 1900 U.S. Census, p. 206, entries 33-36.

[170] *Times Advocate,* October 20, 1916:2.

[171] *Ibid.*

[172] 1900 U.S. Census, entries 37-41.

[173] *Ibid.*, p. 200, entries 37-42.

[174] Register of Voters, 1866-79.

[175] Guinn, *The History of California*: 2210.

[176] Register of Voters, 1880-87.

[177] Homestead Receipts, 1869-91.

[178] Davis, *Valley Center,* circa 1955.

[179] O.S. 24, San Diego County Surveyor's Office.

[180] Davis, *Valley Center,* circa 1955.

[181] Register of Voters, 1866-79.

[182] Homestead Receipts, 1869-91.

[183] 1870 U.S. Census, p. 21, entry 31.

[184] 1880 U.S. Census, p. 22, entry 22.

[185] 1900 U.S. Census, p. 207, entry 22.

[186] 1880 U.S. Census, p. 22, entries 1-7; and Valley Center Cemetery records.
[187] Guinn, *The History of California*: 2210.
[188] *Ibid.*
[189] *Ibid.*
[190] *Ibid.*
[191] 1900 U.S. Census, p. 207, entries 92-95.
[192] *Ibid.*, entry 98.
[193] Davis, *Valley Center,* circa 1955.
[194] Guinn, *The History of California*: 2210.
[195] Homestead Receipts, 1869-91.
[196] *Ibid.*
[197] *Escondido Times,* September 27, 1888:3.
[198] Davis, *Valley Center,* circa 1955.
[199] Guinn, *The History of California*: 2183-2184.
[200] Homestead Receipts, 1869-91.
[201] Homestead, Book 3, p. 260, 277.
[202] Homestead Receipts, 1869-91.
[203] 1870 U.S. Census, p. 21, entry 52.
[204] 1880 U.S. Census, p. 22, entries 42 and 43.
[205] *Ibid.*, entries 29-32.
[206] 1900 U.S. Census, p. 207, entry 84.
[207] Guinn, *The History of California*: 2183-2184.
[208] Davis, *Valley Center,* circa 1955.
[209] Escondido Genealogical Society Surname Register, Escondido Public Library Pioneer Room, Escondido, California.
[210] Homestead Receipts, 1869-91.
[211] Davis, *Valley Center,* circa 1955.
[212] Register of Voters, 1880-87.
[213] 1880 U.S. Census, p. 22, entry line 22.
[214] Homestead Receipts, 1869-91.
[215] 1880 U.S. Census, p. 20, entries 12 and 13.
[216] *Ibid.*, entries 14 and 15.
[217] *Ibid.*, entry 16.
[218] *Escondido Times*, August 23, 1888:1.
[219] 1870 U.S. Census, p. 523, entry 29.
[220] Register of Voters, 1866-79.
[221] Guinn, *The History of California*: 1274.
[222] Homestead Receipts, 1869-91.
[223] 1880 U.S. Census, p. 22, entries 44-47.
[224] Guinn, *The History of California*: 1274.
[225] *Escondido Times,* April 27, 1906:4.
[226] *Daily Times Advocate,* October 2, 1918:1.
[227] *Escondido Times,* March 9, 1893:3.
[228] Homestead Receipts, 1869-91.
[229] *Escondido Times,* February 22, 1894:2.
[230] *Ibid.*, March 8, 1894:3.
[231] 1900 U.S. Census, p. 205, entries 80 and 81.
[232] *Ibid.*, September 8, 1905:4.
[233] Register of Voters, 1866-79.

[234] *Ibid.,* 1880-87.

[235] Homestead Receipts, 1869-91.

[236] Guinn, *The History of California*: 2035.

[237] On the first day of school in Valley Center, Abel Davis told the story of the school registration and "Toad". The older brother, Dave, stated his name to the teacher and gave his age as 12. The next to be registered was his sister, Sally, who did not know her age. When the youngest child was asked her name, she replied "Toad". The teacher asked if this was a nickname or her real name, and the child did not know. She was told to have her mother fill out a registration card and return it the following day. Toad told the teacher that her mother could not write. When asked if her father could write, the answer was, "Oh yes, he knows everything!" The papers were returned the next day. Written on the card was: "Minn Kitchen, age ten, white, not married". Davis, Abel. *Valley Center,* circa 1955.

[238] Naturalization Records, Vol. 6, Application Number 310.

[239] 1900 U.S. Census, p. 203, entry 27.

[240] *Ibid.*

[241] Haskell, E.P. The Bear Story, unpublished document. On file at the Valley Center Branch Library, Local History files.

[242] Homestead Receipts, 1869-91.

[243] Davis, *Valley Center,* circa 1955.

[244] Maps on file at the San Diego County Surveyor's Office.

[245] Personal letter written by Nellie Chandler-Tomkin [nee Shelby], to the Friends of the Library, San Diego County Library, Valley Center Branch, circa 1978. On file, Valley Center Branch Library Local History files.

[246] 1900 U.S. Census, p. 200, entries 24-28.

[247] Chandler-Tomkin, circa 1978.

[248] *Ibid.*

[249] San Diego County Library archives, San Diego County Library Operations Center, San Diego, California.

[250] Chandler-Tomkin, circa 1978.

[251] Valley Center Cemetery records: Records of Deaths and Map of M.E.S. Church Grave Yard, presented to the M.E. Church South, by Charles Moore, Valley Center, California, February 28th, 1899.

[252] Chandler-Tomkin, circa 1978.

[253] 1880 U.S. Census, p. 22, entry 14.

[254] 1900 U.S. Census, p. 207, entry 55.

[255] Valley Center Cemetery records, 1899.

[256] 1870 U.S. Census, p. 522, entries 17-25.

[257] 1880 U.S. Census, p. 20, entries 17-21.

[258] *Ibid.,* entries 22 and 23.

[259] Davis, *Valley Center,* circa 1955.

[260] Homestead Book Two, Page 351.

[261] *Escondido Times,* September 27, 1888:3; *Times Advocate,* August 4, 1911:6.

[262] *Escondido Times,* March 2, 1893:3.

[263] *Ibid.*, December 28, 1893:3.

[264] von Seggern Family records, on file, Valley Center Branch Library, Historical files.

[265] *Times Advocate*, August 4, 1911:6.
[266] Register of Voters, 1866-79.
[267] *Ibid.*
[268] Homestead Receipts, 1869-91.
[269] *Escondido Times,* April 7, 1898:2.
[270] Personal letter written by Opal Bemis, adopted daughter of Abel M. and Sarah Striplin, no date. On file, Valley Center Branch Library Local History files.
[271] *Daily Times Advocate,* June 8, 1916:2.
[272] Valley Center Cemetery records.
[273] *Daily Times Advocate,* June 8, 1916:2; Valley Center Cemetery records; Bear Valley School Census; and *The Directory of San Diego City and County,* 1889-90.
[274] Register of Voters, 1866-79.
[275] 1880 U.S. Census, p. 21, entries 19-21.
[276] *Ibid.,* p. 20, entry 28.
[277] *Daily Times-Advocate,* September 8, 1967.
[278] San Diego County Coroner's Reports, 1853-1905. On file at the San Diego Historical Society Archives, Balboa Park, San Diego, California.
[279] Register of Voters, 1866-79.
[280] Guinn, *The History of California:* 1161-1162; 1707-1708.
[281] *Ibid.*
[282] *Ibid.*
[283] This information was provided by Holden family members in Maine. The census information was retyped and the original was not provided. This information is confusing due to the fact that later documentation, including California census records, voter registration records, biography provided by Guinn, J.M. and personal family records, all state that Ambrose and Austin were twins born in Atchison County, Missouri, in 1845. Another brother, Walter J., was reportedly born in Maine in 1850. If this information is correct, the family moved to Missouri where the twins, Ambrose and Austin, were born, moved back to Maine by 1850 when Walter J. was born, and then moved to Missouri again where two other children were born by 1854.
[284] 1880 U.S. Census, p. 22, entries 9 and 10.
[285] *Ibid.,* entries 11 and 12.
[286] Guinn, *The History of California*: 1161-1162; 1707-1708.
[287] Register of Voters, 1880-87.
[288] Mortuary Records of San Diego County.
[289] *The Directory of San Diego City and County,* 1889-90.
[290] Homestead Receipts, 1869-91.
[291] 1880 U.S. Census, p. 22, entries 17 and 18.
[292] Guinn, *The History of California*: 1707-1708.
[293] 1900 U.S. Census, p. 207, entries 66 and 67.
[294] *Ibid.,* entries 67-72; A story written in the *Escondido Times,* November 5, 1891, p. 3: Austin and Carrie's first son, Noval Augustine, born September 1889, died on October 29, 1891. The child choked to death on a screw which became lodged in his throat. All attempts to revive him failed after Austin rushed the child to the doctor in Escondido. The child was buried in the Catholic cemetery in Escondido on October 30, 1891.

[295] Guinn, *The History of California*: 1707-1708.

[296] Valley Center Cemetery records.

[297] Homestead Receipts, 1869-91.

[298] Register of Voters, 1866-79.

[299] 1880 U.S. Census, p. 22, entries 19 and 20.

[300] Walsh family records. On file Valley Center Branch Library, Local History files.

[301] Homestead Receipts, 1869-91.

[302] *Ibid.*

[303] Davis,. *Valley Center,* circa 1955.

[304] Guinn, *The History of California*: 1161-1162; 1707-1708.

[305] Homestead Receipts, 1869-91.

[306] 1880 U.S. Census, p. 22, entry 13-16.

[307] 1900 U.S. Census, p. 207, entry 55-57.

[308] *Ibid.*, entry line 58.

[309] *Times Advocate,* July 7, 1911:8.

[310] *Escondido Times,* October 19, 1898:8; and August 17, 1906:6.

[311] Walsh family records.

[312] Homestead Receipts, 1869-91..

[313] 1880 U.S. Census, p. 22, entry 12.

[314] 1900 U.S. Census, p. 207, entry 59.

[315] Homestead Receipts, 1869-91.

[316] Register of Voters, 1866-79.

[317] *Ibid.,* 1880-87.

[318] Walsh family records.

[319] Mortuary Records.

[320] *Times Advocate,* October 11, 1912:6. Charles began his career in San Diego working as a steam and electrical engineer. His aerial acrobatics career began when he built a plane and entered an aerial meet in Los Angeles in 1910. He began his career with the largest monoplane in the world at that time. One problem was that the plane could only carry 2 pounds per square inch compared to five pounds per square inch in other monoplanes. Walsh's plane was maneuvered with two control levers - one for the steering, and one for the engine. The equilibrium was controlled with a pendulum device. The seat and engine were positioned below the main plane.

[321] Walsh family records.

[322] Homestead Receipts, 1869-91.

[323] Register of Voters, 1880-88; Charles' older brother, Joseph B., registered to vote on June 1, 1889, stating his age as 32 at the time, born in Michigan, occupation farmer in Escondido. A reference regarding Joe in 1894 was published in the *Escondido Times.* It stated that Joe had moved to San Francisco but was in Escondido visiting his mother and daughter. The *Escondido Times* references a child named Bertha Blackall as a second grade student, approximately seven years old, in an Escondido school in 1894. This suggests a birthdate circa 1887. This child could be Joseph's.

[324] Valley Center School Census records, 1893-96.

[325] *The Directory of San Diego City and County*, 1896 and 1897.

[326] *Escondido Times,* October 19, 1898:8.

[327] *The Directory of San Diego City and County*, 1897; Valley Center School District Census Report, 1898.

[328] 1900 U.S. Census, p. 207, entry 58.

[329] Register of Voters, 1866-79.

[330] Escondido School Census Records, 1891 and 1893.

[331] Homestead Receipts, 1869-91.

[332] *Ibid.*

[333] Register of Voters, 1866-79.

[334] *Ibid.*, 1880-87.

[335] *Ibid.*

[336] Homestead Receipts, 1869-91.

[337] 1880 U.S. Census, p. 20, entry 27.

[338] 1900 U.S. Census, p. 203, entry 14.

[339] School enrollment published in the *Escondido Times*, February 1, 1894:3.

[340] Register of Voters, 1866-79.

[341] *Maxwell's Directory of San Diego City and County*, 1888.

[342] Guinn, *The History of California*: 1155-1156.

[343] 1880 U.S. Census, p. 21, entries 4 and 5.

[344] *Ibid.*, entries 6-10.

[345] 1900 U.S. Census, p. 200, entries 29-31.

[346] *Ibid.*, entries 32 and 33.

[347] *Ibid.*, entries 34-36.

[348] Guinn, *The History of California*: 1155-1156.

[349] 1900 U.S. Census, p. 200, entry 49 and 50.

[350] *Ibid.*, p. 201, entries 51-57.

CHAPTER THREE

VALLEY CENTRE 1880-1889

Advertisements in newspapers enticed settlers and speculators to come to the valley. One advertisement in the *Escondido Times* in 1887 reads:

VALLEY CENTER!!
2,250 ACRES
For Subdivision and Colonization.

A Rare Opportunity for Homeseekers and Speculators.

The very best of the famous BEAR VALLEY region, one of the richest and most productive valleys of all Southern California.

Beautifully situated
1,400 feet above the sea, surrounded by wooded hills abounding in springs of pure mountain water; eight miles northeast of Escondido, eighteen miles from the ocean, sheltered from the damp coast winds, free from fog, possessing the most equable and salubrious climate in Southern California.
Although this section receives twice the average rainfall of the coast, and
Requires no Irrigation,
abundance of water may be supplied from the Bear Valley reservoir of the San Luis Rey Flume Company. The virtues of the fine
Iron Springs
also situated on the tract, will be extolled by thousands of health seekers in the near future.
A Beautiful Townsite
On the tract. The greatest opportunity remaining in the county to make a substantial town. Railroad communications will be established to within a few miles of this valley inside of 90 days. For further particulars apply to

RICHARDS & MCNEIL,
ESCONDIDO, CALIFORNIA.[1]

By the year 1880, there were at least 30 families living in the Bear Valley area. Most of those families had started their farms or ranches on open, unimproved land which they claimed through the Homestead Act of 1862. An individual over the age of 21 could claim up to 160 acres of government land for a $10 filing fee. They received full title to the land after five years if they fulfilled their obligations of either cultivating or ranching the acreage, as well as residing in a house located on the property during that time period.

If the family did not wish to settle on unimproved land, they could claim a parcel previously claimed and abandoned. Provided improvements were made to the property, they could claim the land and all buildings as their own. This caused disputes if a 'claim jumper' tried to live on property someone else had already claimed. These disputes often led to violence. Abandonment of property was not uncommon given the settler had little money invested. If another parcel appealed to them, they simply packed up their private possessions and moved. The population fluctuated as a result of this. Other variables also affected the population in the valley.

The weather and rainfall were also factors in the fluctuating population in the valley. During the dry years in the mid-1870s, many families came into the valley only to leave after a drought later in the decade which made dry-farming or ranching impossible. During wetter years, such as the valley experienced in the 1880s, people would come to settle again. Of course, too much water also caused problems for the settlers, as in 1883-84 when the rain measured 30 inches in 37 hours.[2] And snow was even worse, for the livestock were not accustomed to cold temperatures and many animals did not survive.

Figure 16. Snow in the Valley, ca. 1882.

In the winter of 1882, the settlers felt a cold northern wind and saw the snow fall in the valley for three days, piling up to two feet on the farmers' fields. Oak tree branches, as well as fruit tree branches, broke under the heavy snow. The snow caused such severe destruction in some orchards that they were not able to recover for many years.[3] Figure 16 is a photograph of snow in the valley in 1882. The location of where the photograph was taken is not known.

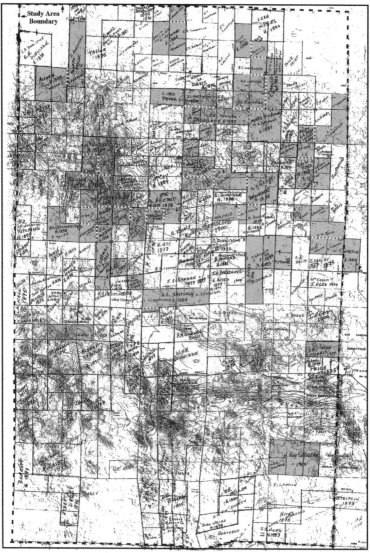

Figure 17. Map Showing Location of Valley Center Pioneers, 1880-89.

The wet years continued into the 1890s. The town of Escondido was being 'colonized' and the need for water was much greater. The San Luis Rey Flume Company was planned to bring water from the San Luis Rey River and channel it in the Escondido Irrigation Canal through the eastern edge of Valley Center. It ended at the Escondido reservoir, known today as Lake Wohlford.

Figure 18. Valley Center School House, ca. 1887.

During the decade of 1880-89 the Valley Center area grew considerably in population. The children of the established families were adults and ready to claim their own property in order to start their families. Almost 40 new families filed homestead claims during this decade. A map showing the location of the new homesteads is provided as Figure 17.

With the influx of people in Valley Center, many new developments occurred during this decade. A new school was built closer to the center of the valley, a post office was established, a community church was built using adobe bricks made on-site, with a community cemetery established beside the church, the railroad had come to southern California via Temecula and Escondido, and a family moved into the valley who had brick making experience, thus changing the housing construction methods within the valley thereafter.

A new wooden frame school house was built in 1887 in Valley Center. It was located on the Walsh property where the Community Hall is located today on Lilac Road. This school, which is included as Figure 18, was the traditional one-room school in which grades one through eight attended. The original Notice of Opening School certificate, dated September 5, 1887, and signed by Mrs. F.M. Curry, is included as Figure 19. This school house burned down later and was replaced by another wooden structure which also burned down before being finally replaced in 1923 by the cement brick structure which serves as the Community Hall today.

An earlier school had reportedly been started in 1876, according to Abel Davis, although no documentation of this fact was found during research for this study. Davis states the school was located on the west end of the Fleishman property and the teacher was Mr. Connally, who was succeeded by Miss Vincent.[4]

The 1880 U.S. census for the Bear Valley District lists the following families known to have lived in the Valley Center study area in Bear Valley:

John Q. Adams	George Hedden
William Adams	Joel C. Hedden
John H. Antes	George Herbst
Samuel G. Antes	John J. Hicks
Daniel E. Bowman	Nancy H. Holcomb
Columbus Breedlove	Augustus C Kitchen [sic]
John H. Breedlove	Jacob T. Reed
William Breedlove	Samuel Striplin
John P. Christenson	George Tracy
James Davis	Goolsby Woods
Columbus C. Dinwiddie	Ambrose Walsh
W.H.H. Dinwiddie	Austin Walsh
Francis Fleshman	Nicholas Walsh
Joseph Fleshman	Walter Walsh
John D. German	William K. Watkins
Edward N. Harrison	William H. Willard

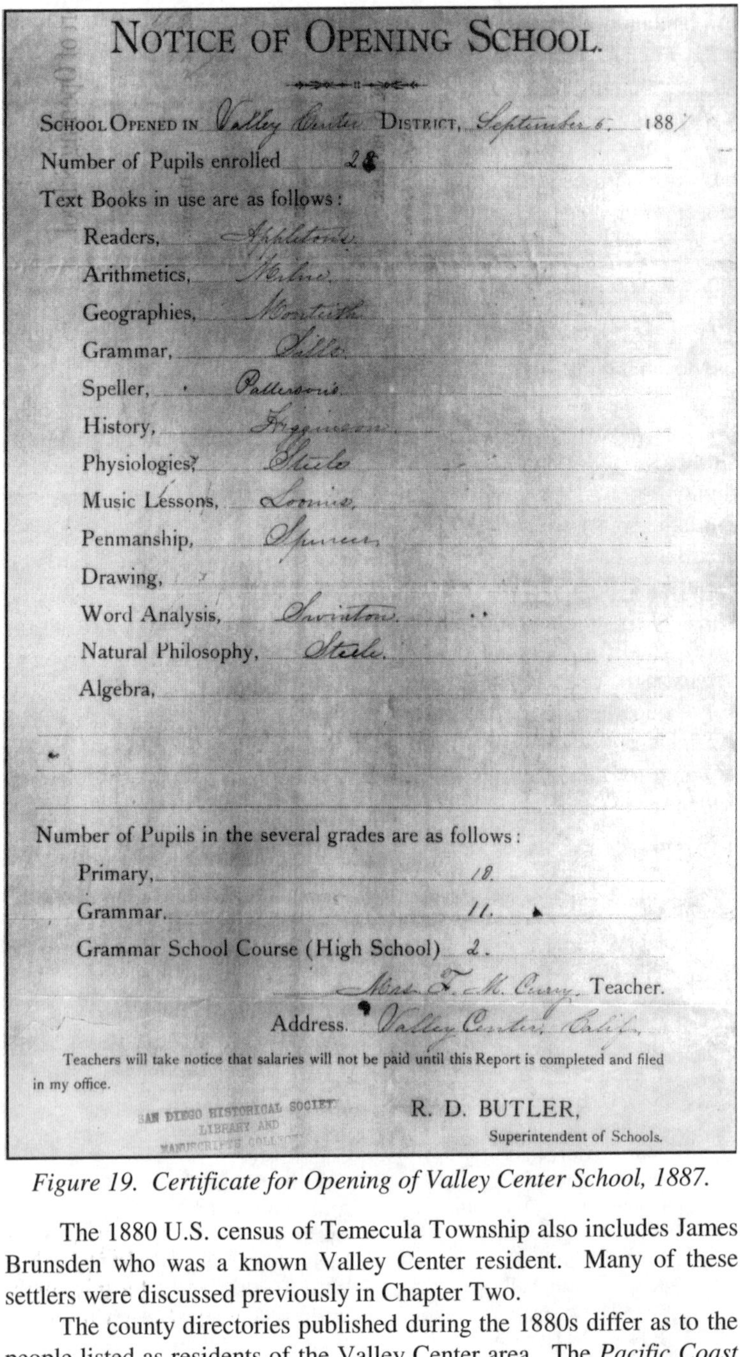

NOTICE OF OPENING SCHOOL.

SCHOOL OPENED IN *Valley Center* DISTRICT, *September 5,* 188*7*

Number of Pupils enrolled   *28*

Text Books in use are as follows:

    Readers, *Appleton's*

    Arithmetics, *Helme*

    Geographies, *Monteith*

    Grammar, *Sill*

    Speller, · *Patterson's*

    History, *Higginson*

    Physiologies? *Steele*

    Music Lessons, *Loomis*

    Penmanship, *Spencer*

    Drawing,

    Word Analysis, *Swinton's*

    Natural Philosophy, *Steele*

    Algebra,

Number of Pupils in the several grades are as follows:

    Primary, *18*

    Grammar, *11* ▸

    Grammar School Course (High School) *2*

                  Mrs. F. M. Curry Teacher.

        Address, *Valley Center, Calif.*

Teachers will take notice that salaries will not be paid until this Report is completed and filed in my office.

SAN DIEGO HISTORICAL SOCIETY
LIBRARY AND
MANUSCRIPTS COLLECTION

           R. D. BUTLER,

             Superintendent of Schools.

Figure 19. Certificate for Opening of Valley Center School, 1887.

    The 1880 U.S. census of Temecula Township also includes James Brunsden who was a known Valley Center resident. Many of these settlers were discussed previously in Chapter Two.

    The county directories published during the 1880s differ as to the people listed as residents of the Valley Center area. The *Pacific Coast*

Directory, 1883-84,[5] only lists nine families living in the valley. It describes Valley Centre as being an agricultural district with a post office, located 40 miles from San Diego and 20 miles from the railroad.

The residents of the area in this directory are listed as:

Beard, SH, justice of peace	McTothlin, D, gen. merchandise
Burchart, JD, gen. merchandise	Miller, Rev. JE, clergyman
German, John D, blacksmith	Reed, JC, brickmaker
Heueldon, Geo, roadmaster	Shelling [sic], JT, blacksmith
Kitching, AC, gen. merchandise and postmaster	

Maxwell's Directory of San Diego City and County,[6] also listed nine families living in the valley at the time. Two of the families are the same as listed earlier in the *Pacific Coast Directory* along with seven new names. Maxwell published the following list of Valley Centre residents in 1887-88:

Adams, John Q., general store	Dinuirddi [sic], W.H.H., Justice of
Beard, A.S., postmaster	the Peace and Deputy County Clerk
Bills & Smith, gen. blacksmiths	Hastings, C.H., physician
Brullon, D.M. constable	Reed, John, constable
Clark, J.H., physician	Woods, G., gen. merchandise store

The biographical profiles of the settlers of Valley Center during the decade 1880-89 are presented alphabetically in this chapter. All locations of their residences were not available for many people did not file homestead claims and either rented or purchased land.

<u>Samuel M. Alcorn</u> filed homestead claim #3504 on August 18, 1887. His claim consisted of 160 acres located in the west half of the northeast quarter, and the east half of the northwest quarter of Section 35, Township 10 South, Range 2 West (see Figure 17).[7] No additional information regarding this person was found during research for this study. It is not known if he remained in the area for he is not listed on the census records or county directories.

<u>William C. Ball</u> filed his homestead claim on November 8, 1888, for 80 acres located in the northern portion of this study area as shown on Figure 17. Claim #4618 included the southeast quarter of the northwest quarter and the northeast quarter of the southwest quarter of Section 29, Township 10 South, Range 1 West, San Bernardino Base Meridian.[8]

William C. Ball immigrated to the United States from Great Britain and became a U.S. citizen on November 20, 1891.[9] His birthdate information was not located during the research for this study, as he did not register to vote in San Diego County and is not listed on the census records.

In 1893 The *Escondido Times* stated that William had bailed 500 tons of hay from his property.[10] The following spring, he planted 250 trees in his orchard, most of which were olive trees.[11]

William, better known as Billy, was a bachelor when he filed his claim. He led the singing in church and Sunday school services and was looked upon by the community as a model, progressive young man.[12] He married Olive Moore on March 20, 1898.[13] Olive had also been active in the church and attended the social events. The couple had no children. Billy died in October 1899, and is buried in the Valley Center Cemetery. Olive did not stay in the area. She moved to Texas after the turn of the century.[14]

D.M. Brullon is listed as constable in the 1887-88 *Maxwell's Directory of San Diego City and County.*[15] No other mention of this person was found during research for this study. It is possible this person's name is incorrectly spelled in the directory, for D.M. Breedlove was the constable during those years.

James Brunsden was a Valley Center resident, even though his name appears on the 1880 U.S. census record for Temecula Township. He filed homestead claim #1624 on March 25, 1884, for 160 acres in the southeast quarter of Section 5, Township 11 South, Range 1 West (see Figure 17).[16]

James and his family are listed on the 1880 census as living in dwelling number 35 in the Temecula Township. James is listed as a white male laborer, 36 years old, married, born in Canada, with his parents both born in England. His wife, Elizabeth, is listed as a white female, occupation keeping house, 29 years old, born in Canada, with her parents both born in Scotland.[17]

Their two children listed include: Sarah, white female, 11 years old, attending school, born in Canada. James and Elizabeth's youngest daughter, Margarite, is listed as a white female, nine years old, attending school, born in Canada.[18]

James filed a petition for citizenship in the United States on February 23, 1886. He stated at that time he was a native of England.[19] He registered to vote in San Diego on the same day, February 23, 1886, and stated his age as 41, his birthplace England, and his occupation as a farmer in Valley Center.[20]

The Brunsden family is listed in the 1900 U.S. census of Bear Valley Township living in dwelling number 59. James is listed as 56 years old, married 31 years, born December 1848, in Canada, both parents born in England, immigrated to the U.S. in 1872, had lived in the U.S. for 28 years, not naturalized, occupation farmer, and owner of his farm.[21]

Elizabeth is listed as 49 years old, born June 1851, in Canada, parents born in Scotland, married 31 years, mother of two children, both living at the time. Living with the Brunsdens is <u>Harry Brunsden</u>, adopted son, white male, eight years old, born February 1892, in California, parents birthplaces unknown, attended school eight months during the year.[22]

According to Abel Davis, James purchased Jack Reed's ranch located at the top of the Rincon incline (see Figure 4, Chapter Two). James built an adobe brick house for his wife and two daughters on the ranch. He also worked with George Reed in cutting the Valley Center grade to Escondido. They used a team of horses hitched to a special wagon to cut the road from an old ox trail used for years to enter the valley from the south.[23]

James cultivated melons, grapes, corn blackberries, barley, and peas in 1888.[24] He was a member in the Alliance Business Association, Orange Glen District Number 9 in 1891.[25]

<u>James B. Burchart</u> was the postmaster in Valley Center in 1881.[26] He married <u>Delia A. Gavin</u> on June 19, 1881, in San Diego.[27] He registered to vote in San Diego on June 3, 1882, under the name "James Bruce Butchart", his age as 30, born in Canada, occupation merchant, residing in the Third Ward in San Diego, a citizen by his father's naturalization.[28] J.D. is also listed in the 1883-84 county directory as in general merchandise.[29]

It is not known where within Valley Center James B. Burchart lived with his family, for a homestead claim was not found during research for this study. He is not listed on the census records for the Valley Center area.

<u>Archibald G. Carpenter</u> is not listed as having filed a homestead claim in Valley Center prior to 1900. His name is not referenced on a map. On his voter registration, dated September 21, 1886, however, he stated his age as 24 years, born in Wisconsin, occupation farmer in Bear Valley.[30]

Abel Davis states that Archie had a ranch on the north rim of Valley Center extending toward the San Luis Rey River (see Figure 4, Chapter Two).[31] Carpenter is not listed on the U.S. census records of Bear Valley for either 1880 or 1900. Albert and Frank J. Carpenter are listed as living in Vista in the 1905 *Directory of San Diego City and County*. It is not known if these two people are related to Archibald Carpenter.

An article in the *Escondido Times,* May 3, 1888, states that certain persons visited A.G. Carpenter at his home south of the reservoir in Beach's Addition. He had planted trees, fruits, and vegetables on two

50x140 foot lots. The article also states that Mr. Carpenter was a bachelor. The visitors were surprised when Carpenter took them into a tent to show them his collectibles. He proudly displayed Indian artifacts, Spanish artifacts, Mexican relics, and many different types of minerals.[32] No additional information regarding Archibald Carpenter was found during research for this study.

Dr. James Harrison Clark and his family arrived in Valley Center in 1885, according to J.M. Guinn, in *The History of California*, published in 1907.[33] Upon arrival, Dr. Clark purchased a farm with an adobe house already built on the property. No record of a homestead claim was found during research for this study. Dr. Clark registered to vote in San Diego on May 6, 1886. He stated his age as 45, born in Missouri, occupation physician in Bear Valley.[34]

Guinn states that James Harrison Clark was born on December 3, 1841, in Cooper County, Missouri. He was the son of Robert Clark, a farmer in Missouri who died in 1852. James traveled across the plains states of the U.S. with two friends in 1864. He arrived in Yuba City, California, where he remained for two years as a teacher. He became interested in the medical field after working in the pharmacy business. He received his Doctor of Medicine degree in 1872. He married Mattie A. Robinson in Missouri in the spring of 1872. They had seven children: Ida DeWilton, William Robinson, Mary Rhoda, Hattie Lewis, James Harrison, Jr., and twins, Horace L. and Martha Amanda.[35]

Dr. Clark worked in various cities in California until he arrived in San Diego in 1885 at which time he purchased 240 acres in Valley Center. He purchased the house and property from Reverend J.H. Sherrard. Rev. Sherrard built a large adobe house in the early 1880s which is still used as a private residence at the time of this study (see Figure 17). He also built a chapel across the road out of the same material. The heavy rains during the mid-1880s caused the adobe to melt, making repairs necessary to both structures. The house was enclosed in red clay bricks to protect it and the chapel was covered with wooden siding. The chapel later became a private residence and a second story added.

The road between the two structures became known as Miller Road, named after the family who purchased the house in the early 1900s. The community cemetery is located beside what used to be the chapel. The cemetery was established in 1883 when the first settler, Silence Dinwiddie was buried.

The property was part of the original homestead claim of George Herbst who died in 1883. When the Clark family moved in, they made improvements to the house and property. Crops raised included pumpkins, golden, yellow, and Egyptian corn.[36] According to Abel Davis, the Clark family also raised wheat, barley, and oats, as well as planted olive trees.[37] Dr. Clark also discovered a rich source of galena on his farm.[38] Galena is a source of lead.

Dr. Clark was a respected man in the Valley Center community. His physician's practices occasionally took him as far as Palomar Mountain and the Rincon Indian Reservation. He made his trips in a horse and buggy wherever roads permitted, and when roads became impassable, Dr. Clark simply unhitched the horse and rode bareback.[39]

The Clark family is listed in the 1900 U.S. census record of the Bear Valley Township as living in dwelling number 63. James is listed as a white male, married 28 years, 58 years old, born December 1841, in Missouri, parents both born in Kentucky, occupation farmer who owns his farm. His wife is listed as M.A., 52 years old, mother of seven living children, born February 1848, birthplace unreadable, father born in South Carolina, mother born in Missouri.

Their seven children listed are: Ida Dee, single, 23 years old, born July 1876, in California; and William is listed as a farm laborer. All information regarding the remaining children, including their names, is unreadable.[40]

Ida DeWilton married Reverend Claude Thompson. She played the church organ during services. She was a school teacher for several years at the Victor School on the Woods property and Orange Glen School in Escondido.[41] Her sister, Mamie, became a teacher in the Bear Valley District.[42]

Hattie Lewis Clark married Walter Buell Holcomb on April 24, 1906.[43] The family moved to San Diego when Walter became a police officer on the San Diego Police Department. He died in 1918, leaving two young children.[44] No further information regarding Hattie was found during research for this study.

The Escondido Genealogical Society Surname Registry lists Mary Clark as having married Alexander Campbell. No further information regarding these two persons was found during research for this study.

The Clark family moved from Valley Center after the turn of the century, at which time the Millers purchased the property.

Thomas S. Coffee was a Valley Center postmaster for several years in the late 1880s.[45] According to Abel Davis, Tom filed a homestead claim on 80 acres located south of the Reed's ranch and adjoining Dr. Clark's property (see Figure 4, Chapter Two). Coffee built a small frame building for use as the post office near where the Community Hall now stands.[46] This information could not be confirmed, for no deed or claim was found during research for this study.

Thomas was married to Louisa J. Coffee [no maiden name given] and they had one daughter, Anna B. While Tom ran the post office,

Louisa is listed in the 1892–97 county directories as selling notions in a variety store.[47]

Tom was born in Tennessee in 1823 according to his voter registration dated April 14, 1888. He listed his occupation as postmaster.[48] In the 1896 Valley Center School census, the Coffee family's residence was listed as Section 13, Township 11 South, Range 2 West.

Tom died on February 2, 1897, and is buried in the Valley Center Cemetery. Cemetery records list his birthplace as New York in 1822.

Louisa later married John Q. Adams in San Diego on March 1, 1900.[49] Louisa's daughter, Anna, is listed as living in the Adams' household on the 1900 census. Louisa was born in Missouri in June 1835, and her parents were born in Tennessee. She stated she had two children, one of whom was living at the time. Anna was born in California in March 1881.[50] The Adams family moved to La Jolla in 1907, selling all holdings in the valley.

Emanuel De Lappe filed homestead claim #4789 on February 9, 1889. The legal description of the 160- acre claim is the southwest quarter of the southeast quarter, the south half of the southwest quarter, and the northeast quarter of the southwest quarter of Section 1, Township 11 South, Range 2 West.[51]

This property is located east of Lilac Road and south of Anthony Road in an area still fairly undeveloped at the time of this study (see Figure 17). A seasonal drainage which runs north/south bisects the property. The name Ames Tyler is shown on this parcel after the turn of the century.

Information regarding Emanuel De Lappe was not found during research for this study. He is not listed in the census records, the county directories, or in the local newspaper during the 1880-90 period.

William S. Dearing filed homestead claim #2358 on July 10, 1885, for 160 acres. The legal description is the northeast quarter of the northwest quarter, the west half of the northeast quarter, and the southeast quarter of the northeast quarter of Section 9, Township 11 South, Range 1 West, (see Figure 17).[52]

Witnesses testifying to his fulfillment of all obligations being satisfied at the time of claiming clear title to the property on June 19, 1891, are listed in the *Escondido Times* as: J.H. Clark, John Reed, C.H. Moore, and W.L. Wilhite.[53]

The property today is located approximately two miles east of Cole Grade Road between Fruitvale and Vesper Road. This parcel was later split, for three separate owners are shown after the turn of the century, including William Bush, S.P. Angle, and C.M. Buck.

Mr. Dearing does not appear on the 1900 census, nor in the county directories. One notation in the *Escondido Times,* on August 10, 1893, stated that Professor Deering [sic], an Orange County teacher, was visiting in the valley and checking on his investments.[54] No additional information was found during research for this study.

John Doane did not file a homestead claim in the Valley Center area. He did work the Antes ranch (see Figure 5, Chapter Two) after his father-in-law, Samuel Antes, died in 1899. D. Griswald appears as the owner of that property as well as several other parcels in the valley after the turn of the century.

The *Escondido Times* mentioned that John was working more than 300 acres on the Antes ranch on February 8, 1894.[55] In 1899, the newspaper stated that John was planning and clearing the land in order to plant an almond orchard.[56]

The family of John Doane appear in the 1900 U.S. census of Bear Valley living in dwelling number 74. John E. is listed as 45-year old, white male, married five years, farmer on his own farm, born 1855 in California, father born in Pennsylvania and mother born in Ohio.

John's wife, Ruby L. is listed as 30 years old, born 1870 in California, married five years, mother of one child who was living at the time, father born in Pennsylvania, mother born in Michigan. Their daughter, Alice, is listed as one-year old, born in December 1898, in California. Also listed living in the house is John's mother-in-law, María Antes, widow of Samuel.

John Doane's family lived on Palomar Mountain, claiming land there. Mr. and Mrs. James Doane are both buried in the Valley Center Cemetery with birth and death dates unknown. It is not known where John Doane and his family moved, for there is no mention of them after María Antes died on December 31, 1903. She is buried in the Valley Center Cemetery.

Hugh F. Doss registered to vote in San Diego on August 16, 1886. He stated his age as 48 years, born in Arkansas, and his occupation was a farmer in Bear Valley.[57] It is not known if this person lived within this study area as no additional information was found during research for this study. His name does not appear in the homestead deed books, the census records, or in county directories.

George W. Fairhurst filed homestead claim #2612 on January 14, 1886. This parcel of 40 acres is described as the northeast quarter of the northeast quarter of Section 13, Township 11 South, Range 2 West.[58] This parcel was claimed the following year by Goolsby Woods. It is located east of Valley Center Road approximately one-quarter mile south of the 90° bend in Valley Center Road (see Figure 17).

No further information was found during the research for this study. Mr. Fairhurst is not listed on the U.S. census records, nor in the county directories.

W.O. Field is not listed as filing a homestead claim, but his name appears on a 1885 survey map in Section 8, Township 11 South, Range 1 West (see Figure 17). His name also appears as having 80 acres in Section 8 on maps after the turn of the century. This parcel was part of Columbus Dinwiddie's original claim (see Figure 5, Chapter Two). Also shown as owner of 80 acres is M.T. Field in another parcel of Dinwiddie's. William A. Fields is shown as having the parcel north of Dinwiddie's claim in the southwest quarter of Section 5.

According to the *Escondido Times*[59] in 1893, Oliver Field filed a claim for land located south of the Antes ranch. This claim was not found during research for this study. The *Escondido Times* mentioned Mark Twain Fields as enjoying his gardening, and that Mrs. M.J. Fields was a teacher from Michigan.[60]

The surname appears both with and without an "S" in various sources. In 1897, O. Fields is listed as a farmer in Valley Center in the county directory.[61] Mr. Field [no first name] is listed in the Escondido Genealogical Society Surname Registry as having married Virginia Dixon.[62]

Further research has uncovered the relationships of the Field family. William Oliver Field is the son of Mary Ann Borden, daughter of Oliver Harrison Borden. Mary Ann married William H. Field in 1867 at Vallonia, Indiana. They had two sons, John Markle (Mark), born 1868, and William Oliver Field (Ollie), born 1869. Mary and William Field divorced when she came to California to be with her parents in Valley Center. She brought her youngest son, Ollie, with her while her oldest son, Mark, stayed in Indiana with his father.

The two brothers were later reunited in Valley Center. Ollie married an unnamed woman with two children in Pasadena in 1911, and moved to Fallbrook where his son, Harry Oliver Field was born in 1914. Harry married Mable Bernice Lackey and they had two daughters, Nancy Gail and Judy Luanne, and two sons, Neil William and Eugene Robert Field.

Oliver Field died in Fallbrook in 1952 and was buried in Odd Fellows Cemetery.

Marcus A. Forster registered to vote in San Diego on August 11, 1880. He stated his age at that time as 40, born in California, occupation farmer in Bear Valley. His name was canceled from the register on August 25, 1880, as having registered twice.

It is not known if this person lived within the study area, as no additional information was found during research for this study. He is not listed on the Valley Center census records, or in county directories nor on any survey maps. A person named John Forster is listed as living in the San Luis Rey area in the 1883-84 *Pacific Coast Directory*.

James S. German filed homestead claim #2548 on November 30, 1885, for 160 acres. The legal description is the northeast quarter of the northwest quarter of Section 13, the east half of the southwest quarter, and the southwest quarter of the southeast quarter of Section 12, Township 11 South, Range 2 West, San Bernardino Base Meridian (see Figure 17).[63]

This parcel was later claimed by John Q. Adams in 1887 (see Figure 5, Chapter Two), and after the turn of the century by W.I. Mundell. It is located west of Valley Center Road at the bend, with Lilac Road cutting through diagonally.

The relationship of James L. German and John D. German is not known. John D. German, is listed as living in dwelling number 182 on the 1880 U.S. census of Bear Valley. He is listed as a white male, 18 years old, married, farmer, born in California, father born in Pennsylvania, mother born in Missouri. His wife, Susie P., is listed as a white female, 16 years old, married, keeping house, born in California, father born in Missouri, mother born in Kentucky.[64] Susie is the daughter of James and Annie Woods, listed in Chapter Two of this study.

Also listed in the German household in 1880 are William P. Belsher, William H. Willard, and Frank Tracy. William Belsher is listed as 22 years old, single, farm laborer, born in California, father's birthplace unknown, mother born in Kentucky. William Willard is listed as 30 years old, married, farmer, born in Wisconsin, father born in Missouri, mother born in Kansas. Frank Tracy is listed as 19 years old, single, farm laborer, born in California, as were his parents.[65]

John D. German is also listed as a blacksmith, in the 1883-84 *Pacific Coast Directory*, town of Valley Centre. James L. German registered to vote in San Diego on October 4, 1884. He stated his age as 21, born in California, occupation wagon maker in Bear Valley. These two individuals could be the same person, or they could be brothers, for their birth years work out to 1863 for James, and 1862 for John.

Neither person is listed on the 1900 U.S. census of Bear Valley. In 1893, an article in the *Escondido Times* mentioned the German family moving to Los Angeles.[66]

Andrew Gillen filed homestead claim #4787 for 80 acres on February 8, 1889. The legal description is the east half of the northeast quarter of Section 12, Township 11 South, Range 2 West.[67] Today this acreage is located west of Miller Road, approximately one-quarter mile north of Valley Center Road. This parcel includes the Clark House shown on Figure 22, for it is directly across the street from the chapel. John Mason is listed as owner of this property after the turn of the century.

Andrew Gillin [sic] registered to vote in San Diego County on September 13, 1886. He stated his age as 58, born in Pennsylvania, occupation shoemaker in Valley Center.[68] He is also listed in the county directories in 1893, 1897, and 1905.[69] Mr. Gillen is not listed in the 1900 U.S. census of Bear Valley Township, and no further information was found during research for this study.

Dr. Hezmer C. Hastings was an early pioneer in the Valley Center area who, unfortunately, met an early death. He left his ten-year old son, Carl, who later took over the property for several years.

Dr. Hastings filed homestead claim #1603 on March 3, 1884. His claim included 161.80 acres located just east of Valley Center Road near the junction of Lilac Road. This parcel was across the street from a garage owned by later Valley Center resident, Al Kuebler (see Figure 17).

The legal description of the property claimed by Dr. Hastings is the south half of the northwest quarter and the south half of the northeast quarter of Section 18, Township 11 South, Range 1 West, San Bernardino Base Meridian (see Figure 17).[70]

According to Abel Davis, Dr. C.H. Hastings' medical practice took him as far as Warner's Ranch, Palomar, Oceanside, Temecula, and Escondido. He never asked for money for services, however, he managed to keep his home repaired and food on the table by bartering his trade. His son usually traveled with him in the light buggy pulled by a small horse.[71]

Hezmer C. Hastings registered to vote in San Diego on September 21, 1886, at which time he stated his age as 38 years, born in Illinois, occupation physician in Bear Valley.[72] A person named Charles H. Hastings appeared on the register to vote in 1867 stating his age as 26 years, born in Boston, occupation mariner.[73] Research could not confirm if these two people were related.

An article in the *Escondido Times* stated that Dr. H.C. Hastings died at the age of 44 years on June 29, 1890. He was found sitting on his porch by his son, who was the only survivor of the family in California. Apparently, there were some brothers of the doctor living in New England.[74]

A coroner's inquest proved Dr. Hastings died of an opium overdose. It was not proven whether the act was intentional, and could not verify suicide. Therefore, it was simply considered an accident.[75]

The property of Dr. Hastings was divided with half of it owned by E.A. Breedlove after the turn of the century. The half closest to Valley Center Road was listed as owned by C. Hastings at that time. Carl is not listed on the county directories or census records of Valley Center.

George Heueldon is listed in the Valley Center section of the 1883-84 county directory.[76] His occupation is listed as roadmaster. It is not known if Mr. Heueldon was in the valley temporarily, for his name is not listed on subsequent directories or census records. No further information was found during research for this study.

James Houses filed homestead claim #2424 on September 2, 1885. His claim included 163.35 acres located in the south half of the southwest quarter and the southwest quarter of the southeast quarter of Section 19, Township 11 South, Range 1 West, San Bernardino Base Meridian (see Figure 17). The total amount paid included $10 filing fee, and $6 commissions at $1.25 per acre. Excess receipt #1629 was issued at that time for $4.19.[77]

According to Abel Davis, the Houses farm was located on the north rim of the valley extending toward the San Luis Rey River (see Figure 4, Chapter Two). They were a large family of mostly females and were active church-goers. The family later moved into town to be closer to the schools for the children.[78]

James registered to vote in San Diego on October 1, 1886. He stated his age at the time as 37 years, born in Mississippi, occupation farmer in Bear Valley.[79] His family is not listed in the county directories nor on the census records for Valley Center.

One person with the surname of House is listed in the 1900 U.S. census living with Joseph Hudspath in dwelling 86. John House is listed as a boarder, single, 55 years old, born August 1844, in Illinois, with his parents born in Pennsylvania. His occupation is listed as farm laborer, and he was out of work for six months during the year.[80] Research did not establish a relationship between these two people.

Mary E. Hughes filed homestead claim #4934 for 121.97 acres on March 7, 1889. The legal description is the east half of the northwest quarter and the northwest quarter of the northwest quarter of Section 1, Township 11 South, Range 2 West. The total fees paid included a $10 filing fee and $4.60 commissions.[81]

This parcel is located in the northern portion of this study area (see Figure 17). The property is east of Lilac Road, north of Anthony

Road. A portion of the parcel was owned by M.M. Lane after the turn of the century.

J. Hughes is listed as living in Valley Center in the 1893-94 *Directory of San Diego City and County*. Charles B. Hughes is listed in Valley Center in the 1897 *Directory of San Diego City and County*.[82] There is no reference as to where these persons lived, or if there is a connection to Mary E. Hughes. No additional information was found regarding Mary or to whom she was related.

It is not known if Lyman C. Jacobs lived within this study area, for his name appears as a farmer in Bear Valley on the San Diego Great Register of Voters, 1880-87. County directories and census records revealed no additional information regarding this person.

William Knight registered to vote in San Diego on June 21, 1884. He stated his age at the time as 44, born in Maine, occupation farmer in Bear Valley.[83]

No homestead claim filed by Mr. Knight was found during research for this study. Abel Davis states that William Knight lived an a ranch north of the Heddens (see Figure 4, Chapter Two). He raised chickens and sold eggs.

Abel Davis relates a story regarding Mr. Knight 'tin-canning' his trees where the chickens roosted. It seems that in order to keep his poultry safe from predators such as coyotes and bobcats, Mr. Knight nailed five-gallon cans around the trunks of the trees after cutting out the bottoms from the cans.[84]

Twenty acres is shown to be property of W. Knight after the turn of the century. This acreage is located in Section 18, Township 11 South, Range 1 West. Today this parcel is located east of Valley Center Road across the street from the Corral Liquor store (see Figure 17).

William M. Knight's name does not appear on the census records for Valley Center. An article in the *Escondido Times* stated that he was raising Spanish corn and white Russian wheat in 1888.[85] He is listed in the 1893-94 *Directory of San Diego City and County* as living in the Valley Center area at that time.[86] No additional information regarding William Knight was found during research for this study.

Aurelius T. Ladd filed homestead claim #2012 on January 12, 1885. His claim included 40 acres located in the southwest quarter of the northwest quarter of Section 1, Township 11 South, Range 2 West. The total fees paid at that time included a $5 filing fee and $1.50 commissions at $1.25 per acre.[87]

This parcel is located southeast of Anthony Road. A large drainage runs diagonally through the property. This area is still mostly undeveloped at the time of this study (see Figure 17).

No additional information was found regarding Mr. Ladd as he is not listed on census records or county directories as living in the Valley Center area.

D. McTothlin is listed in the Valley Center section of the 1883-84 *Directory of San Diego City and County*.[88] His occupation is described as general merchandise. No further information was found during research for this study. It is not known if D. McTothlin was a temporary resident of the valley for his name is not listed on the census records or in subsequent county directories.

John H. Meeks filed homestead claim #2634 on January 10, 1886, for 160 acres. The legal description of this property is the north half of the northwest quarter, the northwest quarter of the northeast quarter, and the southeast quarter of the northwest quarter of Section 12, Township 11 South, Range 2 West of the San Bernardino Base Meridian.[89] This parcel today is located east of Lilac Road and southeast of Anthony Road (see Figure 17).

A large portion of this parcel was claimed by John Q. Adams the following year. Mr. Meeks retained a portion of the parcel. The northwest quarter of the northeast quarter is listed as the property of J.H. Meeks after the turn of the century. Also, Austin Walsh is listed as the owner of the Adams parcel at that time.

John H. Meeks registered to vote in San Diego on December 12, 1883, at which time he stated his age as 43, born in Indiana, occupation photographer in Bear Valley.[90] Mr. Meeks is not listed on the census records as living in the valley. Two male and one female student are listed on the Valley Center School register of 1891. The father, C.H. Meeks, is listed as a grocer. There are also two children, John and Charlie, listed on the school register in 1893.[91]

Abel Davis states that a Mr. Meeks owned the entire section of land in Pala and sold it to the U.S. Government in 1903 when the Pala Indian Reservation was established.[92] Confirmation of this information was not found during research for this study. The Escondido Genealogical Society Surname Registry lists Mr. Meeks [no first name given] as marrying Temperance Freeman, with no date cited. The relationship between John Meeks and the Mr. Meeks who was married could not be determined based on research for this study.

Henry J. Meyer, often misspelled as Myers, Meyers, and even Mers, is listed as living in Valley Center in 1886 according to his voter registration. On June 30th of that year, he stated his age was 58, born in Germany, and his occupation was a carpenter in Valley Center. The registration also stated he was a naturalized citizen who had sworn his oath in Hamilton County, Ohio, Superior Court on October 29, 1856.[93]

Henry is listed in the county directories in the Valley Center area in the years 1892-93, 1893-94, and 1897.[94] He died on April 1, 1899, and is buried in the Valley Center Cemetery. A coroner's inquest proved he died of heart disease.[95] The coroner's report also lists a person named Otto Meyer who committed suicide in Bernardo on Maxcy's ranch on May 21, 1876.[96] It is not known if he was a relative of Henry, for neither person is listed on the census records.

Proof of property ownership under Henry Meyer (or the other spellings) was not conclusive during research for this study. A 40-acre parcel located in Section 32, Township 10 South, Range 1 West, is owned however, by H.C. Meyer after the turn of the century. Family relationship could not be proven between these persons.

Reverend Joseph E. Miller filed homestead claim #623 on August 11, 1880, for 160 acres located in the northern portion of this study area. The legal description is the east half of the northwest quarter and the west half of the northeast quarter of Section 32, Township 10 South, Range 1 West (see Figure 17). Total fees paid at the time included $10 filing fee and $6 in commissions at $1.25 per acre.[97]

The Miller family is firmly attached to the history of Valley Center. Catherine Miller, or "Grandma Miller" as everyone knew her, was responsible for the mail in the valley prior to the establishment of a post office in 1878. The mail was brought up the grade from San Diego on the route through Escondido and put into a bacon packaging box which sat under a pepper tree near the intersection of what is now Woods Valley Road and Valley Center Road. People would collect any new mail for their neighbors and deliver it to them on the way home.[98]

According to Abel Davis and Clyde James, the community only knew her name as "Grandma Miller".[99] An article in the *Escondido Times* dated April 9, 1891, states that Mrs. Catherine "Grandma" Miller was returning to the valley to live. Mrs. Miller was referred to as being the mother of Mrs. George Ogsbury of Escondido.[100] Research also proved Catherine to be the mother of Berthina C. Miller Watkins.

Joseph E. Miller registered to vote in San Diego on October 3, 1882, at which time he stated his age as 71 years, born in Kentucky, occupation farmer in Bear Valley, with no mention of being a minister. Yet, he is listed in the 1883-84 *Pacific Coast Directory* as a minister in Valley Center.[101] The Valley Center Cemetery records list Rev. J.E. Miller died on September 3, 1887, and is buried in the community cemetery.

An obituary written for his son, <u>William H. Miller</u>, states that William was 78 years old at the time of his death, and that he was born in 1837. He is buried in the Valley Center Cemetery along with his father and mother. Mrs. W.H. Miller [no first name given] is also buried in the community cemetery, with birth and death information unknown.[102]

Also listed in Valley Center Cemetery records is <u>Amelia Miller</u>, born 1815, died 1911; <u>William Frank Miller</u>, born 1880, died 1956; <u>Mrs. Bertha Miller</u>, born October 10, 1887, died February 21, 1973; and <u>James K. Miller</u>, born October 5, 1900, died January 3, 1968.

Several Millers are listed as living in the Valley Center area in the county directories, but their family relationships are not known. Their names do not appear on the census of 1900 or in county directories. This includes <u>W.B</u>, 1905 directory; <u>Arthur H.</u>, farmer, 1921 directory, <u>Eugene L.R.</u>, farmer, 1921; and <u>Susie</u>, 1921.[103] It is believed these later Millers are no relation to Rev. J.E. and family. Rather, they were members of the family who came into the valley in 1905 and purchased Dr. Clark's house.

<u>John W. Moore</u> did not file a homestead claim, instead, he purchased the established farm of George Reed, according to Abel Davis. George built a house in 1882 and in 1885 sold the house and property surrounding it to John Moore. A new homestead was then claimed by George Reed a few miles farther east.[104]

The Moore family is not listed on the census records for Bear Valley. John W. Moore registered to vote in San Diego on May 26, 1886. He stated at that time his age was 42, born in Illinois, and his occupation was a farmer in Bear Valley.[105]

John's family members present a question as to whom is related to whom. It is possible these are John's children. Several Moores are listed in the county directory and the Valley Center Cemetery records. This includes: <u>Andrew R. Moore</u>, also listed as a farmer in the 1893-94 and 1897 county directories.[106] The cemetery records state he died in June 1899. <u>Charles Moore</u> appears in the same county directories with Andrew. His occupation is nurseryman. He married <u>Eula Althea Lyle</u> according to the Escondido Genealogical Society Surname Register.[107] <u>J.L. Moore</u> died on March 3, 1891, and is buried in the Valley Center Cemetery. <u>M.L. Moore</u> died on February 15, 1887, and is also buried in the community cemetery.

<u>Olive Moore</u> married William C. Ball in 1898 and lived in the area after her husband's death in 1899. She moved to Texas after the turn of the century.[108] It is not known if she was related to the other Moores in the Valley Center area.

In 1888, John Moore is credited with growing oats,[109] as well as renting 30 acres from Sam Antes to grow some experimental cotton. The experiment was very successful and caused an expansion of cotton growing in California at that time.[110]

John Moore was also instrumental in growing red wheat in the valley. It had not been raised in California before. He received 20 sacks of seed from Texas to begin his test, and it was also very successful.[111] In 1894, he planted five acres in prune trees.[112]

John Moore registered two male and two female students in the Valley Center School in 1891.[113] He was very respected in the community and was named school trustee of Vista in 1894.[114]

John Perrill Morris was a registered voter living in Bear Valley. He registered on September 5, 1882, in San Diego. He stated his age as 44, born in Missouri, and his occupation as farmer.[115] He is not listed on the census records for Bear Valley. He is listed in the 1893-94 county directory as living in the Valley Center area. John P. Morris died in 1898 and is buried in the Valley Center Cemetery.

It is not known if John was married or had a family. There is a J.R. Morris shown on a 1900 plat map as the owner of an 80-acre parcel in the northeast quarter of Section 21, Township 11 South, Range 1 West. This parcel later became part of the San Pasqual Indian Reservation.

There are several persons with the name "Morris" listed in the county directories, newspapers, and census records, but relationships between these people could not be confirmed. These people lived outside of the study area.

A map of Township 10 South, Range 1 West, circa 1900, shows 160 acres owned by L.L. Morrison in the southeast quarter of Section 33. A homestead claim for this land was not found during research for this study. L.L. is listed as a farmer in the 1883-84, 1897, and 1901 county directories.[116]

L.L. Morrison and his family are listed on the 1900 census of Bear Valley Township in dwelling number 55. He is listed as 28 years old, born June 1872, in Illinois, married one year, occupation farmer on his own farm, father born in Pennsylvania, mother born in Iowa. His wife, Alice, is listed as 28 years old, born February 1872, in Kansas, mother of one child, father born at sea, mother born in Iowa. Their daughter, Pearl M., was three months old, born in March 1900, in California.[117]

A map of Township 11 South, Range 1 West, circa 1900, lists J.W. Morrison as owner of 120 acres in Section 4. No homestead claim was found for this parcel during research for this study. No further information was found regarding this individual.

Other Morrisons listed in the Valley Center area include: <u>W.N. Morrison</u>, born 1873, died 1954; and <u>Loretta S. Morrison</u>, born 1877, died 1960, both of whom are listed in the Valley Center Cemetery records. There is also a <u>W.F. Morrison</u> with one female student listed in the Valley Center School census of 1891. A relationship between J.P. Morrison and the others could not be confirmed during research for this study.

<u>William B. Parish</u> filed homestead claim #1040 on June 12, 1882, for 160 acres. The legal description is the south half of the southeast quarter of Section 29, and the east half of the northeast quarter of Section 32, Township 10 South, Range 1 West.[118] This parcel today is located approximately one mile east of Cole Grade Road, south of Hinman Road, and bisected by Cool Valley Road (see Figure 17).

This property was later divided with portions owned by J.C. Woodward, E.H. Wood, J.E. Rohe, and the Pasadena First National Bank.

William Parish was a professional tailor and provided everyone in the valley with their suits, according to Abel Davis. He built his home among huge rocks.[119] William registered to vote in San Diego on June 28, 1886, at which time he stated his age was 57 years, born in North Carolina, and his occupation was a tailor in Bear Valley.[120] He died in Valley Center on September 4, 1886, and is buried in the community cemetery.[121] The coroner's report states that William Parish committed suicide in Bear Valley and died from gunshot wounds.[122]

It is not known if William B. Parish was married or had children, as he is not listed in the census records of Bear Valley.

<u>Reverend John M. Pease</u> did not file a homestead claim that was found during research for this study. According to Abel Davis, however, the family settled on land north of the Davis ranch (see Figure 4, Chapter Two), and later moved into town to be closer to the schools for their many female children. Out of six children, all but one of his daughters became teachers.

John M. Pease registered to vote on May 3, 1886, stating at that time his age was 45 years, born in Maine, and his occupation was a farmer in Bear Valley.[123] He raised brandywine peaches on his farm.[124]

The family is not listed on the census records for Bear Valley. J.M. Pease is listed as the minister of the Methodist Episcopal Church South on the 1893-94, 1897, and 1901 county directories. <u>Charles S.</u>, is listed as the pastor of the M.E. Church in the 1901 directory.[125] A biographical profile of Charles Pease, written by J.M Guinn in 1907, does not confirm the relationship of Charles and John.

The article gives Charles birthdate as July 20, 1865, in Enfield, Maine; therefore, he could be John's son. The article, however, states that Charles received his ministerial training at Hartford Theological Seminary in 1896. In 1899, he attempted to save a drowning man and ended up suffering ill health thereafter. He moved to California in 1900 and from 1905 to 1907 he had served the church in Long Beach, California.[126]

One of Rev. Pease's daughters, Fannie, was hired as the Bear Valley School teacher in 1893 and 1894. Another daughter, Minnie, became the teacher of Pamo School in 1894.[127]

An unpublished biographical story of Minnie Pease, author unknown, is located in the Local History files at the San Diego County Library, Valley Center Branch.[128] In this profile, it states that Minnie was born in Maine and moved to California when young. She received her teaching credentials from the San Diego College of Letters in Pacific Beach, California.

Her first teaching job in San Pasqual was known as the "Hole in the ground" due to the isolation of the school. While teaching there, she lived with one of the local families of her students. She then taught at the Montecito School in Ramona for seven years, through the 1890s. Minnie went on to become the principal of Edison School in San Diego from 1927-1932, and then Florence School from 1932-1935.[129]

Although the Pease family did not file a homestead claim, their presence in the Valley Center area proved to be rewarding to the residents. Many people were married, baptized, and buried in the valley while Reverend J.M. Pease was minister of the M.E. Church and their children educated by his daughters.

The family of Jacob Thomas Reed, Sr. was very influential in the Valley Center area for they brought the brick-building trade with them, and from that day forward, the bricks used in valley were made on-site using the brick kiln built by the Reed family. Many of these buildings are not only still standing, but are used daily. The family members also included a pilot and road engineers, as well as farmers and ranchers. Figure 20 is a photograph of the Reed family and their adobe brick-making machine, circa 1880.

Jacob Reed's family is listed on the 1900 U.S. census of Bear Valley as living in dwelling number 206. Jacob is listed as a 65-year old, married, white male farmer, born in Indiana, father born in South Carolina, and mother born in Virginia. His wife, Martha, is listed as 50 years old, born in Missouri, and her parents born in Virginia.[130]

Their six children listed are: Jacob T., G.W., Wilbern, Austin, Granville, and Emma. Jacob T., Jr., is listed as a single, white male, 23 years old, born in Oregon, occupation farm laborer. G.W. is listed as a single, white male, 19 years old, born in California, occupation farm laborer. Wilbern is listed as a white male, single, 16-year old farm laborer, born in Oregon. Austin is listed as a white male, single, 15-year old farm laborer, born in California. Granville is listed as 12 years old, born in California, with the occupation listed as 'at home'. Jacob and Martha's only daughter, Emma, is listed as 6 years old, born in California.[131]

Source: San Diego Historical Society - Title Insurance and Trust Collection

Figure 20. The Reed Family and Their Brick-making Machine, Making Bricks for the Dr. J.H. Clark House, ca. 1880. Left to right: Jake, Granville, Grandma [Martha], Joe, and Will Reed.

Jacob and Martha married in Oregon, circa 1847. Two of their eleven children were born in Oregon. They moved to the San Francisco area in the late 1840s and remained there for several years before moving to San Diego and taking up government land in Valley Center.[132]

S.T. Black, author of *San Diego County, California*, states that Jacob and Martha had eleven children: <u>Joseph</u>, <u>Benjamin</u>, <u>Samantha</u>, <u>Jacob Thomas</u>, <u>John W</u>., George W., Wilbur [sic], Austin, Granville, Emma, and <u>Malina</u>. Benjamin, Samantha, and Emma had died prior to 1913 when Black's volumes were published. Jacob T., Sr. passed away on March 14, 1884, in Valley Center.[133]

Not surprisingly, the Reed family filed several homestead claims in and around Valley Center. The records also show several 'Reeds' living near Warner's Ranch, Redlands, and Temecula. It is not known if they were relatives of Jacob and family. Jacob's family, however, settled primarily around Valley Center.

A homestead deed to Jacob T., Sr., was not located during research for this study. Several parcels of land were the property of

Martha Reed after the turn of the century. These parcels are located east of Cole Grade Road and between Fruitvale Road and Cool Valley Road (see Figure 17).

Martha filed a homestead claim on one of these parcels in 1885. She filed homestead claim #2439 on September 10, 1885, for 158.94 acres of land. The legal description is the southeast quarter of the southeast quarter of Section 31, Township 10 South, Range 1 West, the west half of the northeast quarter, and the southeast quarter of the northeast quarter of Section 6, Township 11 South, Range 1 West.[134]

An article in the *Escondido Times* written in 1894, states that Mrs. Reed had refused an offer of $20 per acre for her land. The article does not state from whom the offer was made, nor what the true market value was at the time.[135]

The first child to file in Jacob's immediate family was George W. Reed. He filed homestead claim #2212 on April 21, 1885, for 160 acres. The legal description is the southwest quarter of the northeast quarter, the northwest quarter of the southeast quarter, the northeast quarter of the southwest quarter, and the southeast quarter of the northwest quarter of Section 4, Township 11 South, Range 1 West.[136]

Today this property is located north of Fruitvale Road approximately two miles east of Cole Grade Road (see Figure 17). It is situated at the top of the Rincon incline. This is the parcel which George homesteaded after selling his first property to the Moore family when they arrived in the valley in 1885. George lived on this homestead until 1895, at which time he sold it and moved to Fallbrook.[137]

According to Abel Davis, George filed his first homestead claim in 1872. Research for this study could not confirm the date, nor locate the homestead claim.[138]

George W. Reed and Emma Watkins, daughter of W.K. and Berthina Watkins, were married on February 3, 1880. They had no children of their own by 1913. They adopted George's youngest sister's three children, however, upon her death. Details regarding her death were not recovered during research for this study. The children are: Jessie, born 1898, Ray, born 1901, and Floyd, born 1903.[139]

George registered to vote for the first time in San Diego on May 23, 1883. He was 22 years old at the time, stated he was born in California, and was a farmer in Bear Valley.[140] George helped James Brunsden cut the new road from Escondido known as the Valley Center grade.

The second child of Jacob and Martha Reed to file a homestead claim was John W. Reed. He filed claim #3141 on February 8, 1887, for 80 acres located outside of this study area in Section 15, Township 11 South, Range 1 West.[141] John W. Reed registered to vote in San

Diego on October 14, 1882. He stated his age was 23, born in California, and his occupation was a farmer in Bear Valley.[142]

John married <u>Ella Watkins</u> according to Abel Davis.[143] One male child is listed as attending the Valley Center School in 1891.[144] John is listed as a constable in Valley Center during the years 1887-88, and 1905, and farmer or rancher in 1897 and 1901 in the county directories.[145] He is listed as a miner in the mines in Pala in 1913.[146]

Austin was the last of Jacob and Martha's children to file a homestead claim in Valley Center prior to 1900. Austin filed claim #5115 on November 1, 1889, for 118.99 acres. The legal description includes Lots 2 and 3, in Section 4, Township 11 South, Range 1 West, and the southeast half of the southwest quarter of Section 33, Township 10 South, Range 1 West.[147] This parcel today is located approximately two miles east of Cole Grade Road and one-half mile south of Cool Valley Road (see Figure 17).

Austin Y. Reed registered to vote in San Diego on September 23, 1886, stating his age as 21 years, born in California, and his occupation as farmer in Bear Valley.[148] Austin married <u>Anna Watkins</u>.[149] One male child is listed on the 1891 Valley Center School census. According to S.T. Black, Austin and family moved to Garden Grove, California with no date referenced.[150]

Joseph Reed was the aviation specialist in the family. An article in the *Escondido Times* in 1893 stated that Joe, as aviation navigator, had just returned from Australia.[151] Another article in January 1894, stated he was not flying due to the cold weather.[152] Joe registered to vote on July 14, 1882, at which time his age was 33, born in Oregon, and his occupation was farmer in Bear Valley.[153] Joe also operated a saw mill on Palomar Mountain with Sam Striplin and occasionally brought down wagon loads of wood and lumber.[154]

In March of 1893, Joe was building a public road through the Borden ranch, past Brunsden's and Vestal's ranches.[155] According to Black, Joe and his family moved to Fallbrook before 1913.[156]

Wilbern Reed is the only family member who lived in the Valley Center area at the time of the 1900 U.S. census. He is listed with his family in dwelling number 39. Wilburn [sic] is listed as a white male, 35 years old, married 18 years, born October 1864, in Oregon, both parents born in Indiana, and a farmer on his own farm. His wife, <u>Sadie</u>, is listed as 34 years old, born in California February 1866, mother of four children, all living at the time, with both parents born in Indiana.[157]

All of Wilbern and Sadie's children were born in California. The eldest, <u>Frank</u>, was 12 years old, born August 1888, attended school eight months during the year. <u>Carl</u> is listed as 10 years old, born November 1889, attended school eight months during the year. Their youngest son, <u>Robert</u>, seven years old, was born 1873 (no month listed), attended school eight months during the year. Their only daughter, <u>Ivy</u>, was four years old, born in September 1896.[158]

Jacob T. Reed, Jr., registered to vote on July 24, 1880. He stated his age was 23, born in Oregon, occupation farmer in Bear Valley.[159] He was a mail carrier in Escondido during 1889-90.[160]

The other Reed family members moved from the valley after the turn of the century. This includes: Jacob T., Jr., who moved to Huntington Beach; Wilbern moved to Fallbrook; Granville moved to Redlands and moved back to the valley in 1894; and Malina moved to the San Francisco area.[161]

<u>Mary A. Salmon</u> filed homestead claim #3283 on April 23, 1887, for 160 acres located in Valley Center. The legal description is the southeast quarter of Section 32, Township 10 South, Range 1 West, San Bernardino Base Meridian.[162] Today this property is located approximately one mile east of Cole Grade Road and one-quarter mile south of Cool Valley Road (see Figure 17).

Mrs. Mary Salmons [sic] is listed in the 1897 and 1901 county directories as a rancher in Valley Center.[163] She is not listed on the census records for the area, although the name "M.A. Salmons" appears as owner of the property after the turn of the century.

<u>Miss Ora Salmons</u> is listed in the 1901 *Directory of San Diego City and County* as a teacher living in Valley Center.[164] She is also listed on the 1900 census of Bear Valley as living alone in dwelling number 95. She is listed as 44 years old, born in Georgia in November 1855, single, her parents were both born in Georgia, her occupation was the teacher of the Indian School, and she owned her farm.[165]

<u>Miss Hattie Salmons</u> is listed in the 1897 county directory as living in Valley Center. Her occupation is listed as teacher.[166] She is not listed on the census records.

There is also a <u>Lewis Salmons</u> listed in the Pala Township on the 1900 census record. It is not known if he is a relative of Mary or Ora. He lived in dwelling number 135 with his wife and two daughters. He is listed as 28 years old, born in Georgia in May 1872, married four years, parents both born in Georgia, and his occupation listed as a farmer on a rented farm. His wife, <u>Emma</u>, is listed as 25 years old, born in California in February 1874, mother of two live children, father born in Maine, and her mother born in Texas. Daughter <u>Matilda</u> was two years old, born in February 1897, in California, and daughter <u>Rebecca</u>, one year old, was born in February 1899, in California.[167]

<u>Frank Salmons</u> is also listed on the 1900 census of the Pala Township. His age is listed as 34, born in Georgia, September 1866, married five years, parents both born in Georgia, occupation merchant. His wife, <u>Hazel</u>, was 28, born in California in October 1872, mother of two children, both of whom listed as living, her father was born in

South Carolina and her mother was born in Kentucky. Their oldest daughter, <u>Margaret</u>, was four years old, born in California in October 1895, and the youngest daughter, <u>Mildred</u>, was two years old, born in California in December 1897.[168]

It appears the Salmons are related according to the birthdates and places. Mary was probably the mother since she is listed as married, and Ora, Hattie, Lewis, and Frank were her children. No further information regarding the Salmon family was found during research for this study.

<u>Reverend Joseph H. Sherrard</u> and his wife, <u>Hannah</u>, seen in Figure 21, moved into Valley Center during the early 1880s. An early homestead claim was not located during research for this study; however, a newspaper article published in 1889 stated that he had owned 500 acres of the choicest land in Bear Valley only to lose it a few years later through a series of bad trades.[169]

Figure 21. Reverend Joseph H. and Hannah Sherrard, ca. 1885.

In 1883, Rev. Sherrard filed a homestead claim for 42.5 acres of the former Herbst homestead. On this land, Rev. Sherrard built an adobe house and chapel which are currently used as private residences. Homestead claim #1220 was filed on March 16, 1883. The legal description is Lot 1, Section 7, Township 11 South, Range 1 West.[170]

Figure 22. The Clark House Today.

Figure 23. Top Photo: Valley Center Chapel Charter, 1885.
Bottom Photo: Valley Center Chapel During Remodeling,
photo printed in the Valley Roadrunner.

The house was located approximately four miles from the Methodist Episcopal Church South, where Rev. Sherrard served. He built a barn, dug a well, and raised fields of wheat.[171] The house was covered with red brick after the heavy storms of 1883-84 caused the adobe to melt. Dr. J.H. Clark and family bought the house in 1905. The house as it appears today, as well as the keystone above the door, are shown as Figure 22. It is known as the Clark House, even though later owners, the Miller family, have the distinction of having the street in front of the house named in their honor.[172]

The chapel, built across the street from the house, was covered with wooden siding in 1884 to prevent further damage from the adobe bricks melting. The chapel was used as a church for many years by several different denominations and eventually sold as a private residence. A second story was added to the structure at that time. The plot of land used as the community cemetery was donated to the community when Rev. Sherrard sold the property.[173]

A charter was signed on November 8, 1885, the day the chapel first opened as a church. This charter hung in the chapel for many years until it was moved to the Community Church. Photographs of the Sherrards are shown on the charter. A photograph of the charter and a photograph of the chapel after the conversion, are shown as Figure 23.

Rev. Sherrard registered to vote in San Diego on April 25, 1883. He stated his age as 58, born in Ohio, and his occupation was minister in Bear Valley. This registration was canceled and transferred to Los Angeles County by request on September 29, 1886.[174]

Mrs. Hannah Sherrard died on January 7, 1893, at her home in Valley Center. She had been born on July 1, 1816, in Muskinhum County, Ohio, and moved to Texas in 1858. The obituary published in the *Escondido Times Advocate* stated Hannah was a helpful, giving person.[175] She is buried in the Valley Center Cemetery.

Reverend Sherrard moved to the Los Angeles area after Hannah's death and sold his interests in Valley Center. He married Manda McGowan on January 16, 1894, in Ventura County.[176]

Joseph Taylor filed pre-emption claim #6686 for 160 acres located in the northern portion of this study area. He was granted full title to the deed on July 11, 1891, in the Los Angeles Land Office. His witnesses were his neighbors. They testified to the fact that he had fulfilled all obligations over the previous five years. This included: Ransom D. Breedlove, John Reed, W.L. Wilhite, and Donald McGilvray.[177]

The legal description of the claim is the southeast quarter of the northeast quarter and the east half of the southeast quarter of Section 26, and the northeast quarter of the northeast quarter of Section 35, Township 10 South, Range 2 West, San Bernardino Base

Meridian.[178] The property today is located approximately one-mile west of Cole Grade Road with Hilldale Road providing the southern boundary (see Figure 17).

Little information was found regarding Joseph Taylor and his family, for they were not listed in the census records or county directories. Hattie Taylor is listed as a fifth grade student in Escondido in 1894,[179] and C.C. Taylor and family are listed on the 1900 U.S. census of Bear Valley Township. It is not known if these persons are related.

William S. Thomas filed homestead claim #1714 on May 13, 1884. His claim consisted of 168.03 acres located in the south half of the northwest quarter and the north half of the southwest quarter of Section 30, Township 10 South, Range 1 West. Excess receipt #1238 was issued at that time for $10.04.[180] This parcel today is located one-quarter mile north of Hilldale Road with Cole Grade Road providing the western boundary (see Figure 17).

This parcel was later divided with portions owned by C.F. Thompson and the Ransom Independent Home Association after the turn of the century.

William Thomas is not listed in the 1900 U.S. census record of Bear Valley. He is listed in the 1901 *Directory of San Diego City and County* with his occupation listed as a farmer. A person named Henry Thomas is listed also as a farmer in the area.[181]

Also listed in the county directories in the Valley Center area is Genetha Thomas, constable in 1897. Two other persons are listed in the Escondido area.[182] The relationship of these people to William S. Thomas is not known.

Johann Hinrich von Seggern was a naturalized citizen of the U.S. who immigrated from Germany in 1887. He is listed as a 23-year-old on the manifest of the *S.S. Habsburg* which docked in the Port of New York on June 28, 1887.[183] He settled in Valley Center and became known as John Henry von Seggern. His wife, Elise, immigrated from Germany in 1888, and they were married in 1893.

Their five children, Otto Carl, Anna Adeline, Albert Frederick, Henry Erwin, and Ernest Alfred, were born in Bear Valley in 1894, 1897, 1898, 1902, and 1905, respectively. Henry's cousin, Frederick, was the first to immigrate from Germany in the early 1880s, and was living with them in 1900 at the time of the census.

A homestead claim was not found during research for this study. The 1900 U.S. plat map of Township 11 South, Range 1 West, shows 240 acres in Section 28 owned by H. von Seggern. Forty acres of this parcel had been previously owned by W.H.H. Dinwiddie. Today this parcel is located north of Lake Wohlford and west of the San Pasqual Indian Reservation (see Figure 17).

Frederick was the first to file for citizenship. He filed a Declaration of Intention on August 21, 1885, in the Superior Court of San Diego.[184] Johann Heinrich filed on March 7, 1898.[185] The cousins lived in the valley south of Bear Ridge and grew apples and pears which they entered in the San Diego Fair in 1888.[186]

Figure 24. Top: John Henry and Elise von Seggern, 1893.
Bottom: J.H. von Seggern family, 1910:
Top Left to right: Albert, Otto, Anna; Bottom: Ernest, Elise, Henry, and
John Henry. Photos courtesy of Carl von Seggern

The 1900 U.S. census lists the von Seggern family living in dwelling number 81 in the Bear Valley Township. J.H. is listed as the head of the family, age 42 years, born January 1858, in Germany, as were his parents. His wife, listed as 'Albera', is listed as 29 years old, born May 1871, in Germany, married seven years, mother of two children, both of whom were living at the time.[187]

Figure 25. The von Seggern Farm, ca. 1885.
Photo courtesy of Carl von Seggern

Figure 26. "The Old Barn" from 'The Early Days in Escondido.'

Their children are listed as: Otto, six years old, born June 1894, in California; and Anna, one-year old, born August 1898, in California. Henry's cousin, Frederick, is listed as 50 years old, retired, born in 1850 in Germany.[188]

The birth of John's son, Otto, was reported in the *Escondido Times* on January 30, 1894.[189] The Bear Valley School census of 1896 listed one child less than five years old living in the von Seggern household in Section 27, Township 11 South, Range 1 West.

The family members are listed in the *Directory of San Diego City and County* of 1905 and 1921. Henry is listed alone in the 1901 directory. In the 1921 directory, J.H. is listed as a rancher, Albert is listed without an occupation, Annie as a student, and Otto as a farmer.[190]

John Henry von Seggern settled on land purchased by his brother, Freiderich, from J.J. Hicks in 1884, currently underwater in Lake Wohlford. The family ran a dairy business on the property until 1929 when the City of Escondido Irrigation Distirct bought the ranch to expand the Escondido Reservoir.

At that time, the family moved the business to the North Broadway area of Escondido. They continued the dairy at that location until the 1970s, at which time they sold the majority of property for development.

William K. Watkins and his family moved into the Valley Center area and filed a homestead claim in 1880. Claim #574 was filed on March 10, 1880, for 160 acres. The legal description is the west half of the southwest quarter of Section 10, and the north half of the southeast quarter of Section 9, Township 11 South, Range 1 West. Total fees paid included a $10 fee as well as $6 in commissions at $1.25 per acre.[191]

This parcel today is located on the eastern boundary of this study area bordered by Vesper Road on the north and Valley Center Road, Highway S-6, on the south (see Figure 17).

The family of William K. Watkins is listed as living in dwelling number 196 on the 1880 U.S. census of Bear Valley Township. William is listed as a white male, 45 years old, married, his occupation was a farmer, born in Illinois, and his parents both born in Georgia. His wife, Berthina C., is listed as a white female, 37 years old, married, occupation keeping house, born in Arkansas, father born in Illinois, and her mother born in Missouri.[192]

Their ten children were all born in California and are listed as: Charlotte E., 20 years old; Joseph Ewell, 18 years old; Dorcas E., 17 years old; James C., 14 years old; Anna E., 12 years old; William S., ten years old; Martha A., seven years old; John K., five years old; Alabama, three years old; and Lilie, five-month-old baby.[193] W.K. and Berthina also had a son, George E. Watkins, who was born in 1884 and died in 1890. He is buried in the Valley Center Cemetery.[194]

According to J.M. Guinn, William K. Watkins crossed the plains to California in an oxen-drawn wagon in 1853.[195] Also traveling with the wagon train was nine-year old Pathenia [sic] Catherine Miller, whom he later married in 1858. William's father, Ewell Watkins, was a Methodist Episcopal preacher who traveled throughout southern California.

William and his family settled in Valley Center in 1880 and immediately began their farm. William died in 1896 at the age of 66 years. After his death, Berthina moved to Fallbrook, along with several of her children and her mother, Catherine Miller.[196]

The children of William K. and Berthina Watkins married into other pioneering families in Valley Center and surrounding communities. Three of the Watkins' daughters married three of the Reed's sons: Ella married John Reed, Emma married George Reed, and Anna married Austin Reed.[197] Martha married Willliam Fleshman, and James married Ella Bunkerman.

James moved to Fallbrook and began a livery business in 1893. He also operated a transfer line and mail contract business as well as investing in the Fallbrook Hardware Company and the Fallbrook Mercantile Company. According to Guinn, James and his wife, Ella, had one daughter, Anna Izetta. They were both members of the Methodist Episcopal church. James was also a member of the Independent Order of Odd Fellows and a steadfast Democrat.[198]

Alonso S. Westmoreland filed a homestead claim on December 10, 1888, for 160 acres located in Valley Center. Claim #4672 consisted of the south half of the northeast quarter and the northeast quarter of the northeast quarter of Section 11, and the southwest quarter of the northwest quarter of Section 13, Township 11 South, Range 2 West. Total fees paid at the time included a $10 filing fee and $6 in commissions at $1.25 per acre.[199]

This property today is located on both side of Lilac Road and includes the Hideaway Lake (see Figure 17). After the turn of the century, F. Dolan owned a larger portion of the property, while A.S. maintained title to 40 acres. By then, the Westmoreland family had moved into Escondido where A.S. Westmoreland became involved with real estate sales.

According to Guinn, Alonso volunteered to fight in the Civil War for the Confederate Army in the State of Tennessee. He served with the army throughout the war from 1861-65. He married Emma Anna May in Tennessee where their first children were born. They came to California in 1881.[200]

The Westmoreland family was very large. They had 11 children, six of whom are listed on the 1900 U.S. census of Bear Valley

Township. The family is listed as living in dwelling number 109. A.S. is listed as the head of the family. His age was 57, married 31 years, occupation farmer on his own farm, born February 1843, in Tennessee, his father born in North Carolina, and his mother born in Missouri. His wife, Emma A., is listed as 50 years old, born November 1849, in Tennessee, mother of eleven children, all of whom were living, her father born in North Carolina, and mother born in Tennessee.[201]

Their children listed are: Emma, single, 22 years old, born July 1877, in Tennessee, occupation teacher, who was unemployed four months during the year; Allan, single, 18-year old student, born September 1881, in Tennessee, attended school four months during the year; Ida, single, 17-year old student, attended school nine months during the year, born April 1883, in California; Lena, 14 years old, born April 1886, in California, attended school nine months during the year; son, J.S., 12 years old, born May 1888, in California, attended school nine months during the year; and the youngest son, J.M., nine years old, born July 1890, in California, attended school nine months during the year.[202]

Alonso and Emma's older daughter, Ivy L., had married George F. Jacoby in 1894, and was living in Escondido at the time of the census.[203]   The 1905 county directory lists several members of the Westmoreland family: A.S., C.F., Emma, E.M., and J.E.[204]   No additional information regarding these persons was found during research for this study.

Emma Anna Westmoreland died in Escondido on May 3, 1917. The cause of death was reported in the *Escondido Times* as leukemia. They gave her birthdate as November 12, 1849, in Tennessee.[205] Additional information regarding the family members was not found during research for this study.

William L. Wilhite filed homestead claim #1336 on August 23, 1883, for 160 acres. The legal description is the north half of the southeast quarter of Section 31 and the north half of the southwest quarter of Section 32, Township 10 South, Range 1 West, San Bernardino Base Meridian.[206] William received full title to the property in 1888.[207]

This property today is located one-quarter mile south of Cool Valley Road with the western border along Cole Grade Road (see Figure 17). This parcel was divided after the turn of the century with J.C. Ferguson owner of 10 acres and R.E. Jauman the owner of the remaining 150 acres.

William is not listed on the 1880 U.S. census of Bear Valley. He registered to vote in San Diego on September 19, 1884, and he stated his age at the time as 24 years old, born in California, with his occupation as a farmer in Bear Valley.[208]

William worked with Sam Striplin in 1893 at the lumber mill on Palomar Mountain. They transported the lumber to Valley Center, Escondido, and even into San Diego for much-needed building supplies in the fast growing communities in southern California.[209]

William was married twice, according to research material. It is not known if the first wife died, for no reference to her death was found. Abel Davis states that William was married to Laura.[210] The 1900 U.S. census record, however, shows his wife's name as Mary A. She is listed as an 18-year old, married three years, born April 1872, in Iowa, and her parents both born in Illinois. William is listed as 41 years old, married 16 years and three years, born November 1858, in California, his father born in Tennessee and his mother born in Missouri. His occupation is listed as a farmer on his own farm. The Wilhite's are listed in dwelling number 112.[211]

William is listed in the county directories in 1893-94 and 1905 as living in Valley Center.[212] Further information regarding the Wilhite family was not found during research for this study.

Rufus T. Willis filed a pre-emption claim for 40 acres located in the northwest quarter of the southeast quarter of Section 29, Township 10 South, Range 2 West, San Bernardino Base Meridian. He received full title on October 9, 1893, for claim #6634 filed in 1888. His neighbors witnessed his compliance of the five-year requirements under the Homestead Act of 1862. The witnesses included David Huckaby, James Frazier, Richard Coles, and William Ball.[213]

This parcel today is located one-quarter mile south of Juanita Way approximately one mile east of Cole Grade Road (see Figure 17).

Rufus married Miss Myers (no first name given) in January 1894.[214] Mrs. Willis (again, no first name given) died June 6, 1894, and was interred in the Valley Center Cemetery. She was reported to be 48 years old at the time.[215]

It is possible that Rufus married Leah Myers who homesteaded 160 acres adjoining the Willis claim to the north. Leah filed her claim in 1890. No additional information regarding Miss Myers was found during research for this study.

Rufus is not listed on the census records for Bear Valley. His name is listed in the 1893-94 *Directory of San Diego City and County* with no occupation stated.[216] No additional information was found during research for this study.

Sidney J. Willson filed homestead claim #4833 for 80 acres of land in Valley Center on March 7, 1889. The legal description is the northwest quarter of the southwest quarter of Section 1, and the northeast quarter of the southeast quarter of Section 2, Township 11 South, Range 2 West, San Bernardino Base Meridian.[217]

This property today is located east of Lilac Road, approximately two miles northwest of the junction of Lilac Road and Valley Center Road. The western portion is also bisected by Anthony Road (see Figure 17).

No further information regarding Sidney Willson was found during research for this study. He is not listed on the census records, the county directories, or voter registration.

Peter L. Wimmer and his wife, Elizabeth Jane, or Jennie, were very famous, though few people recognize their names.

Before they came to Valley Center in 1882 and filed a homestead claim for more than 164 acres, they had spent some time in the California gold fields. In fact, they were actually very instrumental in the discovery of gold in California. The following story was taken from a small book, *Elizabeth Jane Wimmer, A Georgia Miner.*[218]

Peter Wimmer and his wife, Jennie, had come to California from the Georgia gold mines where they had each lost their spouses to illness in 1843. Peter and Jennie married in 1844 and joined a wagon train to California. The wagons arrived in Sutter's Fort on November 16, 1846, and while Peter helped fight the war against the Californios, Jennie looked after their seven children (his, hers, and theirs).

Figure 27. Jennie and Peter Wimmer, ca. 1870.
Source: Times Advocate, September 8, 1967

After the war was over, Peter joined the rescue team to bring out the survivors of the Donner Party. He then worked for Captain John Sutter and James Marshall as overseer of the sawmill which was providing lumber for the increasing California population. As a ditch was being cut to the American River from the mill site, Marshall and Wimmer were checking the progress when they spotted a gleaming nugget. Marshall picked it up and took it back to camp.

Jennie was in the process of making lye soap in a kettle. Marshall showed her the gold, and they dropped it into the pot to test it. The nugget would tarnish if it was not gold. The gold tested pure and when it was later assayed, it weighed approximately one-third ounce and was worth $5.12. The year was 1848. The Gold Rush of California had begun.

Jennie later showed the miners how to build "shakers" to separate the dirt, rocks, and gold. For this reason, she was referred to as the "Georgia Miner". Marshall later gave her the nugget which she carried in a buckskin pouch on her person for several years. It is now on display in the Bancroft Library at the University of California at Berkeley and is known as the Wimmer Nugget.

After prospecting and traveling down through California for several years, Peter and Jennie ended up settling in Valley Center in 1882. Gold had been discovered nearby, and they simply followed the trail.[219]

Homestead claim #1315 was filed by Peter Wimmer on July 27, 1883. It consisted of 164.87 acres described as the south half of the northwest quarter and the south half of the northeast quarter of Section 31, Township 10 South, Range 1 West. Excess receipt #1098 was issued at the time in the amount of $6.09.[220]

Jennie died the following year and is buried in the Valley Center Cemetery with a simple concrete headstone marked "Weamer." Peter and his sons, Peter L. Wimmer, Jr., and Ira, registered to vote on October 4, 1884. The elder Peter stated his age as 70 years, born in Ohio, and his occupation was a farmer in Bear Valley. His son, Peter, Jr., stated his age as 30, born in California, occupation farmer in Bear Valley. Ira stated his age as 25, born in California, also a farmer in Bear Valley.[221]

Peter, Sr., died in 1892 in Cambria, California. His son, Peter, Jr., remained in Valley Center and married Cornelia Tracy. He is listed in the 1893-94 *Directory of San Diego City and County.*[222]

Although there are several families with the name Young listed in various sources as living in the Valley Center area, George W. Young filed the only homestead claim within this study area. It is assumed these families are related in some way, however, this was not confirmed during research for this study.

George filed homestead claim #4175 on April 19, 1888. His claim consisted of 160 acres located in the south half of the southwest quarter of Section 13, and the south half of the southeast quarter of Section 14, Township 11 South, Range 2 West, San Bernardino Base Meridian.[223]

This property today is located approximately one-half mile west of Valley Center Road and one-half mile south of Lilac Road (see Figure 17). A portion of this parcel was later owned by P. Kreiss.

George is not listed on the census records for Bear Valley Township. He is listed in the 1897 *Directory of San Diego City and County*, with his occupation listed as a farmer.[224] F.M. Young is listed in the 1893-94 *Directory of San Diego City and County*.[225]

George W. Young is listed on the Bear Valley School census during the years 1891-97. The 1891 census shows two male children attending school during that year; 1895 and 1896, lists three male students and two children less than five years old at home; 1897 shows four male students and two children less than five years old at home.

The school census also lists the children of E.E. Young, E.H. Young, J.S. Young, and Scott Young with students attending the Bear Valley School during the years 1891-98.[226] E.E. Young and his family are the only family listed in the 1900 census with the surname Young.

The 44 families discussed in this chapter who settled in the Valley Center area during the decade of 1880-89 were a diverse assortment. Not only were there farmers and ranchers, but also pilots, brickmakers, and goldminers. Many families moved into the valley during the decade only to be forced to move out due to extreme weather conditions.

The city of Escondido was fast becoming a thriving community which would see the railroad and major thoroughfares pass through their town. The settlers in Valley Center became more dependent on the Escondido markets and stores for their supplies instead of traveling into San Diego.

Many of the changes in Escondido and neighboring communities also affected the residents of Valley Center. When the railroad was being built into Temecula through De Luz Canyon, many travelers had to pass through Valley Center to reach Temecula and on into San Bernardino.

The growing population of San Diego and its outlying communities created more need for dairy supplies such as milk, butter, and even ice cream. Many new 'creameries' began in Valley Center in the decade of 1890-1900 as a result of this need. The new inventions of the industrialized cities worked its way into the little valley of the sun. Telephone service came in, and eventually, electricity as well. Automobiles were making their presence known throughout the country, and would change the way-of-life for most people. Many of these new inventions caused the young people to leave the country lifestyle of living on the farm or ranch and seek new adventures in town.

The United States became involved in another war during the next decade. Even though it was not fought on American soil, many young people felt it their duty to enlist their services, many of them not returning. Of those who stayed in the valley, there were still thousands of acres of land unclaimed and waiting for the next homesteaders.

NOTES

[1] *Escondido Times,* November 3, 1887:1.

[2] Kuhn, Gerald G. *Sea Cliffs, beaches, and coastal valleys of San Diego County, California,* University of California Press, Berkeley and Los Angeles, California, 1984:36.

[3] Davis, Abel. *Valley Center, California,* unpublished memoir, circa 1955.

[4] Davis, *Valley Center,* circa 1955.

[5] *Pacific Coast Directory,* San Diego County, California, 1883-84.

[6] *Maxwell's Directory of San Diego City and County,* 1887-88. George D Maxwell, publisher, San Diego, California.

[7] Register of Receipts Issued by the Receiver of Public Monies at Los Angeles, California, for Lands Entered Under the Homestead Act, Vols. I and II, 1869-91, National Archives, Pacific Southwest Region, Laguna Niguel, California.

[8] *Ibid.*

[9] Records of the District Courts, Superior Court, San Diego County Certificates of Citizenship,   Vols. 1-7, 1883-1902: Vol. 6, p.119; also the Index to Naturalized Citizens, Superior Court of San Diego County, California, 1853-1956: Microfilm Roll M-1609, Roll #1, National Archives, Pacific Southwest Region, Laguna Niguel, California.

[10] *Escondido Times,* August 10, 1893:3.

[11] *Ibid.,* March 15, 1894:3.

[12] Davis, *Valley Center,* circa 1955.

[13] San Diego County Marriage Records, published in *Leaves and Saplings*, San Diego Genealogical Society Newsletter. On file at Escondido Public Library Pioneer Room, Escondido, California.

[14] Davis, *Valley Center,* circa 1955.

[15] *Maxwell's Directory of San Diego City and County, 1887-1888.*

[16] Homestead Register, 1869-91.

[17] 1880 U.S. Census, Schedule 1, Inhabitants in Temecula Township, San Diego County, California, p. 11.

[18] *Ibid.*

[19] Records of the District Courts, 1883-1902: Vol. 1, p. 59; also the Index to Naturalized Citizens, 1853-1956.

[20] Register of Voters, 1880-87.

[21] 1900 U.S. Census, Schedule 1, Inhabitants in Bear Valley Township, San Diego County, California, p. 204, entries 54-56.

[22] *Ibid.*

[23] Davis, *Valley Center,* circa 1955.

[24] *Escondido Times,* September 27, 1888:3.

[25] *Ibid.,* June 4, 1891:3.

[26] *San Diego Union Tribune,* February 14, 1987: 11-2.

[27] San Diego County Marriage Records.

[28] Register of Voters, 1880-87.

[29] *Pacific Coast Directory,* 1883-84.

[30] *Ibid.*

[31] Davis, *Valley Center,* circa 1955.

[32] *Escondido Times,* May 3, 1888:3.

[33] J.M. Guinn, *The History of California,* Historical Record Company, Los Angeles, 1907: 1158-1159.

[34] Register of Voters, 1880-87.

[35] *Ibid.*

[36] *Escondido Times,* September 27, 1888:3.

[37] Davis, *Valley Center,* circa 1955.

[38] *Ibid.,* October 12, 1899:2.

[39] Davis, *Valley Center,* circa 1955.

[40] 1900 U.S. Census, p. 204, entries 75-83.

[41] Davis, *Valley Center,* circa 1955.

[42] *Escondido Times,* February 23, 1906:6.

[43] *Ibid.,* April 27, 1906:2.

[44] *Daily Times Advocate,* October 2, 1918:1.

[45] *San Diego Union Tribune,* February 14, 1987:11-2.

[46] Davis, *Valley Center,* circa 1955.

[47] *The Directory of San Diego City and County,* The Olmsted Company, printers, San Diego, California, 1892-93, 1897.

[48] Register of Voters, 1880-87.

[49] San Diego County Marriage Records.

[50] 1900 U.S. Census, p. 204, entries 96-97.

[51] Homestead Register, 1869-91.

[52] *Ibid.*

[53] *Escondido Times,* June 4, 1891:2.

[54] *Ibid.,* August 10, 1893:3.

[55] *Ibid.,* February 8, 1894:3.

[56] *Ibid.,* October 12, 1899:2.

[57] Register of Voters, 1880-87.

[58] Homestead Register, 1869-91.

[59] *Escondido Times,* August 31, 1893:3.

[60] *Ibid.,* February 23, 1906:6.

[61] *The Directory of San Diego City and County,* 1897.

[62] Escondido Genealogical Society Surname Registry. On file in the Escondido Public Library Pioneer Room, Escondido, California.

[63] Homestead Register, 1869-91.

[64] 1880 U.S. Census, p. 20, entries 24, 25.

[65] *Ibid.,* entries 26-28.

[66] *Escondido Times,* August 17, 1893:3.

[67] Homestead Register, 1869-91.

[68] Register of Voters, 1880-1887.

[69] *The Directory of San Diego City and County,* 1893, 1897, 1905.

[70] Homestead Register, 1869-91.

[71] Davis, *Valley Center,* circa 1955.

[72] Register of Voters, 1880-87.

[73] *Ibid.,* 1866-1879.

[74] *Escondido Times,* July 3, 1890:3.

[75] San Diego County Coroner's Reports, 1853-1905. On file at the San Diego Historical Society Archives, Balboa Park, San Diego, California: Document 49-02.
[76] *Pacific Coast Directory,* 1883-84.
[77] Homestead Register, 1869-91.
[78] Davis, *Valley Center,* circa 1955.
[79] Register of Voters, 1880-87.
[80] 1900 U.S. Census, p. 205, entry 65.
[81] Homestead Register, 1869-91.
[82] *The Directory of San Diego City and County,* 1893-94, 1897.
[83] Register of Voters, 1880-87.
[84] Davis, *Valley Center,* circa 1955.
[85] *Escondido Times,* September 27, 1888:3.
[86] *The Directory of San Diego City and County,* 1893-94.
[87] Homestead Register, 1869-91.
[88] *Pacific Coast Directory,* 1883-84.
[89] *Ibid.*
[90] Register of Voters, 1880-87.
[91] Valley Center School records, 1891-93, *Escondido Times,* February 9, 1893:3.
[92] Davis, *Valley Center,* circa 1955.
[93] Register of Voters, 1880-87.
[94] *The Directory of San Diego City, Coronado, and National City,* 1892-93; *The Directory of San Diego City and County,* 1893-94, and 1897.
[95] Coroner's Reports, 1853-1905: Document 119-1.
[96] *Ibid.,* 07-06.
[97] Homestead Register, 1869-91.
[98] *The Southern California Rancher*, October 1945, January 1948; *San Diego Union*, February 14, 1987: 11-2; and *San Diego Union Tribune,* February 14, 1987: 11-2.
[99] Davis, *Valley Center,* circa 1955; and Clyde James, unpublished memoir, circa 1970.
[100] *Escondido Times,* April 9, 1891: 3.
[101] *Pacific Coast Directory*, 1883-84.
[102] *Daily Times Advocate,* November 2, 1915:1.
[103] *The Directory of San Diego City and County,* 1905, 1921.
[104] Davis, *Valley Center,* circa 1955.
[105] Register of Voters, 1880-87.
[106] *The Pacific Coast Directory,* 1883-84; *The Directory of San Diego City and County,* 1905.
[107] Escondido Genealogical Society Surname Register.
[108] Davis, *Valley Center,* circa 1955.
[109] *Escondido Times,* September 27, 1888:2.
[110] Davis, *Valley Center,* circa 1955.
[111] *Ibid.*
[112] *Escondido Times,* March 1, 1894:3.
[113] Valley Center School census, 1891.
[114] *Ibid.,* June 7, 1894:3.

[115] Register of Voters, 1880-87.
[116] *The Pacific Coast Directory,* 1883-84; *The Directory of San Diego City and County,* 1897, 1901.
[117] 1900 U.S. Census, p. 203, entries 32-34.
[118] Homestead Register, 1869-91.
[119] Davis, *Valley Center,* circa 1955.
[120] Register of Voters, 1880-87.
[121] Valley Center Cemetery records.
[122] Coroner's Report, 1853-1905: Doc. 20-03.
[123] Register of Voters, 1880-87.
[124] *Escondido Times,* September 27, 1888:3.
[125] *The Pacific Coast Directory,* 1883-84; *The Directory of San Diego City and County,* 1897, 1901.
[126] Guinn, *The History of California,* 1907: 566-567.
[127] *Escondido Times,* August 24, 1893:3; February 22, 1894:2; March 22, 1894:3.
[128] Anonymous. A Pioneer Teacher, Minnie Pease. On file, San Diego County Library, Valley Center Branch, Local History files.
[129] *Ibid.*
[130] 1880 U.S. Census, p. 22, entries 34, 35.
[131] *Ibid.,* entries 36-41.
[132] S.T. Black, *San Diego County, California, A Record of Settlement, Organization, Progress and Achievement,* Vols. I and II. The S.J. Clarke Publishing Company, Chicago, 1913:504-505.
[133] *Ibid.*
[134] Homestead Register, 1869-91.
[135] *Escondido Times,* January 18, 1894:3.
[136] Homestead Register, 1869-91.
[137] Black, *San Diego County, California,* 1913:504-505.
[138] Davis, *Valley Center,* circa 1955.
[139] Black, *San Diego County, California,* 1913:504-505.
[140] Register of Voters, 1880-87.
[141] Homestead Register, 1869-91.
[142] Register of Voters, 1880-87.
[143] Davis, *Valley Center,* circa 1955.
[144] Valley Center School census, 1891.
[145] *Maxwell's Directory of San Diego City and County,* 1887-88; *The Directory of San Diego City and County,* 1897, 1901
[146] Black, *San Diego County, California,* 1913:504-505.
[147] Homestead Register, 1869-91.
[148] Register of Voters, 1880-87.
[149] Black, *San Diego County, California,* 1913:504-505.
[150] *Ibid.*
[151] *Escondido Times,* December 21, 1893:3.
[152] *Ibid.,* January 18, 1894:3.
[153] Register of Voters, 1880-87.
[154] *Escondido Times,* December 28, 1893:3.
[155] *Ibid.,* March 15, 1894:3.
[156] Black, *San Diego County, California,* 1913:504-505.

[157] 1900 U.S. Census, p. 200, entries 43, 44.
[158] *Ibid.,* entries 45-48.
[159] Register of Voters, 1880-87.
[160] *The Directory of San Diego City and County,* 1889-90.
[161] Black, *San Diego County, California,* 1913:504-505.
[162] Homestead Register, 1869-91.
[163] *The Directory of San Diego City and County,* 1897-1901.
[164] *Ibid.;* 1900 U.S. Census, p. 206, entry 18.
[165] *The Directory of San Diego City and County,* 1897.
[166] *Ibid.*
[167] 1900 U.S. Census, p. 205, entries 77-80.
[168] *Ibid.,* p. 206, entries 44-47.
[169] *Escondido Times,* February 21, 1889:1.
[170] Homestead Register, 1869-91.
[171] *Escondido Times,* February 21, 1889:1.
[172] Personal communication with Jack Watson, November 5, 1996.
[173] Helen Cramer, Sherrard's Chapel, unpublished paper. On file at the San Diego County Library, Valley Center Branch Local History files, n.d.
[174] Register of Voters, 1880-87.
[175] *Escondido Times Advocate,* January 12, 1893:7.
[176] *Ibid.,* January 25, 1894:3.
[177] *Escondido Times,* February 1, 1894:3.
[178] Homestead Register, 1869-91.
[179] *Escondido Times,* Escondido School report: February 1, 1894:3.
[180] Homestead Register, 1869-91.
[181] *The Directory of San Diego City and County,* 1901.
[182] *Ibid.,* 1889-90, 1897.
[183] von Seggern family files on file at the Valley Center Branch Library Historical files.
[184] Index to Declaration of Intention, Superior Court of San Diego, California, 1853-1956, Vol. 2 (old), No. 155: Microfilm #M-1612, Roll #1. On file, National Archives, Pacific Southwest Region, Laguna Niguel, California.
[185] *Ibid.,* Book 6, No. 300
[186] *Escondido Times,* September 27, 1888:3.
[187] 1900 U.S. Census, p. 208, entries 35, 36.
[188] *Ibid.,* entries 37-39.
[189] *Escondido Times,* January 30, 1894:3.
[190] *The Directory of San Diego City and County,* 1905, 1921.
[191] Homestead Register, 1869-91.
[192] 1880 U.S. Census, p. 21, entries 35, 36.
[193] *Ibid.,* entries 37-46.
[194] Valley Center Cemetery records.
[195] Guinn, *The History of California,* 1907: 1829-30.
[196] *Ibid.*
[197] Davis, *Valley Center,* circa 1955.
[198] Guinn, *The History of California,* 1907: 1829-30.
[199] Homestead Register, 1869-91.
[200] Guinn, *The History of California,* 1907: 1280.

[201] 1900 U.S. Census, p. 207, entries 79 and 80.

[202] *Ibid.*, entries 81-86.

[203] *Escondido Times,* July 6, 1894:3.

[204] *The Directory of San Diego City and County,* 1905.

[205] *Escondido Times,* May 4, 1917:1.

[206] Homestead Register, 1869-91.

[207] *Escondido Times,* September 6, 1888:2.

[208] Register of Voters, 1880-87.

[209] *Escondido Times,* March 2, 1893:3.

[210] Davis, *Valley Center,* circa 1955.

[211] 1900 U.S. Census, p. 207, entries 90 and 91.

[212] *The Directory of San Diego City and County,* John Thom, publisher, San Diego, California, 1893-94; and The Olmsted Company, printers, San Diego, California, 1905.

[213] *Escondido Times,* August 10, 1893:3.

[214] *Ibid.,* February 1, 1894:3.

[215] *Ibid.,* June 14, 1894:3.

[216] *The Directory of San Diego City and County,* 1893-94.

[217] Homestead Register, 1869-91.

[218] Olive Engwicht, *Elizabeth Jane Wimmer, A Georgia Miner,* The Daily Press, Paso Robles, California, 48th Pioneer Edition, 1978.

[219] *Ibid.*

[220] Homestead Register, 1869-91.

[221] Register of Voters, 1880-87.

[222] *The Directory of San Diego City and County,* 1893-94.

[223] Homestead Register, 1869-91.

[224] *The Directory of San Diego City and County,* 1897.

[225] *The Directory of San Diego City and County,* 1893-94.

[226] Bear Valley School Census records, 1891-97.

CHAPTER FOUR

VALLEY CENTER 1890-1900

By the end of the 1890s, Valley Center had grown to include over 100 families. Most of the land in the valley had already been homesteaded, but there was still plenty of room for newcomers. Figure 28 is a photograph taken around the turn of the century which shows Valley Center Road on the left side of the picture lined with telephone poles and the fence line bordering Woods Valley Road seen in the foreground.

Figure 28. Valley Center Overview as seen from Woods Valley Road, ca. 1900.

The large, growing city of Escondido to the south had become a major transportation route with up-to-date road systems, stage lines, and the railroad. Business could be conducted in Escondido, alleviating the necessity to travel 40 miles into San Diego. More schools were available in Escondido including a college for higher education.

The editor of the *Escondido Times,* wrote an article about Bear Valley country on June 4, 1891.[1] The article proclaimed the valley as the "Italy of America" where the farmers produced almost everything under the sun in the way of fruits, vegetables, and cereal grains. The citrus and grape vines were "fast covering the earth" making that route "...a most enjoyable drive." The article also stated that at least 150 families lived in the succession of splendid valleys which comprised Valley Center.

Another article, written in January 1893, stated the valley produced "...more wood from Black oak, sycamore, and cottonwood trees than any section below the forest area of the Cuyamaca mountains."[2] The article also stated the prosperous ranchers of the area at that time included J.C. Reed, W.H.H. Dinwiddie, J.H. Breedlove, E.B. Holcomb, and J. Watkins.

Some of the other businesses considered as part of the valley included dairies and creameries, a grist mill, a lumber mill, a stage line which ran through the middle of the community, and blacksmithing. Many of the women in the valley sold eggs and poultry from their family farms.[3]

The Butterfield stage line operated from San Diego to Los Angeles. On its route the stage traveled through the communities of Poway, Bernardo, Valley Center, Pala, and Temecula. There was also a branch which traveled north of Palomar Mountain through Warner's Ranch and on into Arizona.

The Alliance Business Association was formed in the 1890s by the farmers and ranchers of Valley Center, Pauma Valley, San Pasqual, San Marcos, and Escondido. The association was divided into districts sequentially numbered. Valley Center was district number 16. Some of the founding members were Dr. J.H. Clark, Charles McCurdy, George Hedden, William Belshe, Ransom Breedlove, and J.S. Borden.[4] By working together, the farmers and ranchers were able to market their goods through a cooperative measure. This organization, known earlier as the Farmers Alliance, became the Grange in later years.

The farming community which had begun in the 1860s was now enjoying the fruits of their labors. Not only were they able to produce enough goods to feed their families, they were able to make a profit from selling the excess. Thus began a new and prosperous way-of-life for the pioneers who had settled on "free" government land.

The rainfall was measured by Valley Center resident Samuel Antes. He reported over nine inches from one rainstorm in February

1891. In 1892-93, the season total was more than 19 inches.[5] During the season of 1893-94, the valley received more than 50 inches of rain, with more than 15 inches measured during the month of March. A snow storm covered Palomar Mountain from top to bottom on March 20, 1893.[6]

The extraordinary amount of rainfall during the 1893 season resulted in more than twice the amount of goods exported from the valley than in 1892. Included as exported items were: raisins, grapes, oranges, apricots, peaches, watermelon, wheat, barley, oats, hay, and honey. Miscellaneous items such as eggs, butter, vegetables, and wine comprised more than 365,000 pounds of exported items shipped out of Escondido.[7]

Many new developments and inventions came into the valley in the 1890s. This included the telephone, first installed in John Adams' Valley Center Store in 1896. For many years it served the entire community as the single telephone. The post office was also situated in the store at this time.

Mechanized farming equipment was becoming affordable which allowed a farmer to complete many tasks alone instead of depending on neighbors or hired hands for help. Figure 29 shows the method of harvesting hay using horespower prior to the harvesting machines.

Figure 29. Harvesting Hay in Valley Center, ca. 1900.

The dairy business changed considerably during the 1890s due to the invention of a cream separator.[8] The first large-capacity cream separator was installed by W.B. Hage in 1893 at his dairy in San Pasqual. By 1897, five creameries were operating in San Diego

County, one of which was located in Escondido. The following year, three creameries were operating in Escondido.[9]

The creameries processed butter in large quantities to be shipped by stage or train from Escondido to San Diego and Los Angeles. The cream separator at the Daley's Fern Valley Dairy processed 600 pounds of milk per hour from the milk of 30 cows.[10] This method processed much larger quantities of cream than previous methods.

In comparing the beginning of the nineteenth century to the end of the century, it is interesting to note the dramatic changes. The cost of living in the early 1800s consisted of what one family could produce to feed themselves with little profit to be made from the leftovers. By the late 1890s, most of the population did not have to depend on what they could provide for themselves, for many items were available in the markets by then.

Wages in 1800 were approximately 50 cents per day. By the end of the decade, wages tripled to about $1.50 per day. The land which had cost the settlers $10 to file a homestead claim for up to 160 acres, was now worth thousands of dollars. Many people chose to leave the valley at this time and take their profits. They sold their farms and ranches to claim a homestead elsewhere or to simply move into town where they were closer to schools and stores.

The establishment of the Indian reservations around the Valley Center area also provided the settlers with an option to sell their property back to the government for a profit. Water rights also provided a means of selling a portion of homesteaded land to either the United States government, state or local organizations for water storage.

Figure 30. A Postcard Showing The Escondido Reservoir, Prior to 1920s.

The Act of March 3, 1891, signed by Congress provisioned locations of reservoir sites for holding water as well as the right-of-way for ditches, flumes, or canals to distribute this water. Lake Wohlford was one of these reservoirs. The cost of this facility alone was almost $40,000. The irrigation canal through the Valley Center area crossed several settlers land including Woods, Dinwiddie, Reed, Striplin, and von Seggern. Figure 30 is a postcard showing the Escondido Reservoir prior to raising the level in the 1920s.

The population of Valley Center rose considerably in the 1890s. There are 19 persons listed under the Valley Center heading in the 1892-93 county directory. By 1897, there are more than 120 persons listed. After the turn of the century, the number dropped to 66 people.[11] Many of the names listed were members of large families who had become of age and started their own families. The school census records also reflect this population increase.

The Valley Center School in 1893 listed the following students under teacher, Eldora Lee:

Lawrence Walsh	Burt Warner	Nolley Goodwin
Mary Walsh	Ray Holcomb	Henry McKay
Mamie Clark	Clara Holcomb	Asa Goodwin
Robin Clark	Nettie Holcomb	John Mallicoat
John Watkins	Josie Quackenbush	George Young
Allie Watkins	Blanche Adams	Lillian Breedlove
Church Cook	Charlie Meeks	Lulu Breedlove
Belle Cook	John Meeks	Edward Keys
Susie Cook	Emma Westmoreland	

Public land was still available to homesteaders. An article printed in 1893 stated that the southern California district extended 180 miles north from the Mexican border and from the Colorado River to the ocean, about 350 miles. This totaled over 24 million acres of land available as public land. This included forest reserves, railroads, private land grants, military and Indian reservations, state and private holdings, as well as unsurveyed and surveyed land available for claims.[12]

The article continued to state that natural resources available within the southern California region included: gold, silver, copper, iron, tin, asphaltum, petroleum, marble, kaoline, cement, red and gray sandstone, and timber. The principal products consisted of citrus and deciduous fruits, wine, grain, olives, and walnuts.[13]

The homestead records show that at least 13 new family claims were filed in the Valley Center study area during the 1890s. These new claims are shown on Figure 31. The families who filed those claims, as well as those whose residential locations are not known but were known to be in the area at that time, are presented alphabetically.

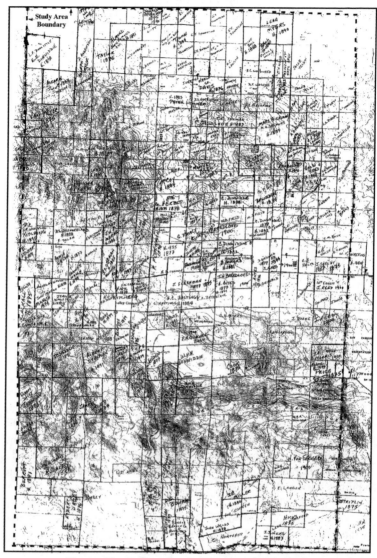

Figure 31. Valley Center Pioneers, 1890-1900.

John Almond filed homestead claim #5899 on April 11, 1891. The claim consisted of 160 acres located in the southwest quarter of the northeast quarter, the southeast quarter of the northwest quarter, and the east half of the southwest quarter of Section 25, Township 10 South,

Range 2 West, San Bernardino Base Meridian.[14] This property today is located with Hilldale Road as the southern boundary and the eastern boundary formed by Mountain View Lane (see Figure 31).

No additional information was found regarding John Almond during research for this study. He is not listed in the county directories, census records, voter registration, or discussed in the Abel Davis book although his name appears on the Davis map of settlers (see Figure 4, Chapter Two). After the turn of the century, the property is shown as an estate, suggesting that Almond had died prior to that date.

Little is known regarding David Anderson or his family. No homestead claim was filed in the San Diego or Los Angeles Land offices prior to 1900. He is, however, listed in the 1897 *San Diego City and County Directory* as living in the Valley Center area.[15]

After the turn of the century, one 40-acre parcel is shown to be the property of B. Anderson, and 120 acres as the property of D. Anderson. These parcels had been claimed by Joseph Taylor earlier. They are located in Sections 26 and 35, Township 10 South, Range 2 West (see Figure 31).

An obituary for Mary, the widow of David Anderson, was printed in the *Daily Times Advocate* in 1915. It states she had been born about 1848 in England and had one son, David, living in Valley Center at the time. Mary died on December 26, 1915, and is buried in the Valley Center Cemetery.[16]

No additional information regarding the Anderson family was found during research for this study. They are not listed in the census or voter registration records.

Robert T. Baines was the postmaster in Valley Center after the turn of the century. According to records, he succeeded John Q. Adams in 1905.[17] Adams had maintained the position for five years out of his general store located in the building where the Corral Liquor Store is presently. The 1897 *San Diego City and County Directory* states that Baines was the sub-mail contractor at the time. His daughter, Mollie, was a dressmaker, and her brothers James and Robert were farmers. The 1905 *San Diego City and County Directory* lists R.T. Baines as the postmaster of Valley Center.[18]

Figure 32 is a photograph of the Robert Baines family. The photograph is on file in the San Diego County Library, Valley Center Branch Local History files. No date is referenced, however, a note attached to the back of the photograph states that Mrs. Baines was the postmaster until 1908, and the building was located at Lilac and Valley Center roads.

A newspaper article from 1906 states that R.T. Baines had completed real estate improvements by providing a new post office sign, new chicken wire on the fence, and ornamental trees and shrubs had been planted in the front yard.[19]   These items are present in the photograph.   Therefore, it is assumed the photograph was taken at approximately the same time, which was 1906.

Figure 32.   The Robert Baines Family, ca. 1906.
Source: San Diego Historical Society Photograph Collection

The Baines family does not appear on the census records and they did not file a homestead claim.   The children, however, are listed as students in the Hidden Dale School in 1893.   This includes Nannie, John, and James.[20]   Nannie is the only student listed in 1894 at the Oak Glen School.   She was a fifth grade student at the time.[21]   No additional information regarding the Baines family was found during research for this study.

Charles Burritt filed homestead claim #6042 on June 24, 1891. His claim consisted of 160 acres in the west half of the southwest quarter of Section 26, and the north half of the northwest quarter of Section 35, Township 11 South, Range 2 West, San Bernardino Base Meridian.[22]

Half of the northern portion of this parcel was claimed by E.E. Dinwiddie in 1888.   After the turn of the century, it appears as the property of L.F. Doolittle.   A section of the southern portion had been claimed by Alcorn in 1887, and later appears as the property of John Mason.   Today this property is located southwest of Keys Creek with Mesa Verde Road crossing through a portion of the property (see Figure 31).

No additional information regarding Charles Burritt was found during research for this study. He is not listed on the census records, voter registration, or county directories.

In 1894, T.B. Campbell was awarded the mail route from Valley Center to Nellie, located on Palomar Mountain. It is not known where Campbell lived, as no additional information was found during research for this study. His name does not appear on the census records, county directories, homestead claim registry, or voter registration.

John A. Craig filed homestead claim #5604 on October 18, 1890. His claim included 158.29 acres located in the west half of the northeast quarter and the east half of the northwest quarter of Section 5, Township 11 South, Range 1 West, San Bernardino Base Meridian.[23] This property today is located approximately one-half mile north of Fruitvale Road and one-half mile east of Cole Grade Road (see Figure 31). The property does not appear on maps after the turn of the century.

John Craig's name does not appear on the county directories or on the 1900 U.S. census record. An article printed in the *Escondido Times* in 1893, however, stated that John had moved into Dr. Hastings house and was going to farm the Cook ranch.[24] Dr. Hastings died six months earlier and was survived by his ten-year old son, Carl. It is not known if Carl Hastings lived in the house with John Craig.

The 1891 Valley Center School census lists one male and one female student enrolled with the surname of Craig during the school year. It is not known if these were children of John Craig. No additional information regarding the Craig family was found during research for this study.

A.G. Crandall did not file a homestead claim in Valley Center before 1900. He is not listed on the 1900 U.S. census of the Bear Valley Township. He is listed on the 1896 Valley Center School census as having one male and one female student enrolled in school during the year. The census shows his residence located in Section 18, Township 11 South, Range 1 West.[25]

The 1897 *San Diego City and County Directory* lists Earl Crandall in the Valley Center region. His occupation was listed as a stage driver.[26] After the turn of the century, newspaper articles in the *Daily Times Advocate* listed H.E. Crandall, H.E. Crandall, Jr., Will W. Crandall, Charles Crandall. All possessions and real estate were being sold at auction and the family members were leaving the area.[27] It is not known if these people are related to A.G. or Earl Crandall, for no further information was found during research for this study.

Spencer Dunphey filed homestead claim #5550 on September 20, 1890. His claim consisted of 160.56 acres in the north half of the northeast quarter and the southeast quarter of the northeast quarter of Section 3, and the southwest quarter of the northwest quarter of Section 2, Township 11 South, Range 2 West.[28] This property is located on the west side of Lilac Road at the junction of Old Castle Road. A portion of this property is outside of this study area (see Figure 31).

Spencer Dunphey is not listed on the 1900 U.S. census record for the Bear Valley Township. He is listed in the 1893-94 and 1897 county directories. His occupation is listed as a farmer.[29] No additional information was found regarding Spencer Dunphey.

David B. Goodwin did not file a homestead claim in the Valley Center study area prior to 1900. A newspaper article written in 1891, however, states that David and his family lived 3.5 miles north of Valley Center.[30] He had two students, Asa and Nolley, enrolled in the Valley Center School in 1893,[31] as well as one student, Charles, enrolled in the Escondido College in 1894.[32]

D.B. Goodwin is listed as a farmer in the 1893-94 and 1897 county directories. The 1897 directory also lists his children as farmers, including Charles B., Asa, and Nolla [sic].[33] No family members are listed in later editions.

Abel Davis writes in his book, *Valley Center,* that the family moved into the area in the 1880s, although this information could not be confirmed. Davis stated the family settled on land in the eastern portion of the study area. Davis also noted that Charles attended the University of Southern California with him and Roy Breedlove before the turn of the century.[34]

In 1909, the *Times Advocate* stated that Charles was moving to Los Angeles and sold 21 acres of his ranch to D.D. Klossen for $10,000.[35]

Floyd L. Hill is listed as a farmer in the 1897 *San Diego City and County Directory,*[36] although no homestead claim was found during research for this study. The location of Floyd's farm is not known, however, an article in the *Escondido Times* reported that Floyd hired George and Austin Reed to manufacture adobe bricks for his new residence in 1894.[37] A later article stated that Floyd had planted 20 acres in fruit trees including prunes, peaches, and olives. Earlier that year he had been reported as putting a crop on Mrs. Reed's property.[38]

L.L. Hill and his family are listed on the 1900 U.S. census as living in dwelling number 62. It is not known if this person is related to Floyd Hill. L.L. is listed as 28 years old, married seven years, born December 1872, in California, his occupation was a farmer on his own

farm. His parents are listed as born in Missouri. His wife, Blanche
[Adams], is listed as 22 years old, born in June 1878, mother of one
child, father born in New York, and mother born in Indiana. Their son,
Reginald, is listed as seven months old, born in October 1899.[39]

An article published in 1905 stated that Blanche Hill had
committed suicide at her home in Freeman, Missouri, in December of
that year. Blanche and her husband, L.L. Hill, had moved to Missouri
in 1903 in hopes of allowing Blanche to recover her health. Blanche
was buried in the Valley Center Cemetery.[40]

Edmond Langer did not file a homestead claim in Valley Center
prior to 1900. His son, Adolph, is listed as a third grade student in the
Bear Valley School in 1894.[41] The 1895 Bear Valley School census
shows the E. Langer family living in Section 35, Township 11 South,
Range 1 West. Three males and two female students are enrolled
during the school year, as well as two additional children at home under
the age of five years.[42]

The 1897 school census lists the Langer family living in Section 28,
of the same township and range. Three male and three female students
enrolled during that year, with one additional child at home less than
five years old. The 1899 and 1900 school census reports show the
Langer family lived in Section 33, with two male and three female
students in school with one additional child at home under the age of
five years. Langer children continued in the Bear Valley School until
1910.[43]

The Langer family is listed in dwelling number 79 in the 1900
U.S. census for the Bear Valley Township. Edmund is listed as the
head of the family. He is listed as a white male, 42 years old, born June
1858, in Austria, married 20 years, both parents born in Austria,
immigrated to the United States in 1885, is a naturalized citizen, his
occupation is farmer on his own farm. His wife, Alvirria, is also listed
as a native of Austria, 41 years old, born June 1858 [sic], mother of 10
children, seven of whom were living at the time.[44]

Their children listed are: Oscar, 18 years old, born October 1881,
in Austria; Adolf [sic], 15 years old, born May 1885, in Austria,
attended school eight months during the year; Mina, 13 years old, born
July 1886, in Arkansas, attended school eight months during the year;
Bertha, 12 years old, born September 1887, in California, attended
school eight months during the year; Frank, 10 years old, born June
1890, in California, attended school eight months during the year;
Anna, eight years old, born August 1891, in California, attended school
eight months during the year; and Lois, five years old, born April 1895,
in California.[45]

Edmund's mother, <u>Anna</u>, is also listed in the Langer household. She is listed as a 67-year old widow, born June 1832, in Austria, unable to read or write English.[46]

Figure 33 includes photographs taken by the Langer's neighbors, the von Seggern's, which show the Langer house in 1911 and Ed Langer picking peaches on the von Seggern farm.

Figure 33. Top photo: The Langer House, 1911;
Bottom photo: Ed Langer Picking Peaches.
Photo courtesy of Carl von Seggern

Benjamin Lesher filed homestead claim #5912 on April 17, 1891, for 160 acres of land in Valley Center. The legal description is the west half of the northwest quarter, the southeast quarter of the northwest quarter, and the northwest quarter of the southwest quarter of Section 11, Township 11 South, Range 2 West.[47] A Homestead Abandonment Deed was filed by F.E. Lesher on May 9, 1902, releasing all interests in the property.[48]

This parcel was later claimed by P.E. Kitching in 1895. After the turn of the century, J.R. Wardlow was the owner. The property is located west of Hideaway Lake, approximately one-half mile west of Lilac Road and one-quarter mile north of Betsworth Road with the western boundary along Aerie Road (see Figure 31).

Benjamin Lesher was born in Pennsylvania. He moved to Minnesota in 1865 and began a successful construction business. He married Annie Gunderson who was born in London, England. They had four children: Samuel M., born November 1, 1868; Jacob C., who was a draftsman in Washington, D.C.; Benjamin, who lived in Los Angeles; and a daughter, Georgianna, who married Edward Keys of Fairbanks, Alaska.[49]

Benjamin's wife died in 1884 in Montana. He moved to Los Angeles in 1888 and later to Valley Center where he settled on his homestead.[50] Benjamin married Valley Center resident, Francis E. Mallicoat on July 26, 1894.[51] Francis had two sons from a previous marriage. Benjamin spent time traveling to visit in Alaska and Washington D.C. before his death in 1902.[52]

The county directories list B. Lesher in 1893-94; B.J. Lester [sic], carpenter, in 1892-93; and Mrs. F.E. Lesher as the postmaster in 1901.[53] Francis is listed as the head of the household on the 1900 U.S. census of Bear Valley Township. She lived in dwelling number 68 with her two sons.[54]

F.E. Lesher is listed as a 51-year old widow, married 30 years, born in Missouri in December 1848, the mother of 10 children, three of whom were living at the time, her occupation was postmaster and farmer on her rented farm, her father was born in Tennessee, and her mother was born in Missouri. Her son, John, is listed as 18 years old, single, born August 1881, in Texas, occupation farm laborer. Her son, Edgar, is listed as 13 years old, born in March 1849, in California, and attended school nine months during that year.[55]

The records indicate that Francis was the widow of Stephen J. Mallicoat, who died in January 1892, in Valley Center. He is buried in the community cemetery. They had three children: John, Edgar, and Fannie, who is also buried in the Valley Center Cemetery.

John T. Lewis filed homestead claim #5933 on April 24, 1891, for 40 acres located in the northeast quarter of the southwest quarter of

Section 18, Township 11 South, Range 1 West, San Bernardino Base Meridian.[56]

No further information was found during research for this study. John Lewis is not listed in the census records, county directories, or voter registration.

Donald McGilvray lived in Section 25, Township 10 South, Range 2 West, as shown on the 1890 U.S. government plat map. "Donald McGilvray's House" in shown in the northeast quarter.[57] However, no record of a homestead claim filed prior to 1900 was found during research for this study.

Donald is listed in the 1893-94 and 1897 county directories as a stone mason. His name is not listed on the 1900 U.S. census record for the Bear Valley Township. He is listed in the Escondido School census report on June 30, 1898. He had five children enrolled in school during the 1897-1898 year. This included three males, two females, and also two additional children at home less than five years old.[58]

Immigration records list four people under "McGillivray," including George B., Robert, John, and Archibald B. The *Times Advocate* printed an obituary for George B. McGillivray who died in Los Angeles on January 29, 1913. The article stated that George had two children, however, it only listed the name Laura. It is not known if these persons are related to Donald. No additional information regarding the McGilvray family was found during research for this study.

According to the *Escondido Times,* D.W. McKay owned the Mount Candado Ranch north of Escondido. He also leased a portion of the Nicholas Walsh ranch for added pasture land and contracted to provide beef to the workers on the Escondido Irrigation Canal project.[59] No homestead claim was found in San Diego or Los Angeles.

Immigration records list D.W. McKay as a naturalized citizen sworn in on October 25, 1889, in the Superior Court of San Diego County.[60]

Henry McKay was a third grade student at the Valley Center School in 1893.[61] D.W. McKay is listed with one male student enrolled in the Valley Center School in 1895, with his residence listed as Section 23, Township 11 South, Range 2 West. In 1897, he is also listed with one male student and the residence is listed as Section 14, Township 11 South, Range 2 West.[62] Henry and D.W. are both listed as farmers in the 1897 county directory.[63] The familial relationship is not known.

William and H.E. Melhuish did not file homestead claims prior to 1900. They lived in the Valley Center area, however, and are listed in the county directories, school census, newspaper articles, and on the 1900 U.S. census.

William was appointed school trustee in the Valley Center District in 1894.[64] He is listed on the 1895 Valley Center School census with one child less than five years old, and his residence is Section 14, Township 11 South, Range 2 West. William is not listed in the county directories or on the census records.

H.E. Melhuish is listed on the 1891 and 1896 Valley Center School census records with one child less than five years old. His residence is listed as Section 10, Township 11 South, Range 2 West. He is also listed in the county directories in 1893-94, 1897, and 1901, with his occupation listed as a carpenter and rancher. H.E. Melhuish's son, Asher, is listed as a farmer in the 1897 and 1901 county directories.[65]

Herbert E. Melhuish is listed on the 1900 U.S. census in dwelling number 107 with his wife, Sarah, and son, Asher. Herbert is listed as 49 years old, married 30 years, born March 1851, in Pennsylvania, father born in England, mother born in Ireland, and his occupation as a farmer on his mortgaged farm. Sarah is listed as the mother of two living children, 49 years old, born in March 1851, in New York, her father born in Germany, and her mother born in Scotland. Asher is listed as 28 years old, single, born in August 1871, in New York.[66]

According to J.M. Guinn, Annie B. Melhuish married John Quincy Adams' son, B.E. Adams.[67] This fact could not be confirmed during research for this study. The 1897 Valley Center School census also listed one female student as the daughter of A.T. Melhuish who lived in Section 10, Township 11 South, Range 2 West. Familial relationships between the Melhuishes could not be determined based on research information.

Leah E. Myers filed homestead claim #5598 on October 17, 1890, for 160 acres located in the northeast quarter of Section 29, Township 10 South, Range 1 West, San Bernardino Base Meridian. Total fees paid included a $10 filing fee, and $6 in commissions.[68] This property is bisected by Juanita Way, approximately one-quarter mile east of Lucas Lane (see Figure 31).

It is possible that Leah E. Myers married Rufus T. Willis, who owned a 40-acre parcel adjoining Leah's on the south. Records show a marriage in 1894, one year after Willis filed his homestead claim. The bride is simply listed as Miss Myers, with no first name given.[69] The Valley Center Cemetery records show that Mrs. Willis [again no first name] died in June 1894.[70]

The cemetery records also show that Henry Myer [sic] died on April 1, 1899. According to Abel Davis, A.J. Myers owned and operated a general store in San Luis Rey until he sold it in 1903 for the establishment of the Pala Indian Reservation.   Davis also states that Reverend E.R. Myers served the Methodist Episcopal Church in Valley Center during the early 1930s.[71]

The familial relationship between these people could not be established during research for this study.

Louis C. Northrop did not file a homestead claim in Valley Center prior to 1900 according to records in San Diego or Los Angeles. His obituary in the *Times Advocate* in 1911, stated that he had lived in the county for 25 years in his home north of the reservoir, [Lake Wohlford].[72] A map from after the turn of the century shows 160 acres owned by L.C. Northrop in Section 32, Township 11 South, Range 1 West. This property is west of Lake Wohlford, not north as described in the obituary.

According to the obituary, Louis C. Northrop was born in Ohio in 1856. He died on January 16, 1911, and is buried in the Valley Center Cemetery.[73] He is listed in the 1900 U.S. census of the Bear Valley Township.   He lived in dwelling number 78 with his wife, D.B. Northrop. Louis is listed as 44 years old, born December 1855, in Illinois, married nine years, occupation farmer on his own farm, and his parents both born in Ohio. His wife is listed as 43 years old, born in April 1857, in Pennsylvania, with both of her parents born in New York. D.B. Northrop is not listed with any children born to her.[74]

References to L.C. Northrop and Clayt Northrop appear in the *Escondido Times* in 1891. One article states that L.C. owned the largest acreage in the "sun-kissed vale." In this same newspaper, the statement appeared that Clayt Northrop had cleared his claim.[75] Another article, printed in June 1891, stated that C. Northrop was a member of the Alliance Business Association in the Striplin District, Number 16.[76]

L.S. Northrop is listed in the 1893-94 *San Diego City and County Directory*.[77] It is not known if L.C. and Clayt are the same person, father and son, or brothers. Research proved inconclusive as to familial relationships.

Charles Z. Peck filed homestead claim #5838 in 1891. His claim of 160 acres was located in Sections 29 and 30, Township 10 South, Range 2 West, San Bernardino Base Meridian.[78] The 1890 U.S. plat map shows "Peck's House" in the northeast quarter of Section 30. This property is shown as owned by J.T. Thompson after the turn of the century.

C.Z. Peck is listed in the 1893-94 *San Diego City and County Directory*.[79] His name does not appear in the school census or U.S. census records. No additional information regarding Charles Peck was found during research for this study.

J.H. Quackenbush did not file a homestead claim in the Valley Center study area prior to 1900. He is listed on the 1900 U.S. plat map in Section 18, Township 11 South, Range 1 West. It is not known if he rented the land.

His daughter, Josie, is listed as a student in the Valley Center School in 1891 and 1893.[80] J.H. Quackenbush is listed in the 1893-94 county directory.[81] He was the mail carrier whose route included Palomar.[82]

The Valley Center Cemetery records list Vance Quackenbush. He was born April 21, 1886, and died on May 22, 1975. It is not known if there is a family relationship to J.H. or Josie Quackenbush for they are not listed on the 1900 U.S. census records.

James M. Quinn filed homestead claim #5170 on January 13, 1890. His claim included 160 acres legally described as the southwest quarter of the northwest quarter, and the northwest quarter of the southwest quarter of Section 13, and the southeast quarter of the northeast quarter and the northeast quarter of the southeast quarter of Section 14, Township 11 South, Range 2 West, San Bernardino Base Meridian.[83] This property is located south of Betsworth Road approximately one-half mile west of Valley Center Road (see Figure 31). This parcel was claimed earlier by Jerome Walsh before his death in 1882. It was owned by F.H. Dolan after the turn of the century.

The Quinn family is not listed in the 1900 U.S. census. James is listed as a carpenter in the 1892 *San Diego, Coronado and National City Directory*. James wife, Mary E. Williams Quinn, died on July 10, 1893. The cause was given as paralysis, from which she had suffered for years. Her obituary stated she was born in 1828 in Flemingsburg, Kentucky. She had five children at the time of death including two children who lived in San Francisco, two other children in Los Angeles, as well as one daughter who lived in Bear Valley and was married to Nicholas Walsh. Mrs. Quinn was buried in the Valley Center Cemetery.[84] No additional information regarding the Quinn family was found during research for this study.

Silas M. Randolph filed homestead claim #5808 on February 24, 1891. His claim consisted of 159.33 acres of land in Valley Center. The legal description is the east half of the northeast quarter of Section 5, the southwest quarter of the northwest quarter and the northwest quarter of the southwest quarter of Section 4, Township 11 South, Range 1 West.[85]

This property is located approximately one-quarter mile north of Fruitvale Road and approximately one mile east of Cole Grade Road (see Figure 31). A portion of this property was owned by D.D. Dodge after the turn of the century.

S.M. Randolf [sic] is listed on the 1891 Valley Center School census with one female student enrolled during that school year.[86] He is also listed on the 1893-94 *San Diego City and County Directory* with his occupation listed as a farmer.[87] No additional information regarding Silas or his family was found during research for this study.

<u>Karl H. Vesper</u> filed for his United States citizenship on July 20, 1900, in the Superior Court of San Diego.[88] He immigrated from Germany, and settled in Valley Center. A homestead claim was not found prior to 1900; however, Vesper School and Vesper Road were named in his honor. No further information was found regarding the Vesper family during research for this study.

<u>George W. Vestal</u> filed homestead claim #5636 on November 7, 1890. His claim consisted of a total of 119.42 acres located in the west half of the southwest quarter of Section 33, Township 10 South, Range 1 West, and Lot 4, Section 4, Township 11 South, Range 1 West, San Bernardino Base Meridian.[89]

This property is located approximately one-half mile south of Cool Valley Road and one and one-half miles east of Cole Grade Road (see Figure 31). A portion of this parcel had been claimed earlier by Austin Reed in 1889. After the turn of the century, the land appears to be the property of A.B. Haight and A.E. Richards.

George and his wife, <u>Ruth,</u> are listed in the 1900 U.S. census record for the Bear Valley Township. They lived in dwelling number 61. George is listed as 55 years old, born February 1845, married 34 years, occupation farmer on his own farm. George and his parents birthplaces are unreadable. Ruth's birth information is also unreadable, except that she was the mother of five children, two of whom were living at the time, her birthplace was Indiana, her father was born in North Carolina, and her mother was born in Ohio.[90]

George is listed in the county directories as a farmer and rancher in 1892-93, 1897, and 1901.[91] He died on April 23, 1912, at the age of 67 years. He had been a resident of Escondido for several years. His obituary stated he had served in the Civil War as a young man before coming to California.[92]

Ruth A. Vestal died on September 3, 1917, at her home in Escondido. She was born on December 11, 1849, in Indiana. She had two sons, one of whom lived in Chicago at the time of her death, and the other son lived in Valley Center.[93] The newspaper article stated the second son's name was <u>Bert,</u> however, an article from the *Escondido Times* in 1892, mentioned <u>Elmer E. Vestal</u> as a young man, 20 years old. Elmer was reported to have walked into Escondido from his home

13 miles distant to attend a concert.[94] It is assumed that Elmer and Bert were children of George and Ruth Vestal based on research material.

The number of families who settled in Valley Center during the decade of 1890-1900 was far less than in previous decades. This is due in part to the fact that there were already at least 100 families in the area who had made large homestead claims prior to 1890. Therefore, land was not as available as it had been in the 1860s when it first opened to homesteaders. Those new families had to claim land farther out from the center of the community, or perhaps file a new claim on land previously claimed and either abandoned or became available upon the person's death.

The newcomers were also fortunate to move into an area which had already suffered through the pains of a fledgling agricultural community. Irrigation was now available to the residents which allowed less desirable land to be farmed. It also allowed a longer harvesting season which translated into additional profit for the farmer. Ranchers also benefited from the irrigation water by allowing more grazing land for their livestock which increased their herd size.

The establishment of the city of Escondido provided the residents of Valley Center a center of business which was 35 miles closer than San Diego and could be traveled to in less than one hour. Railroads and stage lines traveling through Escondido provided excellent shipping options for merchandise or commodities. The modern conveniences of the city also provided a welcome relief from the daily chores of rural life. Recreation, education, and entertainment were available within walking distance.

The lifestyle of the Valley Center community was forever changed with the new inventions of the century. Smaller farms operated with more efficiency producing more profit for less work. The family size also reflected the change. A smaller number of people were needed to operate at an efficient pace. The options available to the children of the latter nineteenth century farmers allowed them to pursue various trades and professions which led them away from the family farm.

Although the community of Valley Center has increased in population since the early days of settlement, the flavor of the area is still rural. It remains an agricultural area with no high-rise buildings and plenty of open space. Horses can be kept in the front yard and ridden down the street without the restrictions of an urban development. Most residents know their neighbors even though they still have large parcels of land. There is a sense of pride in the community that is rarely seen today. Valley Center remains the quiet, beautiful valley that greeted homesteaders in the 1860s.

NOTES

1 *Escondido Times,* April 2, 1891:2.

2 *Ibid.,* January 5, 1893:1.

3 *Ibid.,* September 8, 1905:10.

4 *Ibid.,* May 21, 1891:2.

5 *Ibid.,* March 30, 1893:3.

6 *Ibid.,* March 23, 1893:3.

7 *Ibid.,* February 8, 1894:3.

8 *San Diego Union,* January 1, 1903:22, 1-3.

9 *Ibid.;* November 1, 1897:5,1; June 22, 1898:5,4.

10 *Ibid.*

11 *Directory of San Diego City, Coronado, and National City,* Olmsted and Byron, printers, 1892-93; *Directory of San Diego City and County,* Olmsted Company, printers, 1897, 1901.

12 *Escondido Times,* August 3, 1893:1.

13 *Ibid.*

14 Register of Receipts Issued by the Receiver of Public Monies at Los Angeles, California, for Lands Entered Under the Homestead Act, Vols. I and II, 1869-91, National Archives, Pacific Southwest Region, Laguna Niguel, California.

15 *The Directory of San Diego City and County,* The Olmsted Company, printers, San Diego, California, 1897.

16 *Daily Times Advocate,* December 27, 1915:1.

17 *San Diego Union,* February 14, 1987: 11-2.

18 *San Diego City and County Directory,* 1897, 1905.

19 *Escondido Times,* February 23, 1906:6.

20 *Ibid.*, March 9, 1893:3.

21 *Ibid.*, February 1, 1894:3.

22 Homestead Register, 1869-91.

23 *Ibid.*

24 *Escondido Times,* December 21, 1893:3.

25 Valley Center School Census, 1896.

26 *The Directory of San Diego City and County, 1897.*

27 *Daily Times Advocate,* August 1, 1916:1.

28 Homestead Register, 1869-91.

29 *The Directory of San Diego City and County, 1893-94, 1897.*

30 *Escondido Times,* June 4, 1891:3.

31 *Ibid.,* March 9, 1893:3.

32 *Ibid.,* January 18, 1894:3.

33 *The Directory of San Diego City and County, 1893-94, 1897.*

34 Abel Davis, *Valley Center, California,* unpublished memoir, circa 1955.

35 *Times Advocate,* March 5, 1910:5.

36 *The Directory of San Diego City and County, 1897.*

37 *Escondido Times,* June 7, 1894:3.

38 *Ibid.,* January 18, 1894:3.

[39] 1900 U.S. Census, Schedule 1, Inhabitants in Bear Valley Township, San Diego County, California, p. 204, entries 72-74.

[40] *Times Advocate,* December 8, 1905:3.

[41] *Escondido Times,* February 22, 1894:2.

[42] Bear Valley School Census, June 30, 1895, by L.E. Breedlove.

[43] *Ibid.,* 1896-1910, with various teachers.

[44] 1900 U.S. Census, p. 208, entries 21, 22.

[45] *Ibid.,* entries 23-29.

[46] *Ibid.,* entry 30.

[47] Homestead Register, 1869-91.

[48] *Ibid.,* Book 8, p. 124.

[49] J.M. Guinn, *The History of California,* Historical Record Company, Los Angeles, 1907: 1519.

[50] *Ibid.*

[51] *Escondido Times,* August 2, 1894:3.

[52] Guinn, *The History of California,* 1907: 1519.

[53] *The Directory of San Diego City and County, 1893-94,1901, 1921.*

[54] 1900 U.S. Census, p. 204, entries 92-94.

[55] *Ibid.*

[56] Homestead Register, 1869-91.

[57] U.S. Government Plat Map of Township 10 South, Range 2 West, San Bernardino Base Meridian, 1890. On file at San Diego County Surveyor's Office, County Operations Annex, San Diego, California.

[58] Escondido School Census, June 30, 1898.

[59] *Escondido Times,* September 20, 1894:3.

[60] Records of the District Courts, Superior Court, San Diego County Certificates of Citizenship, Vols. 1 through 7, 1883-1902: Vol. 9, p. 166; also the Index to Naturalized Citizens, Superior Court of San Diego County, California, 1853-1956: Microfilm Roll M-1609, Roll #1, National Archives, Pacific Southwest Region, Laguna Niguel, California.

[61] *Escondido Times,* March 9, 1893:3.

[62] Valley Center School Census, June 30, 1895, 1897. On file at the San Diego Historical Society Archives, Balboa Park, San Diego, California.

[63] *The Directory of San Diego City and County, 1897.*

[64] *Escondido Times,* March 1, 1894:3.

[65] *The Directory of San Diego City and County, 1893-94, 1897, 1901.*

[66] 1900 U.S. Census, p. 207, entries 72-75.

[67] Guinn,, *The History of California,* 1907: 861.

[68] Homestead Register, 1869-91.

[69] *Escondido Times,* February 1, 1894:3.

[70] *Ibid.,* June 14, 1894:3.

[71] Davis, *Valley Center, California,* circa 1955.

[72] *Times Advocate,* January 13, 1911:4.

[73] *Ibid.*

[74] 1900 U.S. Census, p. 208, entries 19, 20.

[75] *Escondido Times,* April 2, 1891:2.

[76] *Ibid.,* June 4, 1891:3.

[77] *The Directory of San Diego City and County, 1893-94.*

[78] Homestead Register, 1869-91.

[79] *The Directory of San Diego City and County, 1893-94.*

[80] Valley Center School Census, 1891; and *Escondido Times,* February 9, 1893:3.

[81] *The Directory of San Diego City and County, 1893-94.*

[82] *Escondido Times,* June 22, 1893:3.

[83] Homestead Register, 1869-91.

[84] *Escondido Times,* July 20, 1893:3.

[85] Homestead Register, 1869-91.

[86] Valley Center School Census, 1891.

[87] *The Directory of San Diego City and County, 1893-94.*

[88] Citizenship records, 1883-1902, Vol. 3, p. 319.

[89] Homestead Register, 1869-91.

[90] 1900 U.S. Census, p. 204, entries 60-61.

[91] *The Directory of San Diego City and County, 1892-93, 1897, 1901.*

[92] *Times Advocate,* April 26, 1912:1.

[93] *Daily Times Advocate,* September 3, 1917:1.

[94] *Escondido Times*, June 23, 1892:3.

CHAPTER FIVE

CONCLUSION

Valley Center, or Bear Valley, is a unique area, not only in San Diego County, but in all of California as well. While most of the land in California was granted to Mexican or Spanish citizens, this secluded valley remained unclaimed. When the Mexican war in California ended in 1848, one condition of the Treaty of Guadalupe Hidalgo was that the United States government honored all previous land grants. Any land not included as part of a grant became U.S. government land.

The Homestead Act of 1862 allowed U.S. citizens to claim this government land by several different means. The most popular method was to simply file a claim for up to 160 acres by paying a minimal filing fee of $10 and agreeing to improve the land by providing a place of residence in which to live and any necessary out-buildings for at least five years, as well as to either cultivate the land or raise livestock. Once these obligations were met, the homesteader was granted full ownership on the property.

Another method of claiming government land was known as pre-emption. The settler simply selected the land and lived on that land until filing the legal claim. At that time, the settler was eligible to purchase the land at a minimum price without competition. A person could claim up to 320 acres in this fashion. This Act of Congress was repealed in 1891 due to corruption and abuse by land speculators.

Other methods of claiming land in California were to file timber or mineral claims. A person could claim up to 160 acres of land provided they planted at least 40 acres in timber to replenish the diminishing stock. Trees were to be planted at least 12 feet apart and maintained in healthy growing condition for ten years. The specifics were later modified and these acts were repealed in 1891.

The people who settled in the valley were from many different states, as well foreign countries. Many families traveled together in wagon trains from the eastern U.S. and established lasting bonds with one another. Their children oftentimes intermarried with the other

families in the valley, tightly weaving the ancestral charts for the Valley
Center descendants.

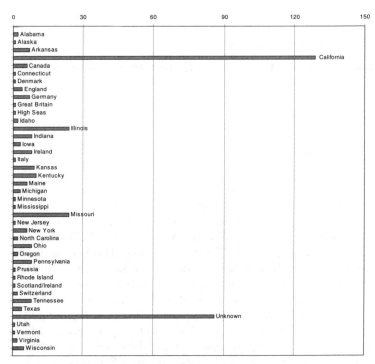

Chart 1. Valley Center Pioneers' Birthplace

The birthplaces of the settlers is shown in Chart 1. The two largest
categories include the native-born Californians (n=129/399) and
unknown birthplaces (n=86/399). The Californians primarily reflect the
children of the settlers born after their emigration. Illinois and Missouri
each have 24 people born in those states. The large number of
unknown birthplaces is due in part to the fact that the majority of the
1890 U.S. Census including California was destroyed in a fire in the
Commerce Department Building in January 1921. Many of the people
in the valley during that time had left the area by the next census
reading in 1900.

The settlers were predominantly farmers who took advantage of
the homestead option. They were not wealthy, in fact, of the 309
homesteaders within the study area with known birthplaces, more than
34 percent were farmers (n=106/309), 24 of whom were native
Californians (n=24/106). Farmers from Missouri and Illinois each had
nine settlers. Also included in this category are farm laborers (6.15%),
or those persons who did not own their land such as young men, and
ranchers (1.29%).

Although many other occupations were also associated with the settlers, farming was their main business. Without farming they could not provide for their families because there were no stores in the region that supplied their daily food. Money was of no object for their primary concern was sustenance. Profits and the need for money came later when there were surplus goods. There were no businesses in the area other than the trades the settlers brought with them. To name a few, this included physicians (fewer than 1%), blacksmiths (fewer than 1%), ministers (fewer than 1%), teachers (fewer than 1%), apiarists (fewer than 2%), merchants (fewer than 2%), and carpenters (fewer than 2%).

The second most popular occupation of the adult settlers in the valley were housekeepers and mothers (n=40/309), the majority of whom were from Missouri (n=8/40). The children of the settlers comprised the greatest percentage. Sixteen percent were students (n=52/309) and 10 percent were classified as living at home (n=31/309).

Based on the known birthdates, the year of birth for the majority of settlers were born in 1865 (n=12/289). Native Californians comprised more than 38 percent (n=110/289), Illinois and Missouri each comprised more than eight percent (n=24/289), and Kentucky was the third highest number with more than three percent (n=10/289).

The settlers between the years 1860-1900 saw many new inventions and developments in the area. The town of Escondido was founded in the 1880s as a planned community. The city attracted many new businesses which offered the residents of Valley Center the opportunity of closer marketplaces and educational facilities. The railroad came into the area in the 1890s which allowed the surplus supplies to be shipped to market. The telephone was first installed in the valley in the 1890s and provided a direct link to the rest of the world.

Inventions during the late 1800s had a profound effect on the farmers and ranchers. One of these was mechanized harvesting equipment. This invention alone allowed one farmer to accomplish what took several persons to do previously. One person could farm more efficiently and economically, thereby increasing profits. This also allowed smaller farms to exist with smaller families.

Another invention which had a large impact on the farmers and ranchers was the cream separator for the dairies. Several dairies operated in the valley and produced much of the milk and butter shipped to San Diego and Los Angeles. The separator produced a greater quantity of cream than previous methods.

The people who settled in Valley Center during the homestead years of 1860-1900 witnessed the birth of a community that is still based in agriculture. Although the population has grown considerably, and the privately owned parcels are no longer comprised of 160 acres or more, the values of the residents remain the same as in the beginning. The residents are proud of their community and its back-country way-of-life, and do not really mind if the heavily traveled highways have not brought them fame and fortune along with large developments and industrialization. Numerous varieties of livestock still outnumber the human population and remain at the heart of this peaceful and beautiful community.

INDEX

A

Abbott, Hugh, 46
acorn-grinding, 9
acorns, 11, 12
Adams family, 104
Adams, Anna B, 31
Adams, B.E., 30, 157
Adams, Blanche, 30, 147
Adams, J.Q., 11, 31, 59, 63
Adams, John, 28, 31, 83, 145
Adams, John Q., 25, 28, 29, 31,
    83, 97, 99, 104, 107, 111, 149
Adams, John Quincy, 28, 157
Adams, John T., 25, 27, 29, 83
Adams, John Thomas, 28
Adams, Louisa Coffee, 104
Adams, Louisa J., 31
Adams, Will H., 31
Adams, William, 97
Adams, William H., 30
adobe, 32, 45, 48, 54, 56, 60, 97,
    101, 102, 116, 121, 124, 152
Advance Planning & Research
    Associates, 10
Aerie Road, 155
agricultural district, 99
Agua Caliente, 11, 59
Agua Hedionda, 9
Aguanga, 11
Aherran, Catherine A., 76
Albuquerque, 47
Alcorn, 150
Alcorn, Samuel M., 99
Allen, Mrs. Jack, 63
Alliance Business Association, 35,
    101, 144, 158
Almond, John, 148, 149
almonds, 38, 54, 105
Alvarado, Juan Bautista, 16
American Pacific Environmental
    Consultants, Inc., 10
American River, 133
Anderson family, 149
Anderson, B., 149

Anderson, D., 149
Anderson, David, 149
Anderson, Mary, 149
Angle, S.P., 104
Antes ranch, 105, 106
Antes, Ada C., 32
Antes, Henry, 38
Antes, John, 25, 32, 33, 57
Antes, John H., 32, 97
Antes, John Henry, 31, 32, 33
Antes, María, 32, 105
Antes, María A., 33
Antes, Ruby D., 32
Antes, S., 32
Antes, Sam, 33, 114
Antes, Samuel, 32, 33, 67, 105,
    144
Antes, Samuel G., 31, 32, 97
Antes, Willie, 33
Anthony Road, 104, 110, 111, 132
apiarist, 36, 55, 169
apiary, 36, 75
apples, 49, 126
apricots, 49, 145
army, 44, 129
artifacts, 8, 102
asphaltum, 147
automobiles, 134
aviation, 119
aviation navigator, 119
avocados, 8

B

Baines family, 149, 150
Baines, James, 149, 150
Baines, John, 150
Baines, Mollie, 149
Baines, Mrs., 149
Baines, Nannie, 150
Baines, R.T., 63, 149
Baines, Robert, 149
Baines, Robert T., 149
Ball, William, 131
Ball, William C., 99, 100, 113

G

T

Y